D1757906

Neoliberalism and Neopanamericanism

Neoliberalism and Neopanamericanism

The View from Latin America

Edited by Gary Prevost and Carlos Oliva Campos

palgrave
macmillan

First published 2002 by
PALGRAVE MACMILLAN™
175 Fifth Avenue, New York, N.Y. 10010 and
Houndmills, Basingstoke, Hampshire, England RG21 6XS.
Companies and representatives throughout the world.

PALGRAVE MACMILLAN IS THE GLOBAL
ACADEMIC IMPRINT OF THE PALGRAVE MACMILLAN
division of St. Martin's Press, LLC and of Palgrave Macmillan Ltd.
Macmillan® is a registered trademark in the United States, United
Kingdom and other countries. Palgrave is a registered trademark in the
European Union and other countries.

ISBN 0-312-29456-5

Library of Congress Cataloging-in-Publication Data
NeoLiberalism and neoPanamericanism : the view from Latin America /
Gary Prevost and Carlos Oliva, editors.
        p.   cm.
    Includes bibliographical references and index.
    ISBN 0-312-29456-5 (cloth)
    1. Latin America—Economic policy.   2. America—Economic
integration.   3. Pan-Americanism.   4. Latin America—Foreign
relations—United States.   5. United States—Foreign relations—Latin
America.   6. Latin America—Foreign economic relations—United
States.   7. United States—Foreign economic relations—Latin America.
8. Latin America—Politics and government—1980–   I. Prevost, Gary.
II. Oliva, Carlos.

HC125.N459   2002
327.7308'09'049—dc21

                                                              2002024605

A catalogue record for this book is available from the British Library.

Design by Letra Libre.

First edition: September 2002
10   9   8   7   6   5   4   3   2   1

Printed in the United States of America

Carlos dedicates this book to his children:
Claudia, Daniela, and Camilo

Gary dedicates this book to his father, Henry, in gratitude for
supporting him in all that he has sought to accomplish.

Contents

Preface

Carlos Oliva Campos and Gary Prevost

In this edited volume, 16 scholars, mostly from Latin America, analyze the current state of relations in the Western hemisphere in a number of sectors—including economic, security, political, and environmental. Particular attention is paid to processes of economic integration that dominated political discussions during the decade of the 1990s—North American Free Trade Agreement (NAFTA), Common Market of the South (MERCOSUR), and the Free Trade Area of the Americas (FTAA). Because most of the scholars are from Latin America, the book has a perspective that is often lacking in books on a similar subject written almost exclusively by scholars from the United States.

Interamerican affairs enter the twenty-first century at a time of both continuity and change. One hundred years ago, at the beginning of the twentieth century, the government of the United States was in the process of establishing a hegemony that had been prematurely declared by President Monroe more than 75 years earlier. In 1900, the United States was consolidating its gains from the recent victorious war with Spain. Cuba was, under U.S. military occupation, on the way to becoming a virtual protectorate. Direct colonial rule had already been established in Puerto Rico, giving the United States a territory that it continues to hold at the start of the new century. One hundred years later, the United States continues its project of hegemony that was begun in earnest under the banner of Panamericanism with the first Panamerican Congress in Washington in 1889. Over the first 50 years of the twentieth century, the United States largely succeeded in establishing its domination of the Caribbean and Central American region using more than 50 armed interventions to project its power. The centerpiece of this influence was the Panama Canal, built by the United States on land granted by a Panamanian government that had little choice in the matter. It is of some significance to the complex contemporary times that the twentieth century ended with the formal return of the canal to Panama by the U.S. government.

In the last decade of the twentieth century, the United States renewed its desire to extend even greater influence over all of the hemisphere. Such desire was not new as evidenced by both the Monroe Doctrine and the Panamericanism of the late nineteenth century. The reasons behind the renewed U.S. push in the 1990s were the end of the Cold War and the decline of revolutionary challenges in Central America and the Caribbean. In the case of the latter, U.S. Latin American policy in the 1980s had been focused almost exclusively on defeating the revolutionary governments of Nicaragua and Grenada while repelling the challenge of revolutionary movements in El Salvador and Guatemala. Latin America as a whole suffered through a "lost decade" of economic stagnation and crippling foreign debt in the 1980s, yet received attention from U.S. policymakers only in moments of crisis (e.g., Mexico's threat to default on its loans in 1982). By 1990, however, the United States was facing a different political situation in Central America and the Caribbean. The revolutionary government in Grenada had been overthrown by a U.S. invasion and in 1990 the Sandinistas lost power in an election following a long and bloody civil war. The new Nicaraguan government pledged strong ties with the United States and a reversal of the Sandinista's revolutionary programs. Meanwhile, the civil wars in El Salvador and Guatemala moved toward negotiated settlements in which the revolutionary forces traded increasingly unlikely victory for political space within the established political processes. These events, combined with a changed international situation, permitted the first Bush administration to cast a new policy for Latin America.

The changed international situation was the end of the Cold War begun by the collapse of the former socialist governments in Eastern Europe in the fall of 1989. This perceived victory over the socialist camp, which culminated with the demise of the USSR at the end of 1991, encouraged the U.S. leaders to view extension of U.S. dominance over all of Latin America with renewed vigor. The U.S. vision took shape over the early years of the decade first with President Bush and then with Clinton. The vision was based on what became known as the Washington Consensus or, as we label it, Neopanamericanism. The U.S. domination was to be based on Latin American governments accepting three principles that ran counter to much of their previous practice. First, the Latin American state was to play a sharply reduced economic role, allowing market forces to run their course. Second, the Latin American governments were to sell off state-owned enterprises and in the process reduce public deficits. Third, the governments were to drastically revise their policies on trade by looking outward for markets rather than primarily inward. In sum, the Washington Consensus advocated the adoption of free market capitalism throughout Latin America.

The U.S. policy initiative quickly took definitive form. First, the United States successfully implemented NAFTA with cooperative governments in Canada and Mexico. The agreement was unveiled in August 1992 and then signed by leaders of Canada, the United States, and Mexico in October 1992 in San Antonio, Texas. After ratification by the legislatures of the three governments, it took effect in January 1994. Building on a bilateral U.S.-Canada agreement initiated in 1989, NAFTA created one of the two largest trading blocs in the world with a population of 370 million and a combined economic production of $6 trillion, a worthy rival to the European Union. Second, the Clinton administration convened the Summit of the Americas in Miami in December 1994, the first such meeting of Western hemisphere heads of state in more than a quarter century. However, not all of the hemisphere was represented, as the Cuban government was excluded on the grounds that it was not democratically elected, a questionable condition given the electoral credentials of several other leaders, especially Fujimori of Peru. The meeting concluded with an agreement to form a FTAA by 2005. President Bill Clinton declared the gathering "a watershed in the history of the continent." Economics had taken center stage in Interamerican affairs.

However, it should be noted that even during this period of reorienting U.S. policy back to a more traditional emphasis on economic issues, the U.S. government did not abandon its security agenda with a primary focus on combating revolutionary forces. Under the guise of a "war on drugs" the Bush administration launched an initiative toward the Andean countries (Bolivia, Columbia, and Peru) that had as its primary concern the growing strength of the revolutionary movements in the region (i.e., Shining Path in Peru and M-19 and the Revolutionary Armed Forces of Columbia [FARC] in Colombia). This initiative, carried out simultaneously with the Enterprise Initiative for the Americas, was continued by the Clinton Administration during the 1990s. Following the defeat of the Shining Path in 1992, U.S. policy in the Andean region refocused almost entirely on Colombia where there is an ongoing U.S. military presence, the largest in Latin America. There is clearly a difference of opinion among U.S. leaders about the level of threat posed by the Colombian revolutionaries but, by the end of the 1990s, it was clearer that the real concern of the United States in Colombia was not drugs but, rather, the stability of the Colombian government in the face of a renewed revolutionary challenge. This focus was reinforced in late 2000 when the U.S. Congress approved Plan Columbia, a $1.3 billion aid package with primary emphasis on military aid.

The new Bush Administration has promised a renewed emphasis on Latin America focused primarily on the achievement of FTAA by 2005. To support this goal, the Bush Administration placed FTAA at the head of the agenda of the Third Summit of the Americas in Quebec City in April 2001 and renewed the drive in the U.S. Congress to obtain Fast Track Authority (FTA), a necessary ingredient in the effort to negotiate a new trade treaty with Latin America.

The book is divided into two sections, the first covering hemispheric-wide issues and the second regional ones. Coeditor Carlos Oliva provides a historical overview of U.S. policy in Latin America by making the case that the guiding principle of U.S. policy has been hemispheric domination from the Monroe Doctrine to FTAA. In the second chapter, Luis Fernando Ayerbe analyzes the perception of Latin America in the debate on national interest in the United States after the Cold War. He argues that U.S. policymakers and their ideological supporters argue that the success of a hemispheric economic integration project is based on the ability of Latin American countries to incorporate themselves in a definite path to the "North American way of life": free markers, democracy, and respect for law. In the third chapter, Carlos Alzugaray Treto challenges the notion that neoliberalism provides the only alternative for Latin American societies. He proposes alternative strategies for governance, integration, and security that emphasize attacking poverty, inequality, and violence. In the fourth chapter, Gary Prevost and Robert Weber analyze the prospects for the successful completion of FTAA by focusing on the nature of the opposition to the project in both the United States and Latin America. The authors also argue that while the project is presented by its supporters as a solution to poverty and inequality, it is primarily designed for easier market access and investments to U.S.-based transnational corporations. In the fifth chapter, Hector Luis Saint-Pierre writes that in the 1990s there was a reduction in the importance of Latin American states and the blurring of internal and external issues. As a result, national armies of Latin America have been reduced, on the one hand, to instruments of internal repression or, on the other hand, to be integrated into an international force of intervention against rebel insurgencies.

The second part of the book contains an article by Dorothea Melcher that provides a theoretical and historical overview of the processes of regional integration in South America. Articles by Armando Lopez Coll and Tullo Vigevani et al. provide analysis of two of the most important regional trading blocs, the Caribbean Common Market (CARICOM) and MERCOSUR. Coll argues that to go beyond its current limited development, CARICOM must fully implement its negotiated treaties and gain independence from the previous system of favoritism and protectionism. Luciana Togeiro, argues against the inclusion of environmental clauses in Interamerican trade treaties on the grounds that they will only serve as veiled protectionism by the United States. Vigevani's article explores the intersection between MERCOSUR's integration and existing political interests in order to verify to what extent this process has incorporated national party interests. In her chapter on Argentine foreign policy, Sandra Colombo analyzes the changes and adjustments in the 1990s during the presidency of Carlos Menem. She argues that Menem pursued as an almost exclusive priority the achievement of a close alliance with the United States in contrast to Argentina's previous priorities. Harry Vanden discusses the impact of neoliberal programs in Nicaragua and Costa Rica in the 1990s, arguing that Costa Rica was more successful in resisting the worst aspects of the programs because of its long history of strong state programs and mobilized popular resistance. In the chapter on Mexico and the United States, Jaime Praciado Coronado argues that Mexico's relationship has changed with the current political circumstances but retains many of its former characteristics based on geography and interdependence.

Hemispheric Issues

The United States, Latin America, and the Caribbean: From Panamericanism to Neopanamericanism

Carlos Oliva Campos

More than two hundred years plagued with convergence and divergence have marked the course of relations between Latin America and the Caribbean. Now is a good opportunity to focus our thoughts on this area given that we are entering a new millennium, particularly if the aim is to evaluate the development of such complex relations in order to project them onto the current scenario. There is no better starting place than the recovery of a series of historical aspects that allow the reader to be located in the context of the matter in question, but not as a simple legacy—rather, as arguments formulated to assess the degree of relevance of early political approaches to interhemispheric dynamics.

To proceed in this direction it will be necessary to reconsider the U.S. hegemonic factor as a key aspect both in terms of the theory and practice of U.S. relations with its southern neighbors. In order to do this, the object of analysis will be Panamericanism, a tool that provides an insight into the degree of interrelation that the United States has aspired to with Latin America and the Caribbean, as well as the bases on which it has been constructed. Panamericanism, not integration, has been the approach adopted by the United States; therein lies what is of interest in analyzing the current hemispheric scenario, the existence of Neopan-american conditions gestated in the heat of the interaction between new global and regional factors predominating today. Throughout the history of Interamerican relations, numerous controversies have emerged as a result of the links between two very different agents. In the first place, we will assess the debated subject of the role and place that Latin America and the Caribbean occupy in U.S. foreign policy. Beyond the logical variations that the question has been subjected to during different historic periods from 1776 until the present there is, above all, a constant for the United States. Latin America and the Caribbean have had an inseparable dimension. On the one hand, it is a geographical area where the United States defines and establishes a system of its particular domination. On the other, it is a platform from which the United States relates to the world. An eloquent example that illustrates this argument has been the controversial theme of U.S. national security.[1]

The description of U.S. national security revolves around two basic axes, the perception of an ongoing threat and the consequent external reaction, and the belief that the "source" of the said threat emanates from beyond the borders of the country. This transnational character of the U.S. doctrine of national security corresponds to the "hegemonic predestination" that is not restricted to territorial borders but to the globalization of U.S. interests.[2]

In contrast to and regardless of the weight that the geopolitical factor may have in the national security doctrines of large countries such as Brazil and Argentina, what is referred to is the preservation of national territory, natural resources, and the defense of sovereignty and national independence.[3] The differences between the approaches were highlighted in the 1983 report of Interamerican Dialogue, stating that when Latin Americans study the subject of national security, the majority think about internal threats to national unity and development, the borders with neighboring states, and, in some cases, in the possibility of U.S. intervention. In the United States, the focus of security is external, global, and strategic. The United States, in general, seeks to ensure political stability abroad, sometimes supporting the status quo in face of internal or regional threats.[4]

One of the authors who has most tackled the theme, defining the perspective as the "reduced relative value" of Latin America and the Caribbean for the United States is Lars Schoultz. In his work *National Security and United States Policy Toward Latin America,* Schoultz argues that the region, in accordance with U.S. national security doctrine, was considered in the bipolar scenario for the Cold War as a passive inert object lacking in intrinsic value.[5]

In the preface of a more recent book, *Beneath the United States: A History of U.S. Policy toward Latin America,* Schoultz speaks of asymmetry as an intrinsic factor in Interamerican relations. He defines hegemony as the model guaranteeing the defense of U.S. interests, "controlling the behavior of its weak neighbors." For Schoultz, the perception of "Latin American inferiority" is a cornerstone of U.S. policy toward Latin America, determining the measures to be taken to protect its interests in the region.[6]

A second historic controversy is the penchant toward analyzing the existence or otherwise of a regional vision in the combined U.S. policy operating at any given moment instead of seeking an answer to this point, a series of characteristics present in the U.S. political decision-making model toward Latin America and the Caribbean. First, it should be understood as a complex process because it is the sum of perceptions and focuses, coinciding and contradictory, of a considerable number of institutional and individual agents that give rise to a combination of specialized policies.[7] The distinction has to be made between the civil servants who are experts in particular areas and matters, almost always anonymous, those who assume a situational role, from those who assume a conjunctional responsibility for reasons of friendship, political trustworthiness, and/or economic interest, with the changeover of government.

Second, levels of priority and interest are established on the basis of areas within the hemispheric geography. It has to be recalled that, for the United States, the Caribbean Basin countries have been the focus of greater influence in comparison to South American nations, owing to the greater level of domination exercised by their powerful neighbor. Last, but of no lesser importance, the variable nature of the process must be recognized, given that priorities are defined as a result of political junctures.

In general, the crisis scenario is that which determines the greater or lesser profile for countries and matters of the hemispheric agenda. What it does not deny is the existence of permanent priorities, because of their strategic nature, such as the case of Mexico.

The third controversy to be mentioned refers to the degree of rationality, of coherence to be found in U.S. policy applied to Latin America. In this regard, it is highly appropriate to stress that rationality and coherence have to be understood in strict and complete accordance with the defined interests and political priorities in a determined historical conjuncture. To this it must be added that these interests and priorities are those of the United States, not those of Latin America and the Caribbean, accepting, of course, an element of ignorance and lack of understanding of the regional reality. By placing the theme in this perspective, decisive historic components can be identified in U.S. policy in the hemisphere, which have transcended time barriers.

Genesis: The Founding Figures of Panamericanism

When history is considered as an endless source of new knowledge, there is a need to go back and review early and transcendental events that gave rise to the American Revolution and the first steps of a new nation in the surrounding world. For a variety of reasons, it was not until the start of the nineteenth century that the United States began to show a growing interest in the affairs of the rest of the hemisphere. This is a logical perception if it is taken into account that the period referred to, approximately from 1776 to 1812 was very much tied up with the survival of the new state. Under a defensive logic, endeavors were made to establish a definitive peace with Great Britain. The privilege of trade, not political, relations with France and Spain was conceived by avoiding the aggravation of conflicts with the former colonial power. In general, U.S. foreign policy sought to create distance from the problems of Europe and to develop a strategy of neutrality.

Nevertheless, the seeds of new policies toward Latin America and the Caribbean had already been sown. When Thomas Paine wrote *Common Sense* in 1776, he described the need for the separation of the United States from Great Britain, like two spheres with two different systems, one European and the other American.[8]

In *The Federalist* (1788), Alexander Hamilton went beyond the idea of the new and old world by perceiving of the world as divided into four systems (Europe, Asia, Africa, and America), each of them having their own interests. For Hamilton, the American system was the Western hemisphere and it was implicitly taken for granted that the young North American nation should construct and lead it.[9]

Thomas Jefferson surpassed the precedents with his reflections, moving from political ideas to concrete policies. Jefferson was a major driving force behind the negotiations between France and Spain for the acquisition of Louisiana and Florida. It was the transition toward a new phase for the nation; from survival it moved toward consolidation and the means indicated was territorial expansion. Another example, one that is well known, of this expansionist thinking was the case of Cuba. The conjunction of commercial and geopolitical interests fed, from very early times, the desire to annex the island to the United States. The aspiration to dominate Cuba was already tangible by 1809, when Jefferson proposed to President Madison that he negotiate with Napoleon, who at that time controlled Spain with his troops, to hand over Cuba in exchange for a "free reign" for France in Hispanic America.[10]

It is useful to refer to an essay written by the U.S. researchers James Petras and Michael Erisman who argue that in the period between the aforementioned Jefferson proposal and the proclamation of the Monroe Doctrine (1823) Spanish colonies in the Caribbean, particularly Cuba, had acquired a commercial priority for the United States. Specifically, in the period from 1821 to 1825, 31 percent of U.S. exports went to Latin America, out of which the Caribbean received 25 percent. In the view of the then secretary of state, John Quincy Adams, Cuba was crucially important for U.S. political and commercial interests.[11]

In the formation of a viewpoint that the United States was constructing on Latin America and the Caribbean, self-perceptions charged with mysticism and messianism assumed increasing strength. The United States began to be seen as a chosen people on the basis of a mixture of philosophical, religious, ethnic, cultural, economic, and political arguments, which would subsequently lead to the so-called idea of Manifest Destiny. In essence, this referred to a mission to be accomplished, a task to be carried out, or rather the need to take the unavoidable and therefore inevitable path.[12] The mysticism that it upholds should be noted. It is claimed that divine providence has especially chosen and guided the U.S. people to develop a higher kind of freedom and civilization, which no other nation had ever achieved.[13] The essence of Manifest Destiny is the expansionist and plundering philosophy of the property and resources of others. Manifest Destiny expresses a dogma of supreme self-confidence and ambition. The idea of the incorporation into the United States of all adjacent regions constituted the carrying out of a virtually inevitable mission assigned to a nation by providence itself.[14]

The first practical expression of Manifest Destiny was the Monroe Doctrine (1823). As Petras and Erisman wrote, the Monroe Doctrine was Washington's response to the ambiguous situation generated by the presence of European powers in the hemisphere and the weakness of the new neighboring republics.[15] Maritime expansion provided a means of defense for the country's security. The Monroe Doctrine has remained the oldest principle of U.S. foreign policy. The fundamental value, however, acquired lies in its application, an unlawful assertion from the beginning. It was the theoretical justification for inviolable U.S. relations with Latin America: control of the presence of extracontinental powers in the hemisphere; not permitting European intervention in the region, a matter that the United States assumed for itself; and noninterference in European affairs as it considered the political systems of the "Old Continent" to be different to the Western hemisphere.[16]

It was for this reason, as Piero Gleijeses argues, that Simón Bolívar, in his concern for the weakness of the new republics, the reigning anarchy, and the danger of military intervention by Spain and the Holy Alliance and, drawing a comparison between the United States and Great Britain, foresaw in the former a potential threat to the territorial integrity of Hispanic-America.[17] Demetrio Boersner explains Bolívarian thinking, considering it in opposition to the unilateral and hegemonic concept contained in the Monroe Doctrine. For Bolívar, the principle of solidarity among all Hispanic-American countries on an equal basis was valid, being the formula applicable to developing collective security in defense of inter- and extraregional aggression.[18]

It is useful to review the discordance between Bolívarian and U.S. political thinking, taking as an example the Amphictyonic Conference that Bolívar called for to be held in Panama in 1826. Bolívar was intending to plan a Hispanic-American confederation with an emphasis on the development of its political-military capacities because of the threats from Spain and the Holy Alliance. It was not his desire nor was he interested in U.S. participation in the conference.

It is worth pointing out that at the outset U.S. political circles showed no interest in participating, but there were numerous debates in Congress. Both in the House of Representatives and in the Senate there were around 60 speeches on the subject over a period of several days. Among the arguments put forward by Congress members, uniformly opposed to an eventual U.S. participation in the Panama Conference, was the determination not to violate the status quo maintained by Spain in America after the wars of independence. There was categorical opposition to Bolívar's intention to fight for Cuba and Puerto Rico's independence. There was support for not participating in the conference, which would be attended by the "black Republic" of Haiti, a comment that was mistaken as Haiti had not been invited. There were concerns about the freedom of religious practice in the new American republics and a denial that American participation in the said conference would imply the obligation to form some type of alliance with Latin American countries.[19]

After reconciling serious concerns, and thanks to the arguments put forward by Secretary of State Henry Clay, President John Quincy Adams accepted the desirability of sending U.S. representatives to the Panama Amphictyonic Conference. On December 6, Adams sent the first message to Congress setting out his new position and, subsequently, sent a special message to the Senate on December 26, 1825, in which he affirmed, "We believe that the time has come to show them the principles of free trade exchange and to insist through disinterested and friendly persuasion, when they are all together, in our determined goal of jointly studying the establishment of such principles, which would be an important means of support for their future well-being."[20] The Clay-Adams thinking is also highly revealing since it endeavors to carve out, as is very primitively logical given the historical context, a free trade area for the United States in the hemisphere. Finally, as a result of the prolonged debates in the U.S. Congress, the two diplomats were sent with some delay; one of them perished on the voyage on contracting yellow fever, and the second arrived scarcely in time for the closure of the Congress.

By 1845, the journalist John O'Sullivan of the *Democratic Review* promoted expansionism under a strong missionary consciousness of the United States. He defined Manifest Destiny for the first time, when one of his articles set out that the fulfillment of Manifest Destiny was to spread throughout the continent assigned to the United States by providence for the free development of millions that annually multiply.[21] On January 3, 1846, Massachusetts state senator Robert C. Winthrop stated, "Ours is a right backed by the Manifest Destiny to spread throughout the entire continent. We appeal to the right of our Manifest Destiny I suppose that a Manifest Destiny's right to expand will not be accorded to any other nation except the universal Yankee nation."[22]

The idea of Manifest Destiny should be approached from three different political phases, responding to the same guiding axis, the search for and establishment of U.S. hegemony in Latin America and the Caribbean. By tackling the question in chronological order, we could say that in the early decades of the nineteenth century, Manifest Destiny was an idea being developed. Then, by 1845, with the process of expansion into Mexico, it was begun to be put into practice. Finally, in the third phase, when it was deployed at full strength, the War of Secession subsequently broke out (1862–1865), with its aim being to strive for a hemispheric hegemonic position.

Writing in this third phase were authors such as John Fiske and Josiah Strong (*Our Country: Its Possible Future and Its Present Crisis,* 1885), a book that sold more than 175,000 copies. For Strong, for example, America's progress was the result of a "natural selection" that should spread the powerful Anglo-Saxon race throughout the hemisphere.[23]

The previous year (1884), the U.S. Congress approved the sending of a special commission to Central and South America with the aim of investigating and obtaining information about the means by which close international and trade relations could be boosted between the United States and Latin America. In their report, the commission proposed three principal measures: holding a Panamerican congress with the aim of creating and strengthening a hemispheric market; a common silver coin; and an agreement on trade reciprocity signed by all American nations, "liberating all the exchange rights of native products transported in ships from either party."[24]

Before making reference to such a major event, however, it is necessary to define the boundaries between Bolívar's concept of Hispanic unity and the Panamericanism of the United States. When Bolívar's writings are re-examined, particularly his well-known Jamaica Charter (1815) in which he sets out his vision of supranational unification, this could have been the main grounds for the U.S. interpretation of Panamericanism, focusing it, as has been reiterated, from an asymmetrical and uneven perspective, on the hegemonic position adopted by the United States.[25]

In the proclamation to the Angostura Congress of 1819, Bolívar argued, "Whatever this government was with regard to the American nation, I have to state that the situation and nature of two states as different as the English-American and the American-Spanish states did not even remotely enter into my similar idea. Would it not be more difficult to apply to Spain England's political freedom, civil and religious code? Because it is more to adapt the laws of North America in Venezuela." In the letter written to General Francisco de Paula Santander on October 27, 1825, the Liberator said, "Simply on account of being foreigners, Americans from the north and Haiti have a heterogeneous character for us. For this reason I will never be of the opinion that they should be invited to take part in our settlements."

Finally, it is important not to overlook a lapidary phrase set out by Bolívar in a letter dated August 5, 1829, sent to Colonel Patrick Campbell, British chargé d'affaires to the Colombian government, "The United States seem to be destined by province to burden America with misery in the name of Freedom."[26]

On October 2, 1829, the First Panamerican Conference was opened in Washington, DC, held and organized by the United States.[27] The well-informed and eloquent reflections put forward by Salvador Morales describe Panamericanism as "a neocolonial version of integration, subjected to constant redefinition on the basis of a model rooted in U.S. leadership."[28]

From Panamericanism to Neopanamericanism

As a starting point for the analysis that we are going to develop, some general observations on U.S. hegemony will be set out, this being the only position accepted by the United States for its relations with its southern neighbors and from which it defines and projects Panamericanism. We will then move on to deal with this phenomena in the present. For the purposes of this chapter and in acknowledgment of the validity of the conceptualization developed by other authors,[29] hegemony is understood to be the capacity of power exercised by the United States (economic, political, military, ideological, technological, cultural) to decisively influence the internal and foreign policies of Latin American and Caribbean countries.

Antonio Gramsci argues that the exercise of hegemony in a determined area is characterized by the existence of a combination of force and consensus, which varies in its reciprocal balance, without force, however, surpassing consensus.[30] In accepting that force is the capacity of power, it is important to specify that in the case of the United States, its hegemony has been constituted and defended on many occasions by combining force with the use of instruments of pressure to attain consensus or even, simply, without the latter to achieve established goals.

In this respect, hegemony's essential components should be considered to be expansionism, understood to be the basic instrument of hegemony—in its economic, political, military, and ideological aspects—and leadership, which is the function, the organizing and controlling "brain." According to the logic set forth, there cannot be hegemony without expansion for the United States; nevertheless, this quantitative dimension requires its qualitative complement, thereby making leadership indispensable through the imposition of a dominant political paradigm.

U.S. expansionism possesses an essential peculiarity. It has been nourished by the two fundamental tendencies that have historically moved within U.S. foreign policy, "isolationism" and "internationalism" or interference, as some authors define it.[31]

"Isolationism" is the tendency to reduce to the absolute minimum the international commitments of the United States, whether it be to avoid involvement in joint actions with other actors to maintain an independence of movement, or for the privilege of dealing with domestic problems in a given conjuncture. It is not a case of not taking on foreign policy actions; rather, it is about translating these into limited agreements and treaties. "Internationalism" is a concept that is as ambiguous as its apparent antonym, by associating it with U.S. foreign relations that translate into the direct participation in agreements or treaties of a mainly multilateral nature.

The "isolationist" tendency was imposed on U.S. foreign policy at the start of the new U.S. state and it focused on relations with European powers. By contrast, the study of Interamerican relations throughout the nineteenth century reveals two complementary tendencies, the sustained effort, direct or undercover, to counter the influence held by Europeans in the Western hemisphere and U.S. dealings with the Caribbean Basin region. Therefore, it can be argued that "isolationism" never predominated as the tendency in U.S. relations with Latin America and the Caribbean. In this respect, we agree with Roberto González Gómez when he argues that "isolationism is a phenomenon resulting from the process of growth and maturity of U.S. imperialism and to some extent signifies the hermetic enclosure within its borders, excluding all expansionist drives."[32] Of particular relevance is the criteria put forward in a similar sense by Arthur Schlesinger Jr., who recognizes the ambiguous nature of the concept, arguing that "the United States has never been 'isolationist' in trade terms, as U.S. traders have plied the seven seas since the first day of independence."[33]

In a more categorical definition, Petras and Erisman write that, "for the United States, national independence was a condition of its own expansion and not a doctrine applicable to other areas of implication. In this way, a bourgeois movement of national liberation was easily able to, in the period following independence, adopt an overseas policy of an expansionist nature, discarding its own national democratic rhetoric."[34] Therefore, in the specific case of relations with Latin America and the Caribbean, U.S. "isolationism" was not only real in terms of agreements and official commitments with its neighbors, but also, projected in the context of U.S. foreign policy, Interamerican relations were the ideal "laboratory" in which to experiment with and create its global hegemonic project.

U.S. expansionism is nourished by isolationism, a claim based on two major historical examples. The first is rooted in our object of study, Interamerican relations; the second, a historical conjuncture that signaled a milestone in U.S. foreign policy, the "isolationist" period designed by President Woodrow Wilson between the two world wars (1918–1940). It is, because of its own nature, essentially opportunistic and, transferred into a simple mathematical context, is expressed in the following way:

expansionism = "isolationism" + "internationalism"
                    (action)   (reaction)

The doubt may arise for the reader as to why "internationalism" should be understood in terms of U.S. reaction. However, this should be interpreted as the result of a decision-making process in which, on the basis of a specific reading of the international context as a whole, the United States reacts by assuming external commitments. In the conjuncture following World War II, it was crucial and necessary for global hegemonic design to construct a system of military alliances throughout the entire planet to surround and control the communist adversary. However, the conjuncture in which the U.S. Congress approved NAFTA turned out to be much more complicated.

It should be borne in mind that NAFTA was a project designed in the final days of the Cold War and required a different international scenario, already visualized, in which new threats to the United States broke the boundaries of the traditional political-military operations theater, and the nation had to take on the defense of a different hegemony and on new bases.[35] This draws attention to how the Democrat president Bill Clinton required Republican support in Congress for the approval of NAFTA. It was not the project of a party but of the system and in the debate this viewpoint predominated.[36]

The process of NAFTA approval in the U.S. Congress resulted from the scenario favorable to a new debate, apparently between "isolationists" and "internationalists." In reality, it served as the context for a confrontation between viewpoints that, having the controversy between protectionism and free trade as their framework, were elucidating the new bases for U.S. hegemony. Nevertheless, before reflecting on changes suffered by the U.S. hegemonic project in Latin America, it is necessary to outline its consequences that substantiate the following argument made by Rosario Green, when she claimed that the U.S. global domination project has been expressed in Latin America and the Caribbean in three classic ways: political imposition, invasion and military intervention, and economic manipulation.[37]

The author makes a very incisive observation when she argues that external domination cannot be successful without the backing of Latin American and Caribbean national sectors that, from a position of power, respond to U.S. interests.[38] U.S. policy toward Latin America and the Caribbean, an example of relations between unequals, is aggravated by the fact that one is the superpower within the system. What prevails are the boundaries within which the countries of the hemisphere have had to move. An astute affirmation in this regard is made by Klaus Schubert when he reflects that Latin American foreign policy has two possibilities: It can adjust its instruments to work in terms of self-sustaining national development, or it can devote itself to thoroughly examining the definition of the ideal instruments to negotiate its dependency. Policy elements of one or the other concept are not entirely exclusive, especially in periods of transition, but they do require a clear hierarchization.[39]

In their relations with the United States, Latin America and the Caribbean have fluctuated between periods of either greater autonomy or pronounced alignment with U.S. policy. Without restricting ourselves to a Manichean view of the matter, we can refer to historic examples that underline the phases of greater alignment and greater autonomy in relation to the United States.

After World War II (1945), when Panamericanism assumed the form of the Interamerican System, in the context of emerging U.S. hegemony worldwide, the hemispheric panorama was interpreted in the following terms:

> Other Latin American states, incapable of dealing with the sudden qualitative change taking place in the world of 1945 and still clinging to the classic concept of sovereignty, fell into contradictions in the face of centralized U.S. power. They were destined to fail because the determinisms of the U.S. imperial system—of a very relentless ideology—turned out to be so rigid in the competition with the Soviet Union, that there was no alternative other than alignment with Washington. It is in this security system, of a bipolar orientation, that Latin America lost its special relation with North America (although it remained tied to it orally) and descended to occupy one of the rungs of a chain of pacts. In this way, it was obvious that all attempts to attain autonomy in foreign policy would appear as a potential victory of one side or another and, hence, as a rebellion. In the act of sovereignty the punishment could be direct or indirect.[40]

The second historical phase (1969 to 1979) was, without a doubt, the most dynamic period to date in Latin American and Caribbean foreign policy and the projection of its national interests. The following may be mentioned among the main traits that characterize this period:

1. The restatement of international relations by the large countries of the region (Mexico, Brazil, Argentina, Venezuela), in a process of making their total alignment with the United States more flexible

through activating their relations with Western Europe, Asia, the Soviet Union, and other European socialist countries.

2. The series of nationalist experiences headed by military sectors, with projects to nationalize foreign companies (mainly U.S. enterprises) and/or gradual processes of agrarian reform (Peru, Panama).

3. The reestablishment of diplomatic links with Cuba on the part of Latin American and Caribbean countries (Venezuela, Colombia, Peru, Panama, Jamaica, Guyana, Trinidad and Tobago).

4. The violent response to changes put forward by the Washington triad—U.S. companies—national oligarchies expressed through bloody military coups (Chile, Argentina, Uruguay, Bolivia).[41] The third historical phase began in the decade of the 1990s, although its roots are located in the so-called lost decade—the 1980s—where there is an intermingling between the consolidation of neoliberalism as an economic policy of governments of the region and the deepening of the processes of democratization.[42]

Economic data on that catastrophic decade speaks for itself:

> In global terms, between 1982 and 1990, the region carried out a net transfer of resources to industrialized countries to the approximate value of $233,000 million USD ($163,000 million USD in foreign debt payment, more than $70,000 million USD in terms of the flight of private capital). As never before, the wealthier part of the world extracted from the poorer part the resources to resolve its own crisis and finance its own growth.

"Between 1983 and 1990, the growth of Latin America lowered to an average of 1.5 percent per year. In view of the fact that the population was increasing at an annual rate of 2.1 percent, low economic growth meant a drop in real income per capita of 0.6 percent per year. The 'lost decade' was not then mere stagnation, but a return to levels scarcely above those of 1970."[43] An essential factor in understanding this third phase is the emergence and development during the 1980s of Latin American mechanisms of political agreements, forerunners of the major forums existing today. The fundamental reason for the emergence of these new initiatives was the operational crisis suffered by the main institutions of the Interamerican system—the Organization of American States (OAS) and The Rio Pact—as a consequence of the alignment of the United States with Britain to reconquer the Malvinas/Falklands Islands.[44]

When the basic tendencies characterizing the hemispheric context of the period following the Cold War are analyzed, it is noticeable how the traditional geopolitical vision was displaced and substituted by another agenda that interacted with the emerging geoeconomic vision that responded to the new global challenges. Therefore, the formation of a new hemispheric agenda is apparent, derived in its turn from the new U.S. global agenda. It should be taken into account that the current international scenario reveals a recomposing of U.S. political-military hegemony at a world level. The economic scenario was changing in a different way, however, given the position that countries such as Germany and Japan were taking up, to form a hegemonic set-up shared by these three major powers.

The 1989–1990 biennium, the final period of the Cold War in fact, revealed to Latin America and the Caribbean the framework of the planned new Interamerican relation:

1. U.S. military intervention in Panama, in defense of the new international consensus themes: democracy, human rights and the struggle against narco-trafficking.
2. Launching of the so-called Initiative for the Americas by President George Bush in June 1990.
3. NAFTA, as a defensive measure in the face of the deepening of the European Union in 1992.

The new U.S. hemispheric project was not aiming to push forward a process of integration similar to that being developed in Western Europe. Unlike Intereuropean relations, more balanced by the economic potential of the majority of member countries, U.S. relations with Latin America and the Caribbean are marked by a clear asymmetry, a factor that, to even further aggravate the scenario, is reproduced in drawing comparisons among the Latin American and Caribbean countries themselves. Nevertheless, it cannot be denied that for changes to have taken place certain convergences had to be generated between both parties. Howard Wiarda put forward the following points about the Washington Consensus developing at the beginning of the decade:

•   It includes Wilsonian idealism (democracy, human rights, free markets) as well as practical national interests (stability, an economic climate that the United States can dominate).
•   It puts an end to fratricidal and politically costly debates (for both parties) in the 1980s decade.

- It has the support of the majority of groups of experts, mass media, Congress, the business sector, religious groups, and so on.
- It provides unity and coherence to a bureaucracy and a process of formulating a foreign policy that is other than antagonistic and conflictive.
- It has the backing of dominant tendencies in both Latin American and U.S. foreign policy. It puts an end to the brutal conflict of the last 40 years between both sides over the agenda and political priorities.[45]

There is no doubt that the region has gradually moved toward a position of consensus with the United States since the end of the 1980s in an agenda conforming to themes ranging from the perceived need to apply First World remedies to the problem of the foreign debt to the identification of opportunities that the FTAA might provide in the new global scenario.

We may move on to the development of some ideas on the new U.S. hemispheric project using the following question as a starting point: Was the FTAA the final goal of the project begun by the Initiative for the Americas and continued with the North American Free Trade Agreement (NAFTA), or did it become an inevitable tendency of the process underway? In other words, is the Free Trade Area of the Americas (FTAA) the American version of the integrationist project or hemispheric scenario necessary for new Interamerican relations?

It does not seem reasonable to accept that the United States, in response to the challenges of the European Union, outlined the need for a continental bloc with similar features and goals to those established by Europe. In no way is the Intereuropean world comparable. In comparison to the relative equalities in the European system, the Western hemisphere is plagued by economies as vulnerable as those existing in Central America and the Caribbean together with the presence of a multiplicity of sociopolitical problems constituting a threat to the democratic stability of the region. One might think that the plan drawn up was to create a strategic program of economic integration, such as NAFTA. In the context of the approval of NAFTA (1993), this is what was behind the imminent incorporation of Chile, at that time proof of eloquent economic dynamism.

Notwithstanding this, in the conjuncture leading to FTAA preparation for the Americas Summit (Miami, December 1994) the agenda visualized by Latin America and the Caribbean was a list of demands, unlikely to be met, as has been proven to date.[46] FTAA has to be accepted more as a framework for current relations between the United States, Latin America, and the Caribbean meeting the requirements of the global economy. It is a hemispheric project from the perspective of U.S. hegemony. It is the historically desired scenario, without tangible extra continental threats, that allows the United States to undertake a hemispheric realignment not only encompassed within the rigid ideological-military parameters of the Cold War but also governed by free trade from the U.S. hegemonic vision.

A similar scenario was that which the United States attempted to prematurely create when it held the First Panamerican Conference in October 1889. Prematurely, it is argued, because for the United States there were two unresolved challenges in that conjuncture; the first was not having geopolitical control over the hemispheric scenario. The second was not having risen to the position scale that it currently occupies in order to participate from a position of advantage and choice in the global geoeconomy. Both challenges were the result of not yet having acquired continental-global hegemonic control. Let us look more deeply into this conjuncture, however, recalling that in 1889 the United States was rapidly advancing in its capitalist economic development, after having resolved with the War of Secession (1862–1865) the hitherto insoluble contradiction between the northern and southern states in the country.

Therefore, the route taken by the emerging unified nation was that of a geoeconomy, and therein lie the basic proposals put to Latin America in October 1889. The poor results taught the U.S. government two important lessons: the first, that there could not be an efficient geoeconomy if it were not complemented by an adequate geopolitical agenda, and the second, the need to reverse the terms and seek, on the basis of a controlled geopolitical scenario, the construction of the desired geoeconomic agenda. These lessons were applied in Cuba and Puerto Rico in 1898 and during the first quarter of the twentieth century, with successive military interventions in Central America and the Caribbean.

History confirms these observations. World War II had to take place, with the emergence of the United States as the main power on the planet, to create the opportunity to install an Interamerican system that would signal a major step forward in relation to the Panamerican conferences held up until the prewar period. However, the Interamerican system that emerged remained captive of the confines in the Cold War, a scenario that circumscribed priorities to strict management of regional geopolitics.

One hundred years after that First Panamerican Conference, the hemispheric situation was highly favorable to the United States. The fall of the Soviet Union and European socialist countries had broken Cuba's main strategic alliances. Cuba was obliged to throw itself into the quest to reinsert itself into the international economy, in the context of a strengthening of the U.S. economic blockade. The invasion of Granada in October 1983 brought about the conditions for a Caribbean realignment with the United States. The electoral defeat of the Sandinistas (February 1990) and the negotiated solutions to the internal conflicts in El Salvador and Guatemala, together with the U.S. invasion of Panama, led to a strengthening of the rigid geopolitical paradigm applied to Central America by Washington. As a generalized context, it was the advance and consolidation of the processes of democratization.

Therefore, moving beyond the Cold War geopolitical scenario allowed the United States to push forward with its geoeconomic agenda as a response to contemporary global threats. Among aspects figuring in the geopolitical agenda are the ongoing matter of Cuba, with the focus not on international relations with the island, but on the deterioration of its internal situation and the search for a "peaceful transition" to a multiparty system under the model of representative democracy. Another of the main themes is narco-trafficking that, in spite of occupying a place on the agenda since the 1980s, had come to acquire the dimension of a global threat with a specific impact on the hemisphere. Likewise, migration is an important issue with particular repercussions in U.S. relations with the Greater Caribbean (a concept including Central America, Mexico, Colombia, and Venezuela, in addition to the Caribbean islands).

The environment is another of the global challenges with notable emphasis on the discussions surrounding the approval of NAFTA on the part of Mexican environmental organizations. Finally, an emerging theme that should not be overlooked is the rise to political power, presidential or parliamentary, of the forces considered to be leftist or simply having nationalist agendas not approved in the United States. Such is the case of Hugo Chávez in Venezuela or the Partido Frente Amplio in Uruguay, as expressions of widespread disillusionment with traditional political parties.

We will not conclude this aspect of the discussion without referring to the astute commentary made by Craig Van Grasstek, international assessor to the permanent secretary to the Latin American Economic System (SELA) in which he states that the United States has recently adopted a more energetic focus with regard to the review of social contracts of other countries. This includes the promotion of changes in labor relations and environmental protection policies, in addition to laws governing competition and sanctions to punish bribery and corruption. Although the United

States presents these themes under the rubric of trade policy, it is impossible to ignore the many delicate political questions they raise. Taken as a whole, these diverse national and international political matters could lead to serious tensions in the negotiation, approval, and execution of the FTAA.[47]

This author endorses the thesis, with which we agree, that political factors may turn out to be decisive for FTAA's success. In this respect, FTAA should be understood as an economic project suited to a hemispheric context that is politically favorable to the United States. And it is precisely at this point in the analysis where the hypothesis of Neopanamericanism is located.

From the outset, Panamericanism was marked by contradictions generated by U.S. policy itself. The supposed Panamerican multilateralism was more questioned, neutralized by the unilateralism of the Monroe Doctrine; the Roosevelt Corollary's interventionism; postwar anticommunism; and the unilateral decision by the United States to support Britain in its reconquest of the Malvinas/Falklands Islands in 1982. This latter event turned out to be the catalyst for a crisis in the Interamerican System that has endured until the present, given that the system's main agent, the United States, violated Article IV of the Charter of the Organization of American States (OAS), referring to the interference of extracontinental powers in hemispheric affairs.

Nevertheless, this crisis activated Latin American political will to seek its own solutions to existing problems. The steps taken by the Contadora Group, the Contadora formula, the Group of Support arising from the Group of Eight should be recalled in this respect, which led to the consolidation of the Rio Group, the entire process being characterized by a central axis, the transition to democracy. This element turns out to be decisive when it comes to understanding why we are speaking of Neopanamericanism. It is the result of:

1. Latin America absorbed in the post Cold–War period and immersed in a process of regional democratization, functional to the interests of the United States.
2. The recognition of the current themes of U.S. foreign policy: democracy, human rights, and a free market.
3. Latin America struggling to overcome the deep social and economic crisis it faces, driven by neoliberal policy that opens its domestic markets to free exchange.
4. The United States responding to economic globalization through the mechanism of its own bloc, NAFTA.

We have, for the first time in history of Interamerican relations, the conditions in which the United States could unfurl the banners of Panamericanism with greater possibilities of achieving established goals, or to be precise, Neopanamericanism. Therefore, there is now a new scenario (Neopanamerican) in which the following conditions are apparent:

1. Economic global-regional interdependence.
2. Essential consensus between the geopolitical and geoeconomic hemispheric agendas.
3. Development of an interactive U.S.-Latin American-Caribbean process that, with NAFTA as its basis and free trade agreements as its instruments, fosters diverse plans for subregional integration, namely CARICOM, the Central American System of Integration (SICA), Community of Andean Countries (CPA) and the Common Market of the South (MERCOSUR).
4. Generalized consensus around the creation of a FTAA.
5. Essential consensus among governments, national oligarchies, and large multinationals.

However, the consensus for the FTAA reached by the United States in the 1994 Miami Summit does not guarantee its construction. That will require the reauthorization of "Fast-Track authority" by the U.S. Congress and successful negotiations with MERCOSUR. As of this writing the prospects for the renewal of Fast Track are brightening, but even with Fast Track, completion of the agreement by 2005 is not certain.

Some Final Considerations

By setting out the existence of a Neopanamerican scenario with all the advantages working in favor of the United States, the thesis of the success of U.S. policy is not automatically endorsed. On the contrary, the essentially conflictive nature of Interamerican relations has to be seriously taken into account, in addition to regional economic vulnerability, political fragility, and social instability. We live in a different Latin America and Caribbean, more conscious of the need to defend our own interests.

Neopanamericanism has become viable insofar as FTAA has proposed, but it is likely to perish if the region loses its incentive and motivation for free trade. This is particularly so if it is taken into account that the application of protectionist formulae continues to be a recurrent strategy in U.S. trade policy.

For this reason, there should be an awareness of the real options to which the region might aspire in a project shaped by U.S. hegemony. Without denying the presence of the United States and its quota of hemispheric power, Latin America and the Caribbean could and should undertake a process of independent regional integration and, as part of this dynamic, work on two fundamental levels that will allow it greater strength in the future: increase the margins of economic and political independence with regard to the United States, and reduce subregional differences to attain a greater degree of compatibility and harmony in their processes of regional integration and global insertion.

Notes

1. According to Dr. Jorge Hernández: "From the US standpoint, 'national security' refers to the necessary attainment of the objectives of each nation-state, both internally as well as externally. It is a process that encounters 'threats' in the face of which it must deploy economic, military, political and ideological forces capable of triumphing over them or neutralizing them. This is the conception which forms the basis of the United States' traditional strategic doctrine. known precisely as the 'national security doctrine.' It was propagated and developed under Truman's government, in the heat of the law (1947 National Security Act) which led to the set up of the Central Intelligence Agency (CIA) and the National Security Council (NSC)." Jorge Hernández Martínez, 'La politica latinoamericana de Estados Unidos ' seguridad nacional y subversión,' in *Revista Universidad de la Habana*, no. 230 (May–August 1987). Havana, Cuba, 180–181.

2. For Kenneth N. Waltz, national security can only be defended by acting against other nation-states. Therefore, the United States suppresses threats to its security undermining other actors and generally sidelining domestic affairs. See: Kenneth N. Waltz, *Teoria de la politica internacional* (Buenos Aires, Argentina: Colección Estudios Internacionales, 1998), 96.

3. Sergio Bitar, "Economics and Security: Contradictions in US Latin American Relations." In Kevin J. Middlebrook and Carlos Rico (ed.), *The United States and Latin America in the 1980s, Contending Perspectives on a Decade of Crisis* (Pittsburgh: University of Pittsburgh Press, 1986), 594.

4. *The Americas at the Cross Roads: Inter-American Dialogue.* Woodrow Wilson International Center for Scholars. Washington, DC (April, 1983), 40–41.

5. Larz Schoultz, *National Security and the United States Policy toward Latin America* (Princeton, NJ: Princeton University Press, 1987), 235.

6. Larz Schoultz, *Beneath the United States. A History of U.S. Policy toward Latin America* (Cambridge: Harvard University Press, 1998), Preface, XV.

7. They are the executive, congress, the departments of state, defense, the treasury, trade and justice, among others; in addition to the so-called Intelligence Community in which the CIA, FBI, National Security Agency, and the DEA, among others, may be highlighted.

8. See Michael H. Hunt, *Ideology and U.S. Foreign Policy* (New Haven:Yale University Press, 1987), 19.

9. Akira Iriye, *From Nationalism to Internationalism: U.S. Foreign Policy to 1914* (Routledge and Kegan Paul, Great Britain, 1977) 5.

10. Jefferson to Madison, April 27, 1809, in H. A. Washington, *The Writings of Thomas Jefferson,* vol. 5 (Washington, DC, 1853), 444.

11. James Petras and Michael Erisman, "La Doctrina Monroe y la hegemonia de Estados Unidos en América Latina," in *Cuadernos de la realidad nacional,* no.16 (April 1973): 42.

12. María del Rosario Rodríguez Díaz, *El Destino Manifiesto en el discurso político norteamericano (1776–1849)* (Hidalgo, MX: Institute of Historical Research, University of San Nicolás de Hidalgo, 1997), 19.

13. James Bryce, "Política, carácter y opinión de los Estados Unidos (1891)," In *EUA: Documentos de su historia política. Volume VI.* (Mexico City: Dr. José María Luís Mora Research Institute, 1988), 191.

14. Albert Weinberg, *Destino Manifiesto* (Buenos Aires: Paidós 1968), 16.

15. James Petras and Michael Erisman, "La Doctrina Monroe y la hegemonía de Estados Unidos en América Latina," op cit., 41.

16. Alexander De Conde, *A History of American Foreign Policy,* 2nd edition (New York: Charles Scribner's Sons, 1971), 303.

17. Piero Gleijeses, "The Limits of Sympathy: The United States and the Independence of Spanish America," in *Journal of Latin American Studies,* no. 24, (S.F.).

18. Demetrio Boersner, *Relaciones Internacionales de América Latina. Breve historia* (Caracas: Editorial Nueva Sociedad, Caracas,Venezuela, 1996) 79.

19. Piero Gleijeses, "The Limits of Sympathy," op cit., 495–502.

20. *E.U.A. Documentos de su historia política,* vol. I, op cit., 396.

21. See John O'Sullivan, "Nuestro Destino Manifiesto" (July 1845), in *E.U.A. Documentos de su historia política. Op cit.,* 592.

22. See: J. Pratt, "The Origin of Manifest Destiny," in *American Historical Review,* vol. 32, no. 4, (July 1927): 798.

23. Alexander De Conde, *A History of American Foreign Policy: Growth to World Power (1700–1914),* 3rd edition (New York: Charles Scribner's Sons, 1978).

24. See Manuel Medina Castro. *Estados Unidos y América Latina, siglo XIX* (Havana: Casa de las Américas, 1968), 652.

25. See a copy of the text of this document in Carlos M. Rama, *La imagen de los Estados Unidos en la América Latina.* (Mexico City: Secretaria de Educación Pública, 1975), 51.

26. Ibid., 52–53.
27. See, in this respect: Gordon Cornell-Smith, *El Sistema Interamericano* (Mexico City: Fondo de Cultura Económica, 1971), 487; and Frank Niess, *A Hemisphere to Itself: A History of U.S.-Latin American Relations* (London: Zed Books Ltd., 1990), 229.
28. Salvador E. Morales, *Primera Conferencia Panamericana: Raices del modelo hegemonista de integración* (Mexico City: Jorge L. Tamayo Scientific Research Centre, A.C., 1994), 120.
29. See Emmanuel Wallerstein, *El moderno sistema mundial,* vol. II (Mexico City: Editiorial Siglo XXI, 1984), 51.
30. Antonio Gramsci, *Quaderne de Cancere* (Torino Einaudi, 1975), 1638. Taken from Alberto Van Klaveren, "La crisis de la hegmonia norteamericana y sus repercusiones en América Latina. Antecedentes y proyecciones futuras," in *Cuadernos Semestrales* CIDE, no. 8, second semester of 1980, 108.
31. Roberto González Gómez, *Política Exterior de Estados Unidos: doctrinas y dilemas* (Havana: Raúl Roa García Superior Institute of International Relations, 1988).
32. Ibid., 3–4.
33. Arthur Schlesinger Jr., "Back to the Womb? Isolationism's Renewed Threat," *Foreign Affairs* (August 1995): 2.
34. James Petras and Michael Erisman, "La Doctrina Monroe," op cit., 42.
35. Margaret M. Cummings, "De la seguridad al comercio en las relaciones entre Estados Unidos y América Latina: como se explica el apoyo estadounidense al tratado de Libre Comercio con Mexico," in *Estados Unidos. Informe Trimestral,* vol. III, no. 1, CIDE (Spring 1993): 5–30.
36. James K. Galbraith, "A oposiçao norteamericano ao NAFTA," in *Política Externa,* vol. 3, no. 2 (September–October–November, 1994): 77–83.
37. Rosario Green, "Carter y el ciclo crisis—acercamiento en las relaciones interamericanas," in *Cuadernos Semestrales* (April 1997): 15.
38. Ibid., 16.
39. Klaus Schubert, "Nación, desarrollo y nacionalismo," in *Teoría y práctica de la política exterior latinoamericano,* ed. Gerhard Drekonja and Juna G. Tokatlián (Bogota: Friedrich Ebert Foundation Colombia, 1983), Prologue xix.
40. Gerhard Drekonja, "Contenidos y metas de la Nueva Política Exterior Latinoamericana," in *Teoría y práctica de la política exterior latinoamericana,* op cit., 131; and Demetrio Boersner, *Relaciones Internacionales de América Latina. Breve Historia,* op cit., 230–235.
41. Alberto Van Klaveren, "El lugar de Estados Unidos en la Política Exterior Latinoamericana," in *Teoría y práctica de la política exterior latinoamericana,* op cit., 131; and Demetrio Boersner, *Relaciones Internacionales de América Latina. Breve Historia,* op cit., 230–235.
42. Carlos Oliva Campos, "Estados Unidos y los procesos de democratization in América Latina" in *Revista Cubana de Ciencias Sociales,* no. 28 (1994): 32–48.

43. Demetrio Boersner, *Relaciones Internacionales de América Latina. Breve historia,* op cit., 266.
44. Carlos Oliva Campos and Juan E. Cruz Cabrera, "Estados Unidos frente al conflicto de las Malvinas," *Documentos,* (Havana: Prensa Latina, 1983).
45. Howard J. Wiarda, "Consenso logrado, consenso perdido. Desfases en la política estadounidense hacia América Latina en el final del siglo," in *Cuadernos de Nueva Sociedad* (Venezuela), 40.
46. Permanent Secretary to the Latin American Economic System (SELA). "Qué agenda para la Cumbre Hemisférica?" in *Notas estratégicas* (Venezuela, January to March 1994): 114–115.
47. Craig Van Grasstek, "El ALCA: Opciones y Perspectivas de Estados Unidos y América Latina y el Caribe," in *Secretaria Permanente del Sela Dinámica de la Relaciones externas de América Latina y el Caribe* (Buenos Aires: Ediciones Corregidor, 1998), 191.

Bibliography

The Americas at the Crossroad. (1983). Woodrow Wilson International Center for Scholars. Washington, DC: Inter American Dialogue. Woodrow Wilson International Center for Scholars.

Bitar, Sergio. (1986). "Economics and Security: Contradictions in U.S. Latin American Relations." In Kevin J. Middlebrook and Carlos Rico (ed.), *The United States and Latin America in the 1980s, Contending Perspectives on a Decade of Crisis.* Pittsburgh: University of Pittsburgh Press.

Boersner, Demetrio. (1996). *Relaciones Internacionales de América Latina. Breve historia.* Caracas: Editorial Nueva Sociedad.

Byrce, James. (1988). "Política, carácter y opinión de los Estados Unidos (1891)." In *EUA: Documentos de su historia política. Volume VI.* Mexico City: Dr. José María Luís Mora Research Institute.

Campos, Carlos Oliva. (1994). "Estados Unidos y los procesos de democratización in América Latina." *Revista Cubana de Ciencias Sociales,* no. 28, pp. 32–48.

Campos, Carlos Oliva and Juan E. Cruz Cabrera. (1983). "Estados Unidos frente al conflicto de las Malvinas." *Documentos.* Havana: Prensa Latina.

Castro, Manuel Medina. (1968). *Estados Unidos y América Latina, siglo XIX.* Havana: Casa de las Américas.

Cornell-Smith, Gordon. (1971). *El Sistema Interamericano.* Mexico City: Fondo de Cultura Económica.

Cummings, Margaret M. (1993). "De la seguridad al comercio en las relaciones entre Estados Unidos y América Latina: como se explica el apoyo estadounidense al tratado de Libre Comercio con Mexico." In *Estados Unidos. Informe Trimestral,* vol. III. no. 1, Spring.

De Conde, Alexander. (1971). *A History of American Foreign Policy.* Second Edition. New York: Charles Scribner's Sons.

De Conde, Alexander. (1978). *A History of American Foreign Policy: Growth to World Power (1700–1914).* Third Edition. New York: Charles Scribner's Sons.

Díaz, María del Rosario Rodríguez. (1997). *El Destino Manifesto en el discurso político norteamericano (1776–1849).* Hidalgo, MX: Institute of Historical Research, University of San Nicolás de Hidalgo.

Galbraith, James K. (1994). "A oposiçao norteamericano ao NAFTA." *Política Externa,* vol. 3, no. 2, pp. 77–83.

Gleijeses, Piero. (1992). "The Limits of Sympathy: The United States and the Independence of Spanish America." *Journal of Latin American Studies,* no. 24. October.

Gómez, Roberto González. (1988). *Política Exterior de Estados Unidos: doctrinas y dilemas.* Havana: Raúl Roa García Superior Institute of International Relations.

Green, Rosario. (1997). "Carter y el ciclo crisis—acercamiento en las relaciones interamericanas." *Cuadernos Semestrales.* April.

Hernández Martínez, Jorge. (1987). "La politica latinoamericana de'Estados Unidos ' seguridad nacional y subversion." *Revista Universidad de la Habana,* no. 230. May-August.

Hunt, Michael H. (1987). *Ideology and U.S. Foreign Policy.* New Haven: Yale University Press.

Iriye, Akira. (1977). *From Nationalism to Internationalism U.S. Foreign Policy to 1914.* London: Routledge and Kegan Paul.

Morales, Salvador E. (1994). *Primera Conferencia Panamericana: Raices del modelo hegemonista de integración.* Mexico City: Jorge L. Tamayo Scientific Research Centre.

Niess, Frank. (1990). *A Hemisphere to Itself: A History of U.S.-Latin American Relations.* London: Zed Books.

Petras, James and Michael Erisman. (1973). "La Doctrina Monroe y la hegemonia de Estados Unidos en América Latina." *Cuadernos de la realidad nacional,* no.16, April.

Pratt, J. (1927). "The Origin of Manifest Destiny," *American Historical Review,* vol. 32, no. 4, July.

Rama, Carlos M. (1975). *La imagen de los Estados Unidos en la América Latina.* Mexico City: Secretaria de Educación Pública.

Schlesinger, Arthur, Jr., (1995). "Back to the Womb? Isolationism's Renewed Threat." *Foreign Affairs,* August.

Schoultz, Larz. (1987). *National Security and the United States Policy toward Latin America.* Princeton, NJ: Princeton University Press.

Schoultz, Larz. (1998). *Beneath the United States. A History of U.S. Policy toward Latin America.* Cambridge: Harvard University Press.

Schubert, Klaus. (1983). "Nación, desarrollo y nacionalismo." In *Teoría y práctica de la política exterior latinoamericano,* ed. Gerhard Drekonja and Juna G. Tokatlián. Bogota: Friedrich Ebert Foundation Colombia.

Van Grasstek, Craig. (1998). "El ALCA: Opciones y Perspectivas de Estados Unidos y América Latina y el Caribe." In Secretaria Permanente del Sela.

Dinámica de la Relaciones externas de América Latina y el Caribe. Buenos Aires: Ediciones Corregidor.

Wallerstein, Emmanuel. (1984). *El moderno sistema mundial,* vol. II. Mexico City: Editiorial Siglo XXI.

Waltz, Kenneth N. (1998). *Teoria de la politica internacional.* Buenos Aires: Colección Estudios Internacionales.

Weinberg, Albert. (1968). *Destino Manifiesto.* Buenos Aires: Paidós.

Chapter 2

Culture and National Interest in the United States: Conservative Perceptions of Latin America

Luis Fernando Ayerbe

The dissolution of the Warsaw Pact, the reunification of Germany, and the disappearance of the Soviet Union stated in a uniquely clear way the victory of the United States in the bipolar dispute, which characterized the structure of the international relations during Cold War. However, the defeat of this great empire was not seen, even by the most optimistic, as a perpetual guarantee of peace. The globalization of economic competition, which promotes levels of social exclusion that cross national borders and the concentration of development in well-fixed boundaries, may generate new sources of conflict among the losers of the new world order in formation.

The potential reaction of the "losers" cannot be compared to the previous powerful Soviet threat, but it is more localized and relatively foreseeable. The spectacle of poverty, although differentiated in its gravity, has no exclusive territory. For workers of rich countries, the ghost of unemployment endangers their hopes of security within advanced capitalism.

For representative sectors of trends of opinion, think tanks and private organizations endowed with sufficient influence to interact with the decision-making system of U.S. foreign policy, the perception of threat concentrates on the potential conflicts generated by the resentment in social sectors, countries, and regions that consider themselves victims of the new order, which can stimulate fundamentalist ideas and behaviors tending to question the principal cultural base of historic supremacy of liberal capitalism and Western civilization.

For some authors, the strategic aspects that derive from the affirmation of cultural identity assume each time a bigger role in the characterization of the new sources of conflict. Values and attitudes related with "advanced" or "regressive" cultures loom as the principal explanatory issues for the uneven levels of development, both among countries and in ethnic groups within national frames. Samuel Huntington,[1] one of the representative authors of this approach, considers that

> the fundamental source of conflict in this new world will not be primarily ideological or primarily economic. The great divisions among humankind and the dominating source of conflict will be cultural. Nation states will remain the most powerful actors in world affairs, but the principal conflicts of global politics will occur between nations and groups of different civilizations. (1993:22)

For Huntington, the challenges to Western political and economic supremacy and the values that characterize its cultural identity define a new international situation in which the conflict between "the West and the rest" assumes the leading role. Seven civilizations integrate "the rest": Japanese, Chinese, Islamic, Latin American, Hindu, Slavic-Orthodox, and African.

In a globalized world, the consolidation of Western hegemony is not exclusively a foreign policy task, the challenges are present within domestic affairs. The victory of a way of life is never permanent and the analogy with the decadence of the Roman Empire, after defeating its great enemies, is one of the ghosts that maintains this state of concern. According to Huntington,

> Given the domestic forces pushing toward heterogeneity, diversity, multiculturalism, and ethnic and racial division, however the United States, perhaps more than most countries, may need an opposing other to maintain its unity. Two millennia ago in 84 B.C., after the Romans had completed their conquest of the known world by defeating the armies of Mithradates, Sulla posed the question: "Now the universe offers us no more enemies, what may be the fate of the Republic?" The answer came quickly; the republic collapsed a few years later. (1997:32)

On commemorating its fiftieth anniversary, *Commentary,* the principal neoconservative organ, surveyed intellectuals of different theoretical and political affiliations as to their position on the following statement:

In the eyes of many observers, the United States, which in 1945 entered upon the postwar era confident in its democratic purposes and serene in the possession of a common culture, is now, fifty years later, moving toward balkanization or even breakdown. Pointing to different sorts of evidence—multiculturalism and/or racial polarization; the effects of unchecked immigration; increased economic and social stratification; distrust of authority; the dissolution of shared moral and religious values—such observers conclude in their various ways that our national project is unraveling. (*Commentary*, 1995:23)

Among the exponents of the conservative[2] perspective who answered this survey, we note three analyses that represent the concern with the future of the West and a diagnosis that attributes the problems to predominant national factors, blaming "elite" sectors for those problems. For Elliot Abrams, assistant secretary of state during Ronald Reagan's presidency,

Those elites are principally a mixture of liberal/Left politicians, members of the media and the academy, with reinforcements from the liberal churches, black leaders, the American Jewish establishment, and (intermittently) the judiciary. In their long march toward victory in remaking American culture, their successes have been great. The amazing proliferation of systems in employment and education, the advent of multiculturalism, and the terrible coarsening of social life in only thirty years all give testimony to what they have wrought. (*Commentary*, 1995:24)

For Zbigniev Brzezinski, national security adviser during Jimmy Carter's presidency, the loss of hegemony of the white, Anglo-Saxon and Protestant (WASP) elite is one of the main causes of this state of disorder:

In recent years, the collapse of the WASP elite and the replacement of the traditional instruments for inoculating values by the TV-Hollywood-Mass-Media cartel has produced in America a new dominant and style-setting culture. It can be called a Mediterranean Sea culture in order to underline its contrast to the North Sea ethic. It stressed self-enjoyment, entertainment, sexual promiscuity, and the almost explicit repudiation of any social norms. Controlled by a cartel that is driven exclusively by material self-interest, TV has replaced the schools, churches, and even the family as the principal mechanism for the transmission of values. (*Commentary*, 1995:38)

Francis Fukuyama, former adviser to the U.S. State Department, attributes the main responsibility to the decline of social capital:

One of the most insidious changes that has taken place in American life over the past couple of generations is the secular decline in what Tocqueville labeled the American art of association—that is, the ability of American to organize their own society in voluntary groups and associations. This falling-off can be measured in a variety of ways: in declining memberships in traditional service organizations like the Red Cross, Elks, or Rotarians; in the decrease between the 1960s and the present in the numbers of Americans who, when polled, say they trust "most people" (from two-thirds to one-third); and in the symptoms of fraying community like rising litigation and violent crime. (*Commentary*, 1995:56)

The arguments issued by these authors represent some of the principal conservative worries concerning the new challenges of post–Cold War reality. In a wider scope of the national political and ideological debate, the defenders of the Western roots of North American identity are concerned that the growing cultural pluralism of the United States threatens to undermine the hold of Western civilization, a process that they call de-Westernization. Within this worry, the ghost of the developing world looms up.

James Kurth,[3] using the Huntington approach as reference, considers that the real clash of civilization is "a clash between Western civilization and a different grand alliance, one composed of the multicultural and the feminist movements. It is, in short, a clash between Western and post-Western civilizations" (1995:19). For Kurth, the feminist movement plays a central role as promoter of multiculturalism: "It provides the numbers, having reached a central mass first in academia and now in the media and the law. It promotes the theories, such as deconstructionism and postmodernism. And it provides much of the energy, the leadership, and the political clout" (1995:26). Closing the essay, he synthesizes the nature of his anguish: "Who, in the United States of the future, will still believe in Western civilization. Most practically, who will believe in it enough to fight, kill and die for it in a clash of civilizations?" (1995:27).

For Irving Kristol, historical leader of neoconservativism,[4] the developing-world component of multiculturalism forms part of an anti-American and anti-Western political and ideological strategy:

It is no exaggeration to say that these campus radicals (professors as well as students) having given up on the "class struggle"—the American workers all being conscientious objectors—have now moved to an agenda of ethnic-racial conflict. The agenda, in its educational dimension, has as its explicit purpose to induce in the minds and sensibilities of minority students a "Third World consciousness"—that is the very phrase they use. What these radicals blandly call multiculturalism is as much a "war against the West" as Nazism and Stalinism ever were. (1995:52)

For Kristol, the racial component associated with the black movement represents the principal political strength of this movement and gives it a differentiated profile in relation to immigration of Latin American origin, further inclined to assimilation: "Multiculturalism is a desperate—and surely self-defeating—strategy for coping with the educational deficiencies, and associated social pathologies, of young blacks. There is no evidence that a substantial number of Hispanic parents would like their children to know more about Símon Bolívar and less about George Washington" (1995:50).

In the report of the 1993 meeting of the Trilateral Commission held in Washington, the concern on American society "thirdworldizing" and the perception of a latent civil war atmosphere also shows up in sessions dedicated to the domestic situation in the United States. According to Marian Wright Edelman, President of the Children's Defense Fund:

> Ironically, as Communism has been collapsing all around the world, the American Dream has been collapsing all around America—for millions of families, youths and children, of all races and classes.
>
> We're in danger of becoming two nations—one of the First World privilege and another of Third World deprivation—struggling against increasing odds to peacefully co-exist, as a beleaguered middle class barely holds on. (*Trialogue,* 1993:15)

Culture and National Interest in the United States

In the U.S. Department of State perspective, the international moment is favorable to place the country's foreign policies at the service of promoting "universal" values of human coexistence. Madeleine Albright, secretary of state under President Clinton, explained in her speech before the U.S. Chamber of Commerce the importance of approving the "fast track" for the negotiation of commercial agreements, the intimate relationship between defending those values and the projection of the country's national interests:

> Since taking office, I have stressed my belief that the United States has a historic opportunity to help bring the world closer together around basic principles of democracy, open markets, law, and a commitment to peace. If we seize this opportunity, we can ensure that our economy will continue to

grow, our workers will have access to better jobs, and our leadership will be felt wherever U.S. interests are engaged. We will also fuel an expanding global economy and give more countries a stake in the international system, thereby denying nourishment to the forces of extremist violence that feed on depravation across our planet.

The best course for our nation is not to curse globalization but to shape it. Because we have the world's most competitive economy and its most productive work force, we're better positioned than any other nation to do so. (1997:6)

The emphasis on defending principles does not represent an option to an idealist approach to international relations. For Clinton's government, the first to be elected in post–Cold War context, the combined defense of democracy and market freedom as guarantees of world peace, expressed hegemonic national objectives. At the same time that it legitimated the Cold War banners, it placed the ideal and real frontiers of coexistence in the world within liberal capitalism, with the United States in the center of this system.

Outside of official discourse, divergence exists among foreign politics analysts on the role to be assumed by the United States. Internationalists and isolationists divide themselves into opposite camps between keeping international relations active or retracting to the domestic arena, concentrating efforts on the political, economic, and cultural strengthening of the nation. On this last position, Huntington's approach stands as one that looks to cultural identity for invaluable support, capable of solidifying domestic and international political alliances that will ensure the survival of the Western way of life. This position questions the validity of strategies guided by "big destinies":

> The national interest is national restraint, and that appears to be the only national interest the American people are willing to support at this time in their history. Hence, instead of formulating unrealistic schemes for grand endeavors abroad, foreign policy elites might well devote their energies to designing plans for lowering American involvement in the world in ways that will safeguard possible future national interests. (1997:49)

Huntington defends limits on immigration and the creation of domestic "Americanization" programs designed to the assimilation of immigrants and solidification of loyalties with national identity: "Reviving a stronger sense of national identity would also require countering the cults of diversity and multiculturalism within the United States. It would probably involve limiting immigration . . . and developing new public and private Americanization programs to counter the factors enhancing diaspora loyalties and to promote the assimilation of immigrants" (1997:48).

The need for an effective strategy adapted to the new challenges, is defended by the critics of isolationism. Zalmay Khalilzad, from the RAND Corporation, considers the global leadership of the United States as the best alternative to hold back eventual hostile powers and avoid the return to the multipolar system previous to World War I. For him, the best of worlds is that in which U.S. hegemony has no rivals:

> First, the global environment will be more open and more receptive to American values: democracy, free markets, and the rule of law. Second, such a world has a better chance of dealing cooperatively with its major problems, such as nuclear proliferation, threat of regional hegemony by renegade states, and low-level conflicts. Finally, U.S. leadership will help preclude the rise of another hostile global rival, enabling the United States and the world to avoid another global cold or hot war and all its dangers, including a global nuclear exchange. It is therefore more conductive to global stability than a bipolar or a multipolar balance-of-power system. (1995:21)

James Kurth, one of the most radical supporters of the thesis of "clash of civilizations," promotes from the same premises as Huntington an opposite position on U.S. international behavior. "America is an artificial nation, not a natural one, a nation that has been 'socially constructed,' not organically grown. America must also be socially reconstructed periodically. Otherwise, it will cease to be a nation" (1996:19). Historically, external and domestic threats to "American Doctrine" represented motivating elements of national cohesion. In the new global order, "the task of the United States is to be the motor and monitor for the international order and the model and mentor for the regional spheres of influence. In short, it is to be the global hegemon of the regional hegemons, the boss of all the bosses" (1996:19). Within a domestic frame, Kurth agrees with Huntington in recognizing threats to the strengthening of national identity:

> Economically, national consolidation is being undermined by an unbalanced pursuit of the global economy, putting at risk "the promise of American life" for a majority of Americans. Culturally, it is being undermined by uncontrolled immigration (especially from neighbors in the original regional sphere) and by the ideology of multiculturalism. . . . These divisions will have to be healed with a new New Deal and an Americanization project, ones suited to the specific conditions of our time. Otherwise we may

degenerate into a new civil war, this time not a "War between the States" but more a war of all against all. (1996:19)

The different positions presented on the new role of the United States in the world reflects certain uneasiness with the realities generated by the realization of the two great aims stated at the end of World War II: (1) an open world economy; and (2) the defeat of the Soviet Union. It is hard to visualize the threats to economic prosperity, social and cultural cohesion, and Western territorial safety presented in those analyses, mainly in a context in which (1) political organizations that defend anticapitalist programs have no backing from nuclear powers with ambitions for international hegemony; (2) in social movements, agendas centered on the banner of citizenship predominate, and they aim at constructive restorations: democratization of economic prosperity benefits, respect for political and cultural plurality; and (3) the majority of countries deregulate their markets and open their doors to global capitalism.

More than an order to be created, the presented analyses are fundamentally worried about the order to be kept. On this field, important coincidences exist in defining the main threats to the "Western way of life": (1) power politics of hostile countries (Arab world and China are mostly mentioned), capable of unleashing armament races, disputes on natural resources, wars; (2) regional instability generated by collapsed states as a consequence of politicization of ethnic differences; (3) mass emigration caused by those same conflicts, by poverty or natural catastrophes; (4) global insecurity generated by imbalances in the stock market, environmental degradation, illness spread, drug traffic, terrorism, or uncontrolled demographic growth. The challenges are localized on the mobile borders with the developing world, threatened by a group of "civilizations" with a common trajectory of difficulties in creating prosperous, democratic, and peaceful nations.

The Ghost of the Third World and Latin America

Although not considered a hostile agent, Latin America looms up, in the ghost of the developing world, as explicit reference to what may represent for the United States the road to decadence. Lawrence Harrison, with an extensive career as director of the U.S. Agency for International Development (USAID) missions in Latin America, emphasizes the effects of the cultural changes in the development of nations, comparing Spanish and U.S. trajectories in the last decades:

Culture changes, for good and for bad. In the span of three decades, Spain has turned away from its traditional, authoritarian, hierarchical value system, which was at the root of both Spain's and Hispanic America's backwardness, and has immersed itself in the progressive Western European mainstream. During the same period, a racial revolution has occurred in America. . . . Yet, in the same three decades, the United States as a nation has experienced economic and political decline, principally, I believe, because of the erosion of the traditional American values—work, frugality, education, excellence, community—that had contributed so much to our earlier success. (1992:1)

Contrasting with Spain, Latin America continues to be dragged down by Iberian cultural heritage: "Traditional Iberian values and attitudes impede progress toward political pluralism, social justice, and economic dynamism" (1992:2). In Harrison's perspective, the regressive Latin American culture does not only represent the mirror that reflects the image of decadence that threatens the United States, but it is one of the responsible factors for the erosion of its traditional values: "The Chinese, the Japanese, and the Koreans who have migrated to the United States have injected a dose of the work ethic, excellence, and merit at a time when those values appear particularly beleaguered in the broader society. In contrast, the Mexicans who migrate to the United States bring with them a regressive culture that is disconcertingly persistent" (1992:223).

In the cultural approaches of Latin American underdevelopment, conceptions and political practices predominant up to the present come up as the chief responsible factors for the unsuccessful trajectory of the region. In the center of its diagnosis, they emphasize the ideas and experiences that marked the criticism of imperialism and dependency during the period of Cold War, which attributed underdevelopment to the exploitation of advanced capitalist countries, especially the United States. This line of argument stands out in David Landes', *The Wealth and Poverty of Nations:* "The failure of Latin American development, all the worse by contrast with North America, has been attributed by local scholars and outside sympathizers to the misdeeds of stronger, richer nations. This vulnerability has been labeled 'dependency,' implying a state of inferiority where one does not control one's fate; one does as others dictate" (1998:327).

In spite of being more precisely addressed to the academic audience, Landes' analysis doesn't lack ideology: "Cynics might even say that dependency doctrines have been Latin America's most successful export. Meanwhile they are bad for effort and morale. By fostering a morbid propensity to find fault with everyone but oneself, they promote economic impotence. *Even if they were true, it would be better to stow them*" (1998:328).

For this approach, the differences between wealth and poverty are not originated in the international division of work or the imperial politics of great powers but from the options and practices adopted by societies. "If we learn anything from the history of economic development, it is that culture makes all the difference. . . . Yet culture, in the sense of the inner values and attitudes that guide a population, frightens scholars" (1998:516). From this perspective, external factors cannot be considered structural determinants of poverty or wealth. "History tells us that the most successful cures for poverty come from within. Foreign aid can help, but windfall wealth, can also hurt. It can discourage effort and plant a crippling sense of incapacity" (1998:523).

Some diagnoses on the endemic character of underdevelopment help to build a picture of uncertainties related to the perception of potential inviability of the developing world. In a recent version of the "pivotal states" concept, on the borders that separate the advanced capitalism from the "developing" world, Latin America appears with two representatives, Brazil and Mexico.

> A pivotal state is so important regionally that its collapse would spell transboundary mayhem: migration, communal violence, pollution, disease, and so on. A pivotal state's steady economic progress and stability, on the other hand, would bolster its region's economic vitality and political soundness and benefit American trade and investment.
>
> For the present, the following should be considered pivotal states: Mexico and Brazil; Algeria, Egypt, and South Africa; Turkey; India and Pakistan; and Indonesia. These states' prospects vary widely. India's potential for success, for example, is considerably greater than Algeria's; Egypt's potential for chaos is greater than Brazil's. But all face a precarious future, and their success or failure will powerfully influence the future of the surrounding areas and affect American interests. (Chase et al. 1995:37)[5]

A Territory Without Utopia

In the analysis presented here, we lay stress on two important dimensions of the debate on the strategic relevance of Latin America for the United States: the impacts on the country of the economic, political, and social evolution of the region and whether state assistance politics are needed or not. The parallel process of political and economic liberalization, which has consolidated in the region since the 1980s, strengthened the hegemony of political forces tuned to the market and private initiative. This forms a breach in the predominant path since World War II. Within this context, the relationships with the United States reach a degree of convergence with few historical antecedents (Ayerbe, 1998).

While praising this situation, Lawrence Harrison criticizes its tardiness, which he attributes to cultural factors:

> That Latin America has not made its peace with democratic capitalism—and the United States—until the last years of the twentieth century is principally the consequence of the incompatibility of traditional Iberian culture with political pluralism and the free market, on the one hand, and the inevitable resentment of the successful by the unsuccessful, on the other. (1997:69)

In spite of the consensus to stand out as positive aspects political democratization, economic liberalization and the good relations with the United States, some fears based on analogies with the recent past prevail. This is what most analysis, explicitly or implicitly, reveal. According to Madeleine Albright:

> For today, with one lonely exception, every government in the hemisphere is freely elected. Every major economy has liberalized its system for investment and trade. With war in Guatemala ended, Central America is without conflict for the first time in decades. As recent progress toward settling the Equador-Peru border dispute reflects, nations are determined to live in security and peace from pole to pole. . . . Despite the many areas of progress, the region still faces serious challenges. Growing population make it harder to translate macroeconomic growth into higher standards of living. For many, the dividends of economic reform are not yet visible, while the costs of the accompanying austerity measures are. The building of democracy remains in all countries a work in progress, with stronger, more independent legal systems an urgent need in most. (1998:18–19)

For Elliot Abrams, the idea of the Western hemisphere must be regained and updated. Latin America will continue being a growing market for U.S. products and remain as a source of energetic resources. The demographic growth, effecting illegal immigration and drug traffic, are aspects of concern that justify keeping on the alert. "For the first time in U.S. history, there is no threat of foreign intervention in this region. The key remaining issue is whether the United States will recognize that with complete economic, military, and political domination comes the responsibility to

help maintain stability in the region through preventive, rather than cura-
tive, actions" (1993:55). Thomas Hirschfeld and Benjamin Schwarz, from
the RAND Corporation, present a pessimistic vision of the future of the
region. According to Hirschfeld, in a report prepared for the Army:

> Today, after billions in loans, endless hours of advice, thousands of plans, and
> a population of skilled and knowledgeable Western university graduates in
> virtually every Latin government, we better understand the problems, but
> we do not have solutions. (1993:45)
> The primary threads to U.S. interests in Latin America are derived from
> continued economic stagnation as populations rise. That combination leads
> to civil strife, authoritarian rule, ecological disaster, increased emigration,
> and disinclination to forgo easy earnings from drugs and arms. (1993:52)

For Schwarz, the arguments that combine endemic instability and the
existence of strategic interests to justify military and economic assistance
to the developing world lose basis with the end of the Cold War.

America's economic interests in the Third World are, in fact, small and
shrinking. These countries simply do not produce enough to supply the
lifeblood of the U.S. economy. The entire Third World, over 100 countries
including the OPEC member's nations, accounts for less than 20 percent of
the gross world product. Africa has a Gross National Product less than of
Great Britain; all of Latin America has a combined GNP smaller than that
of former West Germany. . . . The Third World, now and for the foreseeable future, is not the great untapped market and potential salvation of U.S.
industry that proponents of peacetime engagement believe. (1994:269)

The economic interests of the United States in those countries become
the responsibility of the private sector, which must assume the risks of its
own investments. This dissociates those enterprises from the action of the
armed forces, mainly bearing in mind that the access to those markets and
their mineral resources is protected, notwithstanding eventual internal political changes. "With few opportunities to earn foreign exchange and attract investment, any radical or otherwise unfriendly regimes that might
come to power in the underdeveloped world cannot afford the luxury of
being perverse by denying American business and banks access to markets
and investments" (Schwarz 1994:271).

This questioning of the idea that instability factors associated with underdevelopment demand a coordinated aid action brings forth the example of the Alliance for Progress, issued by the Kennedy Administration in
1961, which brought slight compensation in relation to the amount of ap-

plied resources. "Twenty years later . . . many of the countries that were to have benefits from the Alliance are good candidates for nation assistance" (1994:276). Schwartz associates with cultural factors the inefficiency of the aid: "The most important barriers to development . . . are profoundly and stubbornly rooted in the cultural and political heritage of the underdevelopment countries" (1994:277).

Like Schwarz, Harrison remarks on the insignificant economic relevance of Latin America for the United States:

> Of the number NAFTA total (population) of 363 million, 86 million, or almost a quarter, are Mexicans, with per capita purchasing power one-tenth or less of that of a Canadian or American. In terms of an effective market for U.S. exports, then, 86 million Mexican convert into perhaps 8 million, about the population of Sweden. Similarly, 433 million, or 61 percent, of the FTAA total of 710 million are from Latin America and the Caribbean. Given the fact that Mexico's per capita income is above the Latin American average, those 433 million might convert into an effective market of 35 million, less than the population of Spain.
>
> Thus, the *effective* population of NAFTA in 1990 would be 285 million, of FTAA 312 million, both substantially below the European Community (now "Union") total. (1997:205)

In spite of these facts, which show a part of reality, the analysis of the evolution of trade relations between the United States and Latin America shows a picture closer to Abrams's perspective. Since the first Bush Administration, expansion of trade becomes the principal issue of the Interamerican agenda. The Initiative for the Americas, issued in 1990 proposing the creation of a sole regional market, finds continuity with Clinton. At Miami's summit in December 1994, he proposed creating a Free Trade Area of the Americas for the year 2005.

As the Economic Commission for Latin America and the Caribbean (ECLAC/CEPAL) shows, notwithstanding the differences marked by Harrison between the "nominal population" and the "real population" of Latin America and the Caribbean compared with other regions, what is verified is a high expansive capacity of U.S. exports in the "effective Latin American market," which doesn't happen to Europe, that manages to keep the protection of those sectors that it considers strategic. Concretely, between 1990 and 1994, the U.S. exports to Latin America grew 79 percent, while imports barely grew 38 percent during the same time (CEPAL 1996:3). In this period, the region absorbs 15 percent of U.S. exports, with Brazil importing more than Scandinavian countries, Mexico more than Germany,

France, and Italy together, the Dominican Republic more than India and Indonesia, Chile more than Russia, and Costa Rica more than the whole of Eastern Europe (CEPAL).[6]

The analyses presented, which suggest different positions in U.S. foreign policy for Latin America, share the same vision regarding the precarious balance in which the region stands. The divergence is originated when assessing the effects in the United States of eventual economic and/or political unbalances, in a context where no external powers militarily threaten the region. The definition of the new assistance politics depends on the assessment of variables whose real impact remains within a hypothetical field.

Confronting the absence of systemic threats, the characterization of the American role in keeping regional stability offers two different conceptions: (1) a renewed Western hemisphere, with the United States leading the process of economic and cultural homogenization of the continent (Department of State, Abrams); (2) a neighbor with no "assistance" duties, leaving the private sector and multilateral organisms to make the decisions on politics of development aid (Hirschfeld, Schwartz, Harrison).

In reference to its identity, Latin America is considered a culturally hybrid region. Quoting Huntington:

> Latin America could be considered either a subcivilization within Western civilization or a separate civilization closely affiliated with the West and divided as to whether it belongs in the West. For an analysis focused on the international political implications of civilizations, including the relations between Latin America, on the one hand, and North America and Europe, on the other, the latter is the more appropriate and useful designation. (1996:46)

For Huntington, the politics started by Salinas de Gortari in Mexico represents a positive example of alignment with the West in the "clash of civilizations":

> Salinas dramatically reduced inflation, privatized large numbers of public enterprises, promoted foreign investment, reduced tariffs and subsidies, restructured the foreign debt, challenged the power of labor unions, increased productivity, and brought Mexico into the North American Free Trade Agreement with the United States and Canada. Salinas's reforms were designed to change Mexico from a Latin American country into a North American country. (1996:150)

Latin America and the "New World Order": End of History?

In the different approaches presented in this chapter, the potential contributions of Latin America to the "world disorder" are not originated in political, ideological, or cultural activism; the region represents no threat to Western hegemony. The eventual problems might originate in passive elements, as a result of a systemic collapse, product of an "endemic" incompetence. From the North's territorial vision, the perception of Latin America is clear and explicit: It is slightly relevant as an actor of any world order, prone to be assimilated by the West but with some restraint, not being capable of taking care of itself. Although not considered the West, being part of it represents the only possible utopia of the hegemonic project: political and economic liberalization, entering FTAA, an amplified version of NAFTA. Nevertheless, whatever praise given to the adoption of strategies that view as an inspirational model the capitalist democracies and to the excellent relationship with the United States, Latin America continues unique and lonely: unique in its peculiar culture impervious to progress, lonely in the extreme south of the West, separated by a frontier where the urgent priority is to build contention barriers.

Different from the perception of Latin America, when the glance is directed at the reality of the United States, the idea of nation becomes prominent. The strength of territorial frame as the place of production, circulation, and consumption of goods and services appears as permanent worry. The political projection of the country in the international scene represents a natural unfolding. The cultural values, which are references of the ideological discourse, give shape to the conscience of nationality.

Although fidelity to the principles of liberal capitalism is outside any controversy for the mentioned authors, we perceive a pragmatic concern with the local disintegrating effects of global reality. Intellectuals and representatives of the conservative establishment call on the need of new welfare policies together with clear actions to redeem national culture. By contrast, the government presses the other countries to deregulate their markets and adopt "the Western way of life." This is clearly a realist approach of national interest: within a domestic frame, protection of the economic and cultural space; within an international frame, the globalization discourse. While in the United States the hegemonic groups intensify the debate on the new meanings of national interest, Latin American neoliberals ridicule the "anachronism" to think about the nation, considered a typical behavior of our "perfect idiot." Opposed to this ideological posture, to recuperate the idea of Latin America as a center in which we enrich and protect ourselves from the world continues to be a strategic challenge. With no hegemonic pretensions, there must be a twenty-first century where what will prevail will be dialogue and not conflict between civilizations. To build each one's own way, although an enormous challenge, is a reality that this author considers feasible. In this chapter, we pretend a less ambitious contribution: to present an external glance to stimulate one of the important components in the search for identity—the sentiment of loneliness.

Notes

1. Huntington coordinated the project "The Changing Security Environment and American National Interests," at the John M. Olin Institute for Strategic Studies at Harvard University. Studies on "Clash of Civilizations" are part of that project.
2. We use the term "conservative" as a reference to those analyses that emphasize, when approaching national interest, recovering and strengthening cultural Western roots of the United States.
3. James Kurth, Zbigniev Brzezinski, and Elliot Abrams took part in the security colloquium of the project, coordinated by Huntington.
4. Kristol is the founder of *The Public Interest* and *The National Interest* reviews.
5. Paul Kennedy, one of the authors of this chapter, took part in the security colloquium of the project coordinated by Huntington.
6. Between 1989 and 1994 Latin American trade with the United States moved from a surplus of nearly 3 billion dollars to a deficit of 1.8 billion (CEPAL, 1994). The commercial balance of the United States with the rest of the world in 1997 registered the following results: North America, deficit of 32.4 million dollars; Central and South America: surplus of 9.4 billion dollars; Western Europe, deficit of 17.5 billion; Eastern Europe deficit of 727 million; former USSR, deficit of 284 million; Pacific Basin, deficit of 12.1 billion. (Economic perspectives. USIS, vol. 3, no. 2, March 1998. Information obtained from the Commerce Department of the United States).

Bibliography

Abrams, E. (1993). "The American Hemisphere After the Cold War." Cambridge: John M. Olin Institute for Strategic Studies, Harvard University.

Albright, M. (1997). "Fast-Track Trade Negotiating Authority: Essential for America." *U.S. Department of State Dispatch.* November.

———. (1998). "Ensuring Foreign Policy Tools that Sustain American Leadership." *U.S. Department of State Dispatch.* April.

Ayerby, L. F. (1998). *Neoliberalismo e Política Externa na América Latina. Análise a partir da experiência Argentina recente.* São Paulo: Editora da UNESP.

CEPAL (Comisión Económica para América Latina y el Caribe). (1994). *Balance Preliminar de la Economía Latinoamericana.* Santiago de Chile: CEPAL.

————. (1996). "Notas sobre la economía y el desarrollo." Santiago de Chile: CEPAL, August to September.

Chase, R. S. et al. (1996). "Pivotal States and U.S. Strategy." *Foreign Affairs,* vol. 74, no. 1. January–February.

Harrison, L. E. (1992). *Who Prospers? How Cultural Values Shape Economic and Political Success.* New York: Basic Books.

————. (1997). *The Pan-American Dream.* New York: Basic Books.

Hirschfield, T. J. (1993). *The Declining Threat to U.S. Interests.* Santa Monica, CA: RAND.

Huntington, S. (1993). "The Clash on Civilizations?" *Foreign Affairs,* vol. 72, no. 3. Summer.

————. (1996). *The Clash of Civilizations and the Remaking of World Order.* New York: Simon & Schuster.

————. (1997). "The Erosion of American National Interests." *Foreign Affairs,* vol. 76, no. 5. September–October.

Khalilzad, Z. (1995). *From Containment to Global Leadership: America and the World After the Cold War.* Santa Monica, CA: RAND.

Kristol, I. (1995). *Neoconservatism. The Autobiography of an Idea.* New York: The Free Press.

Kurth, J. (1995). "The Clash in Western Society." *Current,* no. 369. January.

————. (1996). "America's Grand Strategy. A Pattern of History." *The National Interest,* no. 43.

Landes, D. (1998). *The Wealth and Poverty of Nations.* New York: W. W. Norton & Company.

Schwarz, B. C. (1994). *A Dubious Strategy in Pursuit of a Dubious Enemy: A Critique of U.S. Post–Cold War Security Policy in the Third World.* Santa Monica, CA: RAND.

Chapter 3

Governance, Security, and Interamerican Relations: A Critique of the Liberal Paradigm

Carlos Alzugaray Treto[1]

This paper's objective is to contribute to the debate about governance and security in Latin America and the Caribbean, introducing a critical view of the liberal paradigm, undoubtedly predominant both at the academic and political level. That paradigm, which can also be called neoliberal,[2] assumes as its basic element Adam Smith's original hypothesis that "the invisible hand of the market" is the "magic wand" that will bring progress, welfare, and peace for human societies as a whole as well as for its individual members.

An essential component of liberal and neoliberal thought, as formulated by Francis Fukuyama in his well-known article about "the end of history" and restated recently by himself in his text "Thinking about the End of History 10 Years Later" is that, by his own words, "the outright failure . . . of social constructivism . . . reinforced a liberal order based in the market, sustained by obvious truths on 'nature and the God of nature,'" so "there is no alternative viable development model that offers better results, not even after the 1997–1998 crisis" (Fukuyama, 1999). It should be remembered, as Susan George (1999) did recently, that this was the logic used by Margaret Thatcher on introducing her program with the acronym TINA: There is no alternative.

There seems to be universal agreement in the proposition that we live in an era of deep political transformations. Whichever position is adopted about the globalization process (hyperglobalist, skeptical, or transformationalist), there seems to exist a broad consensus in that, on the one side, the correlation between sovereign attributes, state power, and territoriality has become more complex, while, on the other, "governments have become increasingly outward looking as they seek to pursue cooperative strategies and to construct international regulatory regimes to manage more effectively the growing array of cross-border issues which regularly surface on national agendas" (Held, McGrew, Goldblatt, and Perraton, 1999:9).

For the peoples and governments of Latin America and the Caribbean, in particular, this dilemma transforms itself into a difficult and complex turning point in the framework of their relationship with the United States, the most powerful nation-state known by history. A nation-state that, as Henry Kissinger has acknowledged, has no peer in having "influenced international relations as decisively and at the same time as ambivalently" and in insisting more firmly "on the inadmissibility of intervention in the domestic affairs of other states, or more passionately asserted that its own values were universally applicable" (1994:17–18).

Economic, political, military, social, and cultural conditions in Interamerican relations shape outcomes in such a way that governance and security acquire major importance. No matter how superficial, any analysis of the agendas of governmental and nongovernmental meetings and conferences underline it. More than in any other region of the world, the predominant liberal ideology, combined with Washington's unquestionable hegemonic will and capacity, has influenced prevailing approaches on both these issues, at the political as well as at the academic level. This has introduced a tendency that emphasizes the formal elements and the external manifestations of governance and security, with a particular reference to U.S. interests, and avoids addressing the real causes of ungovernability and insecurity and evades the necessities imposed on Latin American and Caribbean countries in their relationship with the powerful neighbor to the north.

The fact is that the liberal discourse has created the misleading notion that there is no viable alternative to its proposition of allowing "the invisible hand of the market" to be the sole provider of decisions that shape the economy, politics, culture, and society. This has been reinforced by the North American belief that "the less government, the better." In this way, the classical caveat of a liberal thinker such as Karl Polanyi has been ignored. In his 1944 book, *The Great Transformation,* the English thinker of Austro-Hungarian descent stated: "To allow the market mechanism to be sole director of the fate of human beings and their natural environment, indeed, even of the amount and use of purchasing power, would result in the demolition of society" (Polanyi, 1944:73). Of course, this was not some sort of dogmatic whim coming out of the pen of such a serious scholar. As his work demonstrates, such assertion was based on solid considerations about human destiny in a period as difficult as the one that humanity was going through at the time, when World War II raged across the planet.

The main challenge faced by the countries of the region at this defining moment in their history consists in finding an alternative policy model that will liberate them from the pernicious upshots of neoliberal strategies followed by many governments in the past decade, in a context in which U.S. imperial domination has been ideologically and instrumentally legitimized through power structures, regimes, and institutions serving its purposes. The tangible and inevitable globalization process, decisively swayed by the liberal paradigm, has resulted in the contradictory emergence of positive and negative phenomena, with the distinctiveness that the latter punish a growing majority of human beings while the former benefit a reduced amount of persons. This development is progressively obvious in the Western hemisphere, where social inequality is a grave problem. Influenced by the "Third Way," proclaimed by some sectors of European Social Democracy, a group of Latin American politicians and academics made the following recent analysis:

> Today Latin American societies, traditionally unequal and fragmented in countless ways, are overwhelmingly more so than ever. In a few countries poverty decreases although injustice persists. In most, the number of citizens condemned to an unrewarding, unacceptable and resentful life increases and, at the same time, the appalling gaps that separate the poor from the rich, the city from the rural areas, the blacks and the browns from the whites and the creoles, the men from the women and the children from the rest of society are amplified. Employment remains stagnant, incomes stay penalized, and expenses in education, health, housing, child care and the future cannot compensate the interminable decades lost. Our incipient democracies are constantly threatened by military coup attempts, meager economic results, by the understandable apathy of a population drained by the daily struggle for survival, and a persistent uprooting. And the unconcluded nature of our national identities is taxed today by a pitiless globalization, at times fictitious, at times exaggerated by the media, and always curtailing of fragile sovereignties constructed less than a century and a half ago. That is everything that we should modify, improve, reform, in a word, change. (Castañeda y Mangabeira Unger, 1998:58)

What is required, therefore, are resolute and determined actions by governments and social actors that would rectify prevailing tendencies that prevent a majority of our peoples from achieving a decorous and decent life in which the democratic ideals, defined since the seventeenth century, it is useful to recall, by the French Revolution as "liberty, equality, fraternity" are not hollow words. A scenario of the first order for these actions should be at the level of the future of Interamerican relations.

Governance

In spite of its recent emergence and growth in the field of the social sciences, the governance notion has rapidly occupied a central place in the current academic and political debate, both in the case of those who are devoted to so-called domestic or internal politics, as for international relations specialists. There are two basic reasons for this. There is not the smallest doubt that we are witnessing a profound and tangible transformation in the way that human societies are managed. Whether labeled as a "control loss" (Sassen, 1996), or a "withdrawal of the State" (Strange, 1996), or a "governance crisis" (Vallespín, 2000:123–130), or a "relocation of authority" (Rosenau, 1997:153–156), or the emergence of "multilevel governance" (Held, McGrew, Goldblatt, and Perraton, 1999:62–77), the only thing about it we can be certain of is that governments face new internal and external challenges, which force them to renovate their "modus operandi."

No matter how superficial, any examination of the agenda of problems present in contemporary world affairs, from the difficulty in regulating migratory flows to the environmental crisis, not forgetting the uncontrolled movements of "casino capitalism," the increase and generalization of ethnic conflicts, and the escalation of international crime, it can be shown that something new is happening and that governments find it ever more difficult to exercise their problem-solving capacity.

Liberal ideology has taken advantage of these objective facts to proclaim the "end of sovereignty" and the installing of a hegemonic system of global governance based on existing hierarchies or institutions (the Security Council of the United Nations or the World Bank) or new ones (the World Economic Forum in Davos). A clear example of this tendency has been the proclaimed "right of humanitarian intervention," as exemplified by NATO's bombing of Yugoslavia without declaring war, ignoring international law and the United Nations Charter. This antistate discourse requires the elaboration of a renovated theoretical foundation. This kind of theorizing can put emphasis in a system of "international regimes" of liberal bent (Krasner, 1983) or in the necessity of creating institutions that respond to the liberal paradigm (March and Olsen, 1995:241–248). It is irrelevant that it may seem absurd, given the main tenets of neoliberalism and its emphasis on market mechanisms, because, as Rosenau has pointed out, to value governance "means to focus on powerful tensions, deep contradictions and disconcerting paradoxes" (1997:144).

As regards governance, liberalism has been based in several central ideas:

1. The disappearance or transformation of the Nation-State (Ohmae, 1995).
2. The substantial erosion and limitation of the concept of State sovereignty (Krasner, 1999).
3. The homogenization of the main constituting elements of governance across borders (Russett, 1998).
4. The active promotion of that homogenization process by the main Western powers and international institutions through the so-called Democracy Protection and Promotion programs (DPP) (Schmitter and Brouwer, 1999).

The application of these ideas in an unequal global order, where the structures of power are polarized, together with the proclamation of the preeminence of market forces as the basic organizing principle of international society, mean in practice the creation of a hegemonic world governance system, where the largest powers (the United States and its main allies) control the mechanisms of authority and promote ideological uniformity, through their domination over mass media, on the basis of liberal values and doctrines.

Liberalism has promoted and applied its viewpoint to all levels of governance, as instituted in the contemporary world, but here we will refer basically to three: national, regional, and global. Although it can be argued that the global one does not correspond strictly to the parameters of this chapter—after all, I am referring to a region—the level of interconnectedness of the current political processes makes it impossible to refer to the other two levels without referring to the third one, which I do at the end of this section, although I will start with the liberal notion of national governance.

The liberal approach to the concept of national governance had its first practical political manifestation in some of the financial institutions of the international system. In 1992, simultaneously with the elaboration of Washington Consensus, a global liberal manifesto if ever there was one, the World Bank published a report under the title "Governance and Development," in which this notion was defined as "the form in which power is exercised in the management of a country's economic and social resources in order to bring about development." Two years later, in another report titled "Governance: The World Bank's Experience," that international institution suggested the rules under which "good governance" should be conducted, placing special emphasis on those that should be applied to the system of governmental decision making (transparency, professional ethics of the bureaucracy, accountability of the executive and a strong participation of civil society in public affairs) (The World Bank, 1994).

It is paradoxical, however, that although the Bank was favorable to the notion that sustainable development could only be possible in "a predictable and transparent framework of rules and institutions in the administration of the public and private business," emphasis was placed in the setting up of rules for the realm of public affairs, while the realm of the private was placed in the free working of the market. The Bank was in favor of "an acutely limited state." It cannot be denied that the notion of governance came into fruition by the hand of "Washington Consensus," which presided over the politics of structural adjustment and of neoliberal reforms, applied in Latin America and the Caribbean in the late 1980s and early 1990s with results that today are generally recognized as unsatisfactory and even disastrous.

The concept of governance, as elaborated by the World Bank, was quickly incorporated into the prevailing democracy discourse, which acquired dogmatic contours when postulating that the essence of the democratic system resided exclusively in the mechanisms of electoral processes, taking as the only valid model only an aspect of the notion proposed by Joseph Schumpeter in 1942: "The democratic philosophy of the XVIII century can be understood from the following definition: the democratic method is that institutional arrangement for arriving at political decisions in the benefit of the common good by letting the people decide by themselves contentious issues through the selection of those individuals who will realize their will" (Schumpeter, 1968:321).

The liberal interpretation of Schumpeter has ignored the central objective of his notion of democracy (to realize the common good) and its essence (that the people decide by themselves the issues, that is to say that they participate) placing emphasis in the instrumentation, for example, in the election of their representatives. Nothing else is more coherent with the idea that it is necessary to leave the "invisible hand" of the market make the most important decisions. Current electoral processes in many countries of Latin America and the Caribbean, following the North American pattern, have become marketing operations, where what determines the results are not the virtues of one or another proposed governmental program but the candidate's political machinery's ability in mobilizing material resources to make a good propaganda campaign. This is the best of the cases, because on many occasions what decides is raw and open electoral fraud. As it has been recognized, these systems do not solve the deficit of civic political participation. Carlos Vilas has summarized it in the following way:

> However it is defined (even in its minimal, procedural sense), democracy is an inclusive regime. It involves participation of all citizens in a polis that is seen as belonging to all—the res public of the Romans or the Anglo-Saxon commonwealth. But the polis can hardly be considered as belonging to everyone when the principle of citizenship (as a synthesis of rights of participation and obligations of contribution) and the underlying idea of equality must coexist with profound and apparently growing inequalities in most countries, and with growing numbers of citizens who fall below the poverty line as a result of the restructuring of economies, changes in labor markets, the reform of the state, and the shifts in public policies. (Vilas, 1997:21)

As regards regional governance, the contributions of liberalism are rather scarce. It is obvious that liberal thinkers prefer a system of global governance. The articulation of a regional level of governance goes against one of the most important elements of neoliberal thought on world order, the creation of a liberalized world market. However, the theoreticians of this vein have contributed heavily to the high degree of confusion that exists among three different notions: regionalism, regional integration, and the creation of free trade areas. This confusion is advantageous to the liberal discourse. Their preference leans toward the last of these models (free trade areas), as demonstrated in two recent works about "hemispheric integration" (Hufbauer and Schott, 1994; Jatar and Weintraub, 1997).

The third pillar of the neoliberal idea of governance is little debated. It refers to the mechanisms of global governance. The progressive interdependence and globalization of economies requires appropriate mechanisms of world governance. It is difficult to argue against that proposition. As David Held has written, "No conception of the modern democratic State can be valid without an analysis of the global system and no analysis of the global system can do without of a conception of the democratic State" (Held, 1997:49). Nevertheless, the neoliberal paradigm prefers a global governance model based on the broadest possible degree of deregulation allowing for a growing liberalization of the market and the free movement of capital, in a progressive limitation of the sovereign attributions of the peripheral States (without affecting, of course, that of the large central powers) and in decision-making processes that are as little transparent as possible (as they were tried in the unsuccessful negotiation of the Multilateral Agreement on Investments). To that must be added an elitist conception of the decision-making process, either by means of the Group of 7 (transformed formally to 8 with the addition of Russia) or at the World Economic Forum of Davos.

The global system of international relations is profoundly antidemocratic, even if the analysis is based on the existing institutions and an abstraction is made of the violations that take place against that same institutionalization by the great powers, as it happened recently in the case of the aggression of NATO countries against Yugoslavia, adducing a supposed right "of humanitarian intervention." As the Cuban President, Fidel Castro, has recently pointed out, "If it is necessary to speak about democracy, then we have to begin to democratize the United Nations Organization," where "the irritant privilege of the veto in the Security Council should disappear because it is anachronistic, dangerous and unjustified" (Castro, 1996:14).

But the problem is still deeper. The present international regimes—the "principles, norms, rules, and decision-making procedures around which actor expectations converge in a given issue-area," as defined by Krasner (1983:1), have been completely incapable in predicting, preventing, and solving the crises to which countries are subjected, even the great powers. This reality also was underlined by the President of Brazil, Fernando Henrique Cardoso, when he emphasized that "the main thing is that, indeed, at the same time that this globalization process exists, there does not exist at the political level a simultaneous process of creation of legitimizing and implementing rules of governance" (Demos, 1997).

In Latin America and the Caribbean, two preponderant risk factors have negatively influenced the creation of democratic governance regimes. The adoption by Latin America and the Caribbean of the three basic precepts of Washington Consensus—reduction of the State, development of the private sector and trade liberalization—far from benefiting the democratic processes, have weakened them by increasing poverty and inequality (Smith, 2000:255–256). The lack of social equity, made worse by neoliberal policies, impedes an effective civic participation in decision-making processes and they are the ultimate cause of an entire series of political crises in Argentina,

Brazil, Ecuador, Venezuela, Peru, Paraguay, Chile, Mexico, and Colombia, to mention alone the most significant cases (Einaudi, 1999:1–2).

The second risk factor is determined by the unequal nature of the Interamerican system of interstate relations and the U.S. inclination to act unilaterally. The fact that Washington still exercises an ostensible hegemony in the region, at the same time that it acts as a superpower determined to establish a world order to its image and likeness, requires of a special effort on the part of the countries of Latin America and the Caribbean who are its more immediate neighbors. As Jorge Domínguez, Director of the Center for International Affairs of Harvard University, has recently remembered, it can be affirmed that "a central problem in inter-American relations has been the propensity of United States to act unilaterally, as . . . George Kennan had preferred, and in so doing to presume that its own vision of the hemisphere is widely shared by other governments and peoples of the Americas" (Domínguez, 2000:24).

This unequal nature of the Interamerican system has been reflected in the supremacy that the United States has exercised over the whole agenda related to the topic of the Democracy Promotion and Protection (DPP) with the purpose of using that mechanism to consolidate its hegemony in the region, at the expense of regional institutions (Robinson, 1996). The consequences are visible. It is not surprising that the Interamerican Dialogue has affirmed recently that the Interamerican relationships is going through "a time of testing," complaining that while one notices setbacks in the will for expanding economic and political cooperation, little interest has been expressed in strengthening the Organization of American States and other hemispheric institutions. (Interamerican Dialogue, 1999:2). The diagnosis could not be more somber:

> The opportunity to build productive cooperation in Western Hemisphere affairs is fading. It can be revived, but renewed progress must be made soon on several fronts. The challenge for the United States and every other nation of the hemisphere is straightforward: they must take action to fulfill their stated commitments to protect and reinforce democracy, integrate their economies, raise the living standards of the poor, and improve regional institutions. (Interamerican Dialogue, 1999:15)

Security

The theory and practice of security in international relations has been the object of more than one debate since Arnold Wolfers defined it as an "ambiguous symbol" in 1952 (Wolfers, 1952). It has been so controversial that in 1983 the Secretary General of the UN, at the request of the General Assembly, asked a group of experts to study the topic in order to come up with an acceptable and clear definition. The experts produced *A Study on the Concepts of Security* (1985), in which they recognized the difficulties in defining a consensual notion (United Nations, 1985). In the 1940s and 1950s, the United States used the so-called national security doctrine as the legitimizing and organizing idea for its global imperial ambitions. In the 1960s and 1970s, the military dictatorships in Latin America developed their own "national security doctrines" to justify the most appalling repressive campaigns in which, with the support of the United States, systematic, persistent, and flagrant violations of human rights took place. All these conceptions put emphasis in the repressive military and police content of the idea of security.

Nevertheless, by the end of the 1960s, at the international level, it began to be recognized that security and development were two topics indissolubly bound to each other. Paradoxically, Robert McNamara, at the time the secretary of defense of the United States and one of the main architects of the war against Vietnam, was among the first to accept that relationship, when he declared in 1968 that "in a society that is modernizing, security means development" (McNamara, 1968:49). This notion about the linkage between security and development, in which the economic and social aspects of security began to be considered, was consolidated in the 1980s, together with the acceptance of the developing world's demand about the "right to development." Maybe a bigger tribute should be paid to the Independent Commission on Questions of Disarmament and Security, presided over by the former prime minister of Sweden, Olof Palme, for their clear definition in this respect, elaborated in 1982, but of whose current soundness there should be very few doubts:

> The present condition of the world economy threatens the security of every country. The Commission believes that just as countries cannot achieve security at each other's expense, so too they cannot achieve security through military strength alone. Common security requires that people live in dignity and peace, that they have enough to eat and are able to find work and live in a world without poverty and destitution. (Palme and others, 1982:182)

Shortly after the fall of the Berlin Wall and the end of strategic bipolarity, the linkage between security and development was recognized as "inextricable" in an article written by Boutros Boutros Ghali, the secretary general of the UN, in the Winter 1992 to 1993 issue of *Foreign Affairs*.[3]

However, development, considered as a key concept of contemporary international relations, and the right to development, as one of the main achievements of the countries from the South in their struggles during the 1960s, 1970s, and 1980s, have been the victims of the globalizing process and of the predominance of the neoliberal paradigm in the 1990s. The spread of liberal ideas and their transformation into a dogmatic "pensée unique" has produced a major setback in security studies, undoing most of what had been achieved in previous decades, pushing them back to the prevailing notions in the 1940s and 1950s when security, at its different levels (international, national, and personal), centered in its repressive military and police aspects, contributing as the only new element a biased vision of human or individual security, which, among other things, is sought after in order to legitimize the so-called right of humanitarian intervention and the curbing, if not the total abolition, of the concept of state sovereignty.

However, as Barry Buzan and Ole Waever have pointed out, the central notion of liberalism, the emphasis in the market, is intrinsically insecurity-generating: "Actors in a market are supposed to feel insecure: If they don't the market doesn't produce its efficiencies. This fundamental axiom of liberal economic theory and praxis sharply limits the scope of economic security in liberal systems" (Buzan and Weaver, 1998:19). By contrast, the neoliberal paradigm has searched and found its oldest and most noteworthy antecedent in the German classic philosopher Immanuel Kant and its work about perpetual peace. According to this theory, war is impossible between liberal democracies, which in turn have the right to intervene against countries that do not share their governmental system (Doyle, 1986:280). The United States government has elaborated a "doctrine of democratic enlargement" that is based on these premises, in order to impose its hegemony at a world scale but specifically in Latin America and the Caribbean (Talbott, 1996).

In Latin America and the Caribbean, this paradigm has been assumed in practice and theory with considerable enthusiasm, at the expense of the principle of the sovereignty (Farer, 1996). However, more than enough reasons exist to question this model if collaboration as regards security has any chance of being achieved. This analysis is shared by political scientists such as Mónica Hirst, who has written the following when referring to the case of the Southern Cone:

> In fact, expectations held that security cooperation, together with economic integration and political coordination, would become an irreversible process.

In this context, it became appropriate to make use of Kant's interdemocratic peace approach to explain cooperative enterprises en the region, particularly those initiated between Argentina an Brazil.[4]

Though these prospects have not suffered a complete reversal, expectations regarding the "dovish" vocations of the newborn democracies of the Southern Cone have diminished. Pessimistic predictions have suggested that democratic consolidation in the subregion could signify a movement back to a classic security dilemma environment. (Hirst, 1998:102)[5]

Just as in the pre-1989 period, the current agenda on security in the Americas is dominated by the United States. As Isabel Jaramillo has pointed out, "On the basis of the argument about the transnationalization of security issues, an attempt has been made to legitimize policies that encroach on the sovereign interests of countries, thereby creating elements of insecurity" (Jaramillo, 1998:2). By contrast, there is an inclination to accept, practically without any debate at all, that the challenges to hemisphere security that are commonly shared by Washington and the Latin American capitals (drug trafficking, terrorism, organized crime, corruption, and other) are autonomous or independent of the prevailing policies in the economic and social sphere (Rojas Aravena, 1999; Mares, 2000). According to the August 25, 1999, edition of Ciudad Mexico's journal *Excélsior,* Professor Jorge Domínguez, Director of the Center of International Affairs of Harvard University, has stated that "the situation of violence and drug trafficking in Latin America is a consequence of the processes of demobilization of the armies and of guerrillas in Central America, as the specialists in violence lost their jobs."

It is not perceived (or it is not admitted) that the neoliberal paradigm, by increasing inequality, poverty, destitution, and the neglect of broad masses, provides the dangerous environment in which violence in its different manifestations is born. As Vilas has pointed out:

The inefficiency of policies designed and executed by States to deal with poverty have generated more social dissatisfaction in societies characterized by relatively high levels of social homogeneity until the 60s and 70s—for example Argentina, Costa Rica, Uruguay—than in those traditionally characterized by precariousness and social exclusion. In every society there exists a legitimate margin of inequality that, in the end, is linked to the capacity of that society to offer explanations or collectively accepted justifications for the existing levels of social inequality. When, due to causes that can vary from country to country, the levels of inequality increase objectively or the explanations and justifications of that inequality lose or reduce their credibility, the processes of impoverishment and social fragmentation are usually accompanied by tension and social uneasiness, and even enhanced violent reactions on the part of those that consider themselves wrongly harmed. That is the origin of the violence that usually accompanies moments of additional impoverishment, that is not necessarily carried out by those who are worse, but by those who lose levels or integration margins. The violence that has accompanied in recent years what we call "new poverty" is much more the result of the new insolvency of certain groups than of the magnitude of their impoverishment. (Vilas, 1999:12)

In this context, and not recognizing the real causes behind the developments that encompass the regional security agenda, the U.S. government is appealing more and more to the old formula of unilateral military interventionism. The issue of drug trafficking is a case in point. Although it is not new and has deep historical and structural roots (Walker, 1996), the United States, whose society is one of those most affected by the terrible consequences of drug addiction and trade, has oscillated between the lack of interest and the adoption of short-term policies that do not address the problem in depth. Although at times it has seemed that U.S. policymakers are ready to adopt new policies, more multilateral in scope and more multifaceted in implementation, focusing on aspects of the problem that have never before been tackled, as is the case with domestic strategies for the control or diminution of consumption, they are still thinking above all in terms of the use of the repressive instrument, as is the case with "Plan Colombia."

The Colombian case and the possibility of a direct military intervention of the United States, in spite of all the official protests of Washington and the warnings of North American academic experts on Latin America, continue to be the object of concern for the whole Hemisphere. The approval of the current "Plan Colombia," valued at U.S.$1.3 billion, has made many observers point out the danger of an escalation very similar to the one that took place more than a quarter of a century ago in Vietnam.

It should be remembered that, after the end of the Cold War, the United States has launched two military interventions in Latin America and the Caribbean: the invasion of Panama in 1989 and the occupation of Haiti in 1995. Both actions demonstrated that Washington can put aside the principle of the inviolability of sovereignty when it suits its interests or its perception of them, both were legitimated by the prevalent discourse about the "restoration of the democracy," both were successful, both had as backdrop the problem of "personalities" (Noriega and

Cédras) and both underlined the crushing power of North American domination of the continent (Smith, 2000:315–317).

After the aggression of the NATO member countries against Yugoslavia, the proclaimed "New Strategic Concept" of that organization that expands and enlarges its military mandate and sphere, and the certain fact that this alliance transgressed the obligations to which it was subject by the United Nations Charter, it is necessary to ask, as the Cuban President, Fidel Castro, did at the Rio Summit between Latin America and the Caribbean and the European Union, when he questioned his European colleagues about the possibility that a country of Latin America and the Caribbean could be subjected in the future to a similar military intervention.[6]

This question is not rhetoric in any way. The so-called right of humanitarian intervention constitutes a serious threat for any country, but in particular for those in Latin America and the Caribbean. In a world context as the existent one, in which ostensible unipolarity prevails in the military sphere, exercised by a superpower like the United States, whose leaders do not hesitate to proclaim their faith in the notion that their nation is "irreplaceable" and that it is called by history to preside over the destiny of the world, it is clear that that "right," if enacted as a recognized rule of the international security regime, would be the perfect alibi to subject by force any country that opposed those designs of Pax Americana. Latin America and the Caribbean know from their experience that a unilateral military intervention by the United States is not an impossibility, as the cases of Panama and Haiti demonstrate.

Facing these realities, the concern expressed by President Fidel Castro at the Ibero-American Summit in Guadalajara carries special weight: "Never before has it been so important to proclaim and to defend uncompromisingly the principle that the independence and the sovereignty of each State are sacred" (Castro, 1996:14).

However, the defense of the principle of national sovereignty as the irreplaceable cornerstone of the international system and for the establishment of a stable and fair regime of international security does not mean that the lack of harmony that can exist between national and individual security should be ignored as a valid issue, as Barry Buzan has pointed out (1991:50). Nevertheless, the emphasis placed by neoliberal thought on the direct threats to individual and human security on the part of the state (evident mainly in the cases of the military dictatorships that Latin America and the Caribbean suffered in the past) does not take into account that many forms of personal insecurity exist, and that the most extended in our region are the ones that arise from destitution and misery, which are the central causes of violence and of its spiraling out of control as the result of the repressive response against the popular movements that demand fairness and social justice. In the face of this insecurity, the construction of a robust national state that would have as its main objective the protection of the common good and that would serve as a counterbalancing force against the power of the market and of the forces that control it (the transnational companies, for example) is an imperious necessity.

A security agenda for the region has necessarily to consider these aspects of the problem, ignored and disregarded by the liberal paradigm: the violence-generating social inequality and the threat represented by the military unipolarity of the United States and its propensity to unilateral interventionism that questions the validity of the principle of national sovereignty and its parallel precept, the sovereign equality of states.

Conclusion

The neoliberal paradigm has dominated the governance and security agenda and discourse in Interamerican relations. Its basic precepts are: the preeminence of the market, the reduction of the state, and the promotion and protection of the liberal democratic model. In political practice, these have been accompanied by a powerful homogenizing project, imposed by the international financial mechanisms and centers of power, in particular the United States, based also on the limitation of the sovereign attributes of the national states in Latin America and the Caribbean. It is presupposed that a future of peace, well-being, and progress for the region will automatically come about with the application of these concepts.

However, this project worsens the two main risk factors in Interamerican relations: the domestic social inequalities in each nation and the massive asymmetry of power prevalent in the interstate system of the hemisphere between the United States, the biggest superpower in the contemporary world, with a clear will of imperial hegemonism, and the rest of the countries of the region. That translates, on the one hand, in a strengthening of violence-generating social tensions facing nation-states whose authority has been considerably diminished by neoliberal policies. On the other hand, by weakening the concept of sovereignty and legitimizing North American interventionism, the liberal paradigm has strengthened U.S. hegemony, whose security interests continue dominating the Hemispheric agenda. This will have pernicious effects in Interamerican affairs.

Notes

1. Professor, Instituto Superior de Relaciones Internacionales "Raúl Roa García" ("Raúl Roa García" Higher Institute of International Relations), Calle 22 No. 111, Miramar, Playa, La Habana 11300, Cuba. Email: calzugaray@ minrex.gov.cu.
2. For the author, there is no substantial difference between what most authors today call "neoliberalism" and classical liberalism. Therefore, both terms will be used on the assumption that they refer to the same basic theoretical outlook.
3. I have discussed these issues in three previous essays. See references.
4. See Philippe Schmitter, "Idealism, Regime Change, and Regional Cooperation: Lessons from the Southern Cone of Latin America," *The New Interdependence in the Americas: Challenges to Economic Restructuring, Political Redemocratization and Foreign Policy* (Stanford: Stanford University Press, 1991). For general analysis of Kant's theory of liberal internationalism, see Michael Doyle, "Liberalism and World Politics," *American Political Science Review* 80 (1986): 1151–1169 (Hirst's note).
5. See Carlos Acuña and William Smith, "The Politics of 'Military Economics' in the Southern Cone: Comparative Perspectives on Democracy, Armas Production and the Armas Race Among Argentina, Brazil and Chile," mimeo, CEDES, Buenos Aires, 1994 (Hirst's note).
6. The full text of Fidel Castro's speech at the Summit can be checked in "Preguntas y reflexiones sobre el nuevo concepto estratégico de la OTAN," in *Granma,* La Habana, June 26, 1999.

Bibliography

Alzugaray, Carlos. (1989). "Problems of National Security in the Cuban-U.S. Historic Breach." In Jorge I. Domínguez and Rafael Hernández (editors): *U.S.-Cuban Relations in the 1990s.* Boulder, CO: Westview Press.

———. (1992). "Seguridad Nacional en la Cuenca del Caribe." In Asociación Latinoamericana de Sociología (ALAS) and Centro de Estudios de América (editors), *Sistemas políticos: Poder y Sociedad (Estudios de Casos en América Latina).* Caracas: Editorial Nueva Sociedad.

———. (1995). "Cuban Security in the Post–Cold War World: Old and New Challenges and Opportunities." In A. R. M. Ritter and J. M. Kirk (eds.), *Cuba in the International System: Normalization and Integration.* London: Macmillan Press.

Buzan, Barry. (1991). *People, States, and Fear: An Agenda for International Security Studies in the Post–Cold War Era.* Second Edition. New York: Harvester Wheatsheaf.

Buzan, Barry, and Ole Waever. (1998). *Liberalism and Security: The Contradictions of the Liberal Leviathan. Working Paper No. 23—1998.* Copenhagen, Denmark: Copenhagen Peace Research Institute (COPRI).

Camilleri, J. A., and J. Falk. (1992). *The End of Sovereignty? The Politics of a Shrinking and Fragmenting World.* Aldershot: Edward Elgar.

Castañeda, Jorge G., and Roberto Mangabeira Unger. (1998). "Después del neoliberalismo: un nuevo camino." In Nexos, Ciudad México, March 1998. (This is a document elaborated by a group of Latin American politicians and intellectuals who, summoned by Castañeda and Mangabeira Unger, have circulated it also under the title "The Latin American alternative.")

Castro, Fidel. (1996). "Speech at the I Iberoamerican Summit—Guadalajara, México, 18 de julio de 1991." In *Por un mundo de paz, justicia y dignidad: discursos en conferencias cumbre 1991–1996.* La Habana: Oficina de Publicaciones del Consejo de Estado.

Demos. (1997). *Gobernar la globalización. La política de inclusión: el cambio de responsabilidad compartida, Informe sobre los principios democráticos y la gobernabilidad.* Cumbre Regional para el Desarrollo Político y los Principios Democráticos, Brasilia, julio de 1997. (Published under the auspices of UNESCO.)

Domínguez, Jorge I. (2000). "The Future of Inter-American Relations: States, Challenges, and Likely Responses." In Jorge I. Domínguez, ed. *The Future of Inter-American Relations.*

———, ed. (2000). *The Future of Inter-American Relations. An Inter-American Dialogue Book.* New York: Routledge.

Doyle, Michael. (1986). "Liberalism and World Politics," *American Political Science Review,* vol. 80, no. 4, December 1986. Abstract reproduced in P. R. Viotti and M. V. Kauppi, *International Relations Theory: Realism, Pluralism, Globalism.* Second edition. Boston: Allyn and Bacon, 1993.

Einaudi, Luigi R. (1999). The Common Defense of Democracy in the Americas. Policy Brief of the Inter-American Dialogue, Washington: Inter-American Dialogue, June 1999.

Farer, Tom, ed. (1996). *Beyond Sovereignty: Collectively Defending Democracy in the Americas.* Baltimore, MD: The Johns Hopkins University Press.

Fukuyama, Francis. (1999). "Pensando en el fin de la historia diez años después," *El País Digital,* Madrid, June 17, 1999, no. 1140.

George, Susan. (1999). *A Short History of Neo-Liberalism: Twenty Years of Elite Economics and Emerging Opportunities for Structural Change. Lecture on Economic Sovereignty in a Globalized World.* Bangkok, Thailand, 24 Marzo 1999, retrieved from http://www.millennium-round.org/.

Held, David. (1997). *La democracia y el orden global: Del Estado moderno al gobierno cosmopolita.* Barcelona: Paidós.

Held, David, Anthony McGrew, David Goldblatt, and Jonathan Perraton. (1999). *Global Transformations: Politics, Economics and Culture.* Cambridge, MA: Polity Press.

Hirst, Mónica. (1998). "Security Policies, Democratization, and Regional Integration in the Southern Cone." In Jorge Domínguez, ed., *International Security and Democracy: Latin America and the Caribbean in the Post–Cold War Era.* Pittsburgh, PA: University of Pittsburgh Press.

Hufbauer, Gary C. and Jeffrey J. Schott, assisted by Diana Clark. (1994). *Western Hemisphere Integration.* Washington, DC: Institute for International Economics.

Inter-American Dialogue. (1999). *The Americas at the Millennium: A Time of Testing. A Report of the Sol M. Linowitz Forum.* Washington, DC: Inter-American Dialogue.

Jaramillo, Isabel. (1998). "Seguridad Hemisférica: Los Retos de la Responsabilidad Compartida." Draft of a paper presented at the LASA Congress in Chicago, Illinois, September 25.

Jatar, Ana Julia, and Sidney Weintraub, ed. (1997). *Integrating the Hemisphere: Perspectives from Latin America and the Caribbean.* Washington, DC: Inter-American Dialogue.

Kissinger, Henry. (1994). *Diplomacy.* New York: Simon & Schuster.

Krasner, Stephen, ed. (1983). *International Regimes.* Ithaca, NY: Cornell University Press.

———.(1999). *Sovereignty: Organized Hipocrisy.* Princeton, NJ: Princeton University Press.

McNamara, Robert. (1968). *The Essence of Security: Reflections in Office.* New York: Harper and Row.

March, J. G. and J. P. Olsen (1995). *Democratic Governance.* New York: The Free Press.

Mares, David R. (2000). "Securing Peace in the Americas en the Next Decade," in Jorge I Domínguez, ed. *The Future of Inter-American Relations.*

Moneta, Carlos Juan. (1999). "América Latina y el Caribe frente a la UNCTAD X." Speech by Ambassador Embajador Carlos Moneta, Permanente Secretary of the Latin American Economic System (SELA), during the ceremony instituting the Coordinating Meeting of the Latin American and Caribbean Countries, August 5–6, 1999, in the Dominican Republic, before the Tenth United Nations Conference on Trade and Development, which took place in Bangkok, Thailand, in 2000. Retrieved from http://www.lanic.utexas.edu/project/sela/documento.htm.

Ohmae, Keinichi. (1995). *The End of the Nation-State.* New York: The Free Press.

Palme, Oof et al. (1982). *Common Security: A Blueprint for Survival.* New York: Simon & Schuster.

Polanyi, Karl. (1944). *The Great Transformation.* New York: Farrar & Rinehart.

Robinson, William. (1996). *Promoting Polyarchy: Globalization, US Intervention, and Hegemony.* Cambridge: Cambridge University Press.

Rojas Aravena, Francisco, ed. (1999). *Cooperación y Seguridad Internacional en las Américas.* Caracas: Editorial Nueva Sociedad.

Russett, Bruce. (1998). "A structure for peace: A democratica, interdependent, and institutionalized order." In T. Inoguchi, E. Newman, and J. Keane, *The Changing Nature of Democracy.* Tokyo: United Nations University Press.

Sassen, Saskia. (1996). *Losing Control? Sovereignty in an Age of Globalization.* New York: Cambridge University Press.

Schmitter, Philippe C. and Imco Brouwer. (1999). *Conceptualizing, Researching and Evaluating Democracy Promotion and Protection. EUI Working Paper SPS No. 99/9.* Florence: European University Institute.

Schumpeter, Joseph A. (1968). *Capitalismo, Socialismo y Democracia.* Madrid: Aguilar.

Smith, Peter H. (2000). *Talons of the Eagle: Dynamics of U.S.-Latin American Relations.* Second edition. New York: Oxford University Press.

Strange, Susan (1996). *The Retreat of the State: The Diffusion of Power in the World Economy.* Cambridge: Cambridge University Press.

Talbott, Strobe. (1996). "Democracy and the National Interest," in *Foreign Affairs,* vol. 75, no. 6. November/December.

United Nations General Assembly. (1985). *Estudio sobre los conceptos de seguridad: Informe al Secretario General. Documento A/40/553.* New York: United Nations Organization.

Vallespín, Fernando. (2000). *El futuro de la política.* Madrid: Taurus.

Vilas, Carlos M. (1997). "Participation, Inequality, and the Whereabouts of Democracy." In Douglas Chalmers, Carlos M. Vilas et al., eds. *The New Politics of Inequality in Latin America: Rethinking Participation and Representation.* Oxford: Oxford University Press.

⸻. (1999, January). *Pobreza, inequidad social y deterioro laboral en América Latina: ¿"Asignaturas pendientes" o resultados sistémicos?* Paper presented at the First International Conference on Globalization and Problems of Development, La Habana.

Walker III, William O. (1996). *Drugs in the Western Hemisphere: An Odyssey of Cultures in Conflict.* Wilmington, DE: Scholarly Resources.

Wolfers, Arnold. (1952). "National Security as an Ambiguous Symbol," *Political Science Quarterly,* vol. 67, no. 4, (December): 481–502.

The World Bank. (1994). *Governance: The World Bank's Experience.* Washington: The World Bank.

Chapter 4

The Prospects for the Free Trade Area of the Americas in the Bush Administration

Gary Prevost and Robert Weber

The Free Trade Area of the Americas (FTAA) is an international trade agreement that aims to eliminate the remaining barriers to the free flow of money, goods, and services across borders in the Western hemisphere (excluding Cuba), to create one large integrated open market. If successful the FTAA would encompass 655 million people and a combined gross domestic product of $9 trillion. The stated goals of the FTAA, according to the Organization of American States (OAS) and the Interamerican Development Bank (IDB) are to provide "free market access to goods and services for the entire continent," to link less open and less developed economies in a spirit of solidarity and commercial interdependence, promoting modernization, efficiency and "more open, competitive and stronger democratic societies in Latin America and the Caribbean."[1] The FTAA falls within the wider free trade and free markets approach promoted by the World Bank, International Monetary Fund (IMF), and World Trade Organization (WTO) to be part of a solution to poverty and inequity. In reality, the rules and policies of free trade are designed to create a stable and profitable environment for corporations and investors. Like other previous economic integration projects, the primary backers are the business community and the politicians over which they have the most influence. Not surprisingly, the opponents of the FTAA can be found among groups concerned with labor rights, human rights, the environment, and indigenous concerns.

The FTAA intends to gradually eliminate tariff and nontariff barriers that restrict or regulate the flow of trade between countries to make all markets more "accessible" to foreign goods and investment. Tariffs, which give favoritism to domestically produced products also provide significant revenue to governments that must be replaced by other taxes, if eliminated. Nontariff barriers are any government policy that may affect trade such as regulations that protect workers and the environment.

Most commentators see 2002 as a crucial year for the FTAA project. In its report, entitled *A Time for Decisions,* delivered to incoming U.S. president George Bush, the Interamerican Dialogue states: "The new administration must confront whether and how to negotiate hemisphere-wide trade agreements and move toward broader economic integration with Latin America, the Caribbean, and Canada."[2] This recommendation is listed first among all others regarding Latin America. This positioning is an accurate reflection of the interest that this project is receiving, but it is not yet clear on how 2002 will unfold for the FTAA. The Summit of the Americas meeting in Quebec was an important step forward. The stance of key Latin American countries, especially Brazil, is important but without the renewal of the Fast Track Authority (FTA) for President Bush the entire project may stall. FTA is a process that grants to the U.S. president the right to negotiate international agreements and then to submit them to the U.S. Congress for a yes or no vote with no amendments. Foreign governments are unlikely to make any agreements with the United States in the absence of the FTA. President Clinton's loss of the FTA was crucial in the lack of significant FTAA progress in the last four years. As a result, later in this chapter we will provide some detailed thoughts on possible congressional action on FTA.

The effort to unite the economies of the Western hemisphere into a single free trade arrangement was initiated at the first Summit of the Americas, held in December 1994 in Miami. The Heads of State of 34 Western hemisphere nations, excluding Cuba, agreed to construct the FTAA and to complete negotiations for the agreement by 2005. To achieve that goal, a work plan was established for the trade ministers of the 34 countries involving periodic conferences and the creation of 12 working groups that were to gather and compile information on the current status of trading relations in the hemisphere. These 12 working groups were later transformed into nine negotiating groups. On a formal basis the process has moved forward; the trade ministers have met regularly as planned— 1995 in Denver, 1996 in Cartegena, 1997 in Belo Horizonte, 1998 in San Jose, 1999 in Toronto, and 2001 in Buenos Aires.

The key progress made at the San Jose meeting was the creation of a Trade Negotiating Committee (TNC), which was charged with guiding the work of the negotiating groups and overseeing the overall progress toward the goal of achieving the 2005 goal. The TNC was also charged with the task of ensuring full participation of all countries in the FTAA process with particular attention to the concerns of the smaller economies and concerns related to countries with different levels of development. Canada was selected to chair the TNC for an 18-month term and to prepare for the next Western Hemisphere Trade Ministerial held in Toronto in November 1999. The TNC operates at the vice ministerial level and met five times prior to Toronto.

The Toronto meeting of the 34 finance ministers of the FTAA process was held November 3–4, 1999. No great breakthroughs were made at this meeting, largely the result of President Clinton's lack of FTA and Brazilian desire to focus more on the deepening of the Common Market of the South (MERCOSUR). However, the meeting did produce an upbeat declaration that proclaimed the process on track for reaching its 2005 deadline. The primary focus of the Toronto Declaration was to acknowledge the ongoing work of the Trade Negotiations Committee (TNC) formed at the San Jose meeting and to charge the TNC and the nine negotiating groups that it oversees to complete drafts of their respective sections of the proposed FTAA charter by the next convening of the ministerial meeting. The negotiating groups were given specific guidelines for preparing their drafts. The drafts were charged with being "frames of reference, not as definitive or exclusive outlines of an agreement."[3] Recognizing the likely difficult nature of the process the negotiating groups were charged with "preparing a text that is comprehensive in scope and that contains the texts on which consensus was reached and places the texts on which consensus could not be reached between brackets."[4] The TNC was charged with the task of assembling the reports and preparing a report for the next ministerial meeting with advice on how to move forward.

Argentina took over from Canada as the chair of the TNC and the ministerial meeting was set for Buenos Aires for April 2001. Interim meetings were scheduled and completed in Guatemala, Barbados, in January 2001 in Lima, Peru. During this time period the work of the negotiating committees—market access, investment, services, dispute settlement, agriculture, intellectual property rights, subsidies, and competition policy—moved forward tackling many different issues. In addition to the negotiating committees, additional structures were created as the process of negotiating the FTAA quickened. The most important institutions being the Consultative Group on Smaller Economies, the Committee of Government Representatives on the Participation of Civil Society, the Joint Government-Private Sector Committee of Experts on Electronic Commerce, and the Administrative

Secretariat (established in Miami). The Secretariat was formed, supported by the resources of several long-standing Interamerican organizations including the United Nations Economic Commission for Latin America and the Caribbean (ECLAC), OAS, and IDB. These organizations are known as the Tripartite Committee.

Another organization that emerged as important in the FTAA process is the Summit Implementation Review Group (SIRG), which was created following the 1994 Miami Summit to oversee the process of institutionalizing the Summit of the Americas process. The SIRG most recently met in Washington, DC, in November 2000 to plan the Third Summit of the Americas held in Quebec City April 20–22, 2001. Canada's role as host of the summit culminated a process of greater Canadian involvement in Interamerican affairs highlighted by its hosting of the Panamerican Games in Winnipeg in July 1999 and the General Assembly of the Organization of American States in Windsor, Ontario, in June 2000.

Another organization that has emerged as an important player in the FTAA process is the Business Forum of the Americas. Made up of private sector leaders from throughout the hemisphere, the Forum was created in 1996 and convened first in Denver, Colorado, in July of that year. Its subsequent gatherings have been coordinated with the trade ministerial meetings convening in the same city as the minister in the days proceeding the governmental meeting. This schedule was carried out in 1996 in Cartegena, 1997 in Belo Horizonte, 1998 in San Jose, and 1999 in Toronto. The sixth Business Forum convened in Buenos Aires in April 2001 just prior to the ministerial meeting. The level of integration of the business community into the FTAA process is underscored by the fact that its meetings are included in the official chronology of the FTAA process presented in the FTAA official website. This unprecedented access is significant because all other nongovernmental, labor, and human rights groups are only represented indirectly through the Committee of Government Representatives on the Participation of Civil Society. This latter committee is the first such group included in the negotiating process for an international trade agreement, but it seems unlikely to give environmental, labor, and human rights groups any significant input compared to the central role being granted to the Business Forum.

Key Issues

During the past three years, serious negotiations have occurred within the working groups on a wide range of issues. A review of some of the most contentious issues provides a window on some of the challenges that must be overcome in the coming years if the FTAA is to be achieved by its target date of 2005. The list is by no means an exhaustive one, but these are issues that have emerged as especially important to forces that are skeptical about the free trade project.

One key element of the FTAA plan is the concept of national treatment. National treatment is the requirement that corporations be treated at least as well as domestic investors. In addition, the FTAA is expected to impose a policy of "nondiscrimination" forbidding governments from having policies that favor locally produced goods and services. Such a provision, while seemingly fair on the surface, is actually quite problematic. Looking past the single indicator of efficiency, domestic industry and agriculture carry many advantages such as providing a stable source of employment, creating and maintaining domestic markets and providing a product that is more suited to local needs. Examples of this factor can be found in the contemporary Caribbean. In Haiti, the domestic rice industry has been almost completely wiped out by competition from U.S.-produced rice. The U.S. rice can be produced more efficiently, but the end result has been to devastate the economy of many of the rice growing parts of the country. The FTAA would likely also restrict subsidies for small farmers and eliminate price controls for commodities like corn and rice. An example of this likely impact on Latin American farmers can be seen with the results from the NAFTA agreement.

Before NAFTA, small farmers in Mexico produced mostly corn. The corn was consumed by the Mexican people mainly in the form of tortillas. The Mexican government, under NAFTA, reduced tariffs on corn, price supports for growers, and subsidies on tortillas. Lower tariffs caused U.S. corn, which is subsidized, to push Mexican prices down further, forcing more than one million small farmers out of business since 1994. However, lower corn prices did not benefit consumers because of the elimination of tortilla subsidies. The price of tortillas quadrupled in some places.

Another area of controversial negotiation in the proposed FTAA treaty is investment. Foreign investment has traditionally referred to the purchase of stocks, bonds, and national industries by foreign corporations. There have been calls for an expansion of the definition of investment and thus an expansion of what will be available on the free market. The expanded definition would include anything that can be given a monetary value like a nation's forests, oil reserves, the administration of hospitals, health care, energy, or water provision. This expanded definition of investment was included in the recently defeated Multilateral Agreement on Investment (MAI), but it is likely to resurface in the FTAA.

Related to the issue of investment is the deregulation of capital controls. Involved is the ability of states to control the amount of speculative trading that occurs within their country. Such short-term investing, which makes up 90 percent of the transactions worldwide, consists of gambling on things like currencies, stock options, and commodity futures (i.e., the future prices of crops and precious metals). National governments have sought to gain control over such speculation, but organizations such as the WTO, IMF, and the World Bank have argued that such controls would impede the wider strategy of investment liberalization. The battle of over this issue may be a strong one in the FTAA negotiations. In 1994 and 1995, the Mexican "Peso Crisis" underscored the vulnerability of a lesser-developed economy. Before the crisis Mexico had been widely praised by the IMF for taking measures to make its economy attractive to short-term investors. However, U.S. interests rates went up, which made it more attractive to invest in the United States and when combined with uncertainty over a new Mexican president investors bailed out. Mexican businesses went bankrupt, unemployment and interest rates skyrocketed.

Privatization is another key component of the investment liberalization strategy. Because of its legacy of Import Substitution Industrialization (ISI) from the 1950s, Latin America has a long history of state-owned industries and public services. Structural adjustment programs in the 1990s resulted in a wave of sell-offs of these enterprises to private investors, but many still remain under government control in defiance of the neoliberal principle that government control breeds inefficiency. Some governments, such as Costa Rica, have restricted privatization of public services in the face of citizens fearing higher costs and government workers fearing unemployment. Governments have also feared that private investors have no accountability to the population they are serving but are principally accountable to their foreign stockholders. Privatization can also result in the weakening of trade unions, as demonstrated in El Salvador. The privatization of public services there is a joint project of the IDB and the World Bank. Following the privatization of the telecommunications sector in 1998, scores of union leaders were fired and previous union contracts were unilaterally abrogated. Efforts by the unions to resist their destruction have been strongly resisted by the new management and the Salvadoran Ministry of Labor. The Salvadoran privatization program has also denied the government important revenue sources with resulting cuts in health care and education.

The FTAA is expected to limit the ability of governments to put conditions or performance requirements on foreign investments. Historically, many countries have had laws restricting the percentage of a business that can be foreign owned or requiring that some percentage of the profit be reinvested in the host country. These laws often require the use of local materials and local labor or require that a new factory operate for a minimum number of years. Elimination of such provisions has long been a goal of transnational corporations and the proposed MAI would have banned performance requirements outright; similar bans are in some WTO agreements.

Investor-to-state dispute resolution is designed to give special legal protections to corporations that invest in another country. Under the WTO's Dispute Settlement Body, disputes over trade are settled between governments. However, investor-to-state dispute resolution, a feature of NAFTA and the proposed MAI, allows a corporation to sue a government directly if they assert that a national, state, or local law threatens corporate profits or even the company's reputation. This allows companies to challenge democratically enacted laws and force governments to pay compensation, privileging profits over national sovereignty. Such a provision is under strong consideration in the FTAA treaty. If enacted it would make legislatures throughout the Americas consider the possibility of being sued as they discuss policies that would protect the environment or human rights.

Regulatory takings have traditionally meant that a government needs to compensate a company for a "taking," such as forced relocation of a building in order to build a road. The proposed FTAA would expand the rules on regulatory takings so that a corporation could demand compensation for any government action that directly or indirectly limits the value of an investment or decreases present or future profits. If enacted, legitimate nondiscriminatory government laws on things like pollution, toxic chemicals, land use, environment and consumer protection can be challenged by a corporation. For example, if a government passes a law requiring strict pollution controls, a transnational corporation that owns a polluting factory can demand compensation if the clean-up cuts into its profits. Such a provision can limit a government's ability to protect its citizens.

A Canadian case tried under NAFTA provisions illustrates this point. In April 1997 the Canadian Parliament banned the importation and trade between provinces of Methylcyclopentadienyl Manganese Tricarbonyl (MMT), a gasoline additive used a substitute for lead. However, because of its toxic qualities it is banned in many U.S. states. The Virginia-based Ethyl Corporation produced the additive and exported it to Canada. The

Canadian government passed the ban over threats by the corporation. Soon after the ban was in place Ethyl sued the Canadian government for $250 million claiming the ban was "indirectly expropriating their anticipated profits" and damaging their reputation. The NAFTA tribunal ruled that Canada would have to pay the Ethyl Corporation fees and overturn the ban. This ruling set an important precedent for the power of corporation over national sovereignty.

Intellectual property rights are intended to encourage and reward innovation and new ideas. Before the WTO, governments were free to balance between patent rights and the public good depending on the benefit to society that an invention might have. For example, they might limit patent protections to ensure that life-saving medicines and technologies are made available and affordable to the general public, or to enable response in the case of a public health emergency. This issue was recently litigated in South Africa over AIDS drugs. Under the proposed FTAA treaty the ability to make these exceptions would be removed. Patent protections would become grants of monopoly for extended periods of time, with the likely result of preventing the production of cheaper generic equivalents. There is also a desire by some corporations to expand these protections to include seeds that rural people used for generations, medicines that indigenous cultures have developed and genes unique to particular populations. A likely result of these measures would be greater technological dependence of lesser-developed countries.

The issue of genetically modified organisms (GMOs) is a controversial one worldwide. In opposition to many of its European allies, the U.S. government is seeking to expand the market for GMOs and other biotechnology. The FTAA treaty is likely to include provisions that require countries to remove regulations or restrictions on the sale, importation, or production of GMOs. The debate over the safety of these organisms is worldwide, but is especially acute in the lesser-developed world. A large percentage of the population in the LDCs work in agriculture and on small, marginal farms. The widespread use of GMOs would push farmers to use expensive, patented, genetically engineered seed that must be bought every year. This would replace the subsistence farmer's traditional method of saving some seeds to plant the next season. For example, Monsanto Corporation developed the "terminator technology," a crop seed that becomes sterile at harvest time requiring farmers to repurchase seeds every season. In the face of a widespread protest campaign, Monsanto has agreed not to commercialize this particular product, but the existence of such technology may not keep it out of the marketplace for long in the atmosphere of potential FTAA regulations limiting local government regulation in the biotech arena.

Anti-FTAA Movement

The renewed drive for the FTAA began to galvanize an anti-FTAA movement emerging from the wider movement against globalization that has been a prominent actor at most major, international economic forums in the last two years, especially the December 1999 meeting of the WTO in Seattle and the 2001 Summit of the Americas in Quebec. It is a disparate coalition that includes labor organizations, human rights groups, and environmental activists but does not have any clear agreement on tactics. The opposition ranges from system-oriented groups that seek dialogue with governmental authorities, to civil disobedience activists, to a small core of anarchist organizations that seek to create chaos at the site of any major international economic forum. It was the latter, although a small minority of the protestors in Seattle and Quebec, that succeeded in gaining the greatest amount of media attention.

As was the case in Seattle, the hemispheric leaders who met in Quebec were met with tens of thousands of demonstrators. The protestors were met by more than five thousand police officers and the barricading of downtown Quebec City to prevent the protestors from reaching the conference site. A wide range of Canadian and U.S. organizations came together to organize the protests. Some of the organizations included the Canadian Labor Congress and several of its individual unions including communication workers, airline employees, energy and paper workers, and nurses. U.S.-based organizations in the anti-FTAA coalition included the Alliance for Global Justice, Campaign for Labor Rights, School of the Americas Watch, Texas Fair Trade Coalition, Nicaragua Network, Jobs with Justice, the Mexico Solidarity Network, and Action for Community and Ecology in the Regions of Central America.

The breadth of the opposition to the FTAA was underscored when it became a focal point of organizing at the World Social Forum, a gathering of 5,000 antiglobalization activists meeting in Porto Alegre, Brazil, in January 2001. These veterans of the massive protests at previous international economic meetings in Seattle and Prague made the Quebec City Summit the next major focus of street demonstrations. One evidence of the small, but growing, anti-FTAA movement is a resolution against the FTAA passed on a 6 to 1 vote by the City Council of Santa Cruz, California. It should be noted that the resolution was introduced by the city's Green Party mayor, Tim Fitzmaurice.

A key actor in the political activities opposing the quick passage of the FTAA is the leadership of the U.S. trade union movement. At its Executive Council meeting in Los Angeles in February 2001, the AFL-CIO issued a lengthy statement on the FTAA. The statement begins by noting that in 2000 the AFL-CIO launched the Campaign for Global Fairness: "A multi-year, multi-issue campaign to build international solidarity, educate our members, incorporate workers' rights into international trade and investment agreements and hold corporation accountable for their actions globally and locally."[5]

The statement notes that 2001–2002 will be crucial years in the development of the FTAA and promises to be involved through teach-ins, corporate tribunals, and street demonstrations. Cooperation with groups both inside and outside of the labor movement is emphasized, especially the cooperation with ORIT, the Western hemisphere federation of trade unions. The union federation is expressly concerned about what it calls "the secrecy and exclusivity of the FTAA negotiations." The AFL-CIO laments that in spite of its attempts to communicate concerns to the negotiating groups, "There is no evidence that any of these concerns have been addressed in the negotiations to date."[6]

The concerns are summed up by the following, "If the negotiations continue along their current path, they will yield an agreement that undermines workers' rights and environmental protection, and exacerbates inequality in the hemisphere."[7] As evidence of this pessimistic assessment, the AFL-CIO focuses on NAFTA, which is declared to be a model "that has utterly failed to deliver the promised benefits to ordinary citizens in any of the three North American countries."[8] The negative results cited include the strengthening of the bargaining clout of transnational corporations and the extension of corporate rights to sue governments. The AFL-CIO also opposes the inclusion in the FTAA of the WTO's General Agreement on Trade in Services (GATS), which could increase pressure on governments to privatize public services.

The starting point of the AFL-CIO position is not to work for the outright defeat of the FTAA project but, rather, to fight for the inclusion of certain agreements within its framework. Provisions that it seeks to include in a final draft treaty would include enforceable workers' rights and environmental standards, protection of migrant workers, protection of nation-state rights to regulated speculative capital, debt relief to poorer countries, inclusion of WHO standards putting a priority on public health in trade disputes, and equitable and transparent market access rules. The AFL-CIO and other mainstream political opponents of the FTAA will likely focus their opposition on the U.S. Congress where the renewal of FTA shapes up to be a major battle during the 2002 Congressional session. The outcome of this legislative debate on FTA may well determine the fate of the FTAA. How is that legislative battle likely to unfold?

U.S. Congress and Fast Track

Most students of congressional behavior remain convinced that policy and procedure are intimately related. In fact, the defeat of Fast Track legislation at the initial step of the reauthorization process in 1998 testifies to the accuracy of the adage "rules are seldom neutral." Although scholars and parliamentarians cannot always predict who or which interests are likely to be advantaged by the adoption of specific procedures, this choice is likely to be a significant factor in making public policy.[9] To dismiss debates about arcane procedures as much ado about nothing, furthermore, ignores the complexity of these relationships and their significance in the policy making process, a significance that loomed large in the 1998 defeat of "fast track" legislation and is likely to play a similar role in 2002.

Unlike many chief executives, an American president cannot negotiate trade agreements and be certain that these commitments will be sustained. The American Constitution, as it allocates authority between the executive and legislative branches, establishes that Congress will be a major player in this process, ultimately possessing a veto over trade policy if it wishes to exercise it. Indeed, the constitutional basis for congressional participation in making trade policy firmly rests on two key provisions in Article 1, Section 8. In particular, the first provision gives Congress the power "to lay and collect Taxes, Duties, Imposts and Excises." Since most efforts to promote free trade involve modifying or removing taxes and tariffs, the taxing authority remains a relevant justification for congressional involvement. The second provision, also found in Article 1, Section 8, specifically assigns Congress the power "to regulate Commerce with Foreign Nations." In addition, if new trade agreements require the expenditure of federal funds for implementation, congressional involvement is assured because of the requirement of that "No money shall be drawn from the Treasury, but in consequence of appropriations made by law" (Article 1, Section 9). In all, these grants of constitutional authority permit Congress to play a formidable role in the foreign policy making process, a role that Cecil Crab and Pat Holt describe as "more power to influence foreign affairs than any other national legislature in the world."[10]

While the American Congress enjoys a unique set of constitutional prerogatives, the task of drafting trade polices is problematic under the best of conditions. Since the earliest years of the Republic, trade policy in general and the tariff in particular, have been controversial parts of American political life. It is not hard to understand why.[11] Citizens are likely to express different preferences for different trade policies.[12] For example, a citizen, whose livelihood depends on the sale of a particular product, may seek protection from foreign competition. Another may prefer to purchase that same product at a cheaper price. Both preferences normally could not be satisfied simultaneously and the member of Congress must choose between them. Trade policy, primarily because of its effects on employment decisions, has the potential to disrupt the lives of many citizens. To many Americans, a job may merely be a job, a way of earning a living as gracefully as possible. Yet, the fear of losing that job can raise the specter of changing homes, neighborhoods, and cities—changes that imply more than mere changes about routine working conditions.

For the Member of Congress, especially one who places a high premium on winning reelection, the chief task is to estimate the incidence of program costs and benefits of a trade policy on his/her constituents and to vote accordingly. Those members who find the costs outweighing the benefits for their constituents have incentives to join with other similarly situated members to try to defeat or to amend the objectionable proposal. One possible basis for this cooperation is some form of mutual accommodation such as "I'll support your amendment, if you support mine." When enough of these kind of bargains are successfully completed, the final result is either a policy that has undergone major substantive changes or a policy that results in the defeat of the original proposal by the creation of a cyclical majority.[13] Proponents of enhanced free trade are apt to find neither result particularly satisfying.

The political problem of passing new trade initiatives is further complicated by the fact that programmic costs and benefits are likely to show up in constituents' lives at different times. More specifically, unemployment rates initially are likely to rise much faster than the creation of new employment opportunities spurred by expanding overseas markets, a situation that greatly complicates the voting calculus for Members in an institution that was designed to be uniquely sensitive to constituency interests. Expanded international trade may produce net benefits overall, but these benefits are apt to be of little consolation to newly unemployed workers who are anxious to redress this grievance. Moreover, the stakes in this dispute have different political repercussions. The distribution of program costs and benefits are not perfectly symmetrical and Douglas Arnold has argued that "depriving someone of one thousand dollars produces a reaction far more intense (and politically dangerous) than delivering a thousand dollars in the first place."[14] What some psychologists have termed "loss aversion"—a willingness to evaluate losses of a certain magnitude more unfavorably than gains of a corresponding amount—places supporters of liberalized trade pacts at a substantial disadvantage.

Over the years, proponents of free trade have resorted to a variety of methods designed to minimize the political difficulties of passing trade bills intact. For many years, Congress, for example, simply authorized the President to negotiate tariff reductions within specified limits, a delegation of authority that deflected political pressures from the legislature to the executive branch. In recent years, the chief device has been the creation of Fast Track authority, that is, the enactment of a law that requires Congress to act on proposed agreements within 90 days in an up or down vote. Under this statute, no amendments were permitted and agreements, as negotiated by the president, were submitted to Congress for its approval or rejection in their entirety.[15] This statute—used successfully in the adoption of the 1979 Trade Act, the 1988 Canadian Free Trade, and NAFTA—expired in 1994. It was on the question of whether Congress would reinstate this procedure that the House of Representatives derailed Fast Track in 1998.

Procedures like Fast Track or the delegation of this authority to the executive branch probably offer the best hope for ultimately enacting controversial trade policies. These and similar devices are not cost-free measures. In return for a favorable policy such as liberalized trade, a measure of the ability of constituents to hold a Member of Congress accountable for his or her actions is sacrificed. In particular, the effect of both procedures is to make it difficult for constituents to identify governmental actions and to trace these actions to the voting choices of their Member. A candidate for office can, for example, express sympathy for a popular exemption to a trade proposal, but this representative will never have to answer to his constituents for his failure to support this exemption if the original proposal does not contain the exemption and if amendments are not permitted. Constituents can neither reward nor punish their representatives if they cannot reasonably connect their Member's contribution to the enactment or defeat of a specific policy.

The NAFTA Victory: "A Fighter, Not a Fumbler"

In the House of Representatives in 1993, President Clinton prevailed on NAFTA by a slim 16-vote margin, a victory that he described as a "defining moment for our nation" and that the press heralded as "one of the biggest triumphs of his Presidency."[16] Even if one adjusts for inflated rhetoric in the euthphoria of a hard-won victory, the NAFTA decision was an important policy milestone. More important, however, this decision can serve as a useful baseline for analyzing the 1998 Fast Track decision. Although the two issues differ in some important respects, there is sufficient similarity between the two situations to make valid comparisons. Most of the key actors were deeply involved in the resolution of both issues and, while Republicans commanded majorities in both the House and the Senate in 1998, the political skill of the incumbent President remained constant.

Despite nearly 50 years of a free trade policy, President Clinton's success in securing House approval of NAFTA in 1993 surprised participants and observers alike. In July of that year, Speaker Thomas Foley, one of the most cautious Speakers in the twentieth century, believed that the bill "was dead and that there was nothing he or President Clinton 'or anyone on the planet' could do to revive it." The *New York Times* reporter R. W. Apple Jr., in "A High Stakes Gamble That Paid Off," wrote that a top Clinton aide observed that "the private judgment of most senior members of the White House staff was that the President should abandon the trade accord, doing the best he could 'to cover his tracks.'"[17] Only on the day before the vote did supporters of NAFTA begin to voice confidence in the eventual victory, even though neither side had a majority of House Members publicly committed to its cause. "We're going to get it," President Clinton joked: "It's going to be another landslide in paradise."[18] The president's performance in this successful fight also helped to restore some of the luster to his tarnished reputation. "He did not look like Jimmy Carter, tripping and slipping in his relations with Congress," Apple observed, "but like the Lyndon Johnson of 1964 and 1965: relentless and resourceful, a fighter and not a fumbler."[19]

To students of American politics, public opinion is an important, though rarely decisive factor in most legislative battles. In the two fights for liberalized trade pacts, public opinion about the desirability of free trade legislation fluctuated across the nation, never tilting decisively to one side or the other. Several days prior to the NAFTA vote the *New York Times* published a poll that showed the nation almost evenly split on this issue:

37 percent favored NAFTA, 41 percent opposed it, and 22 percent "didn't know." Even though rank-and-file Democrats and Republicans divided almost evenly in their support for and opposition to this trade accord, class differences proved to be a significant factor. In particular, individuals with high incomes and college educations generally favored this proposal, while blue collar workers, those with high school educations or less, and low incomes typically opposed it.[20]

NAFTA opponents also enjoyed a slight edge in the intensity with which they held their views: 24 percent of the public strongly opposed NAFTA, while only 18 percent expressed strong support for this agreement. No doubt it was far easier to mobilize intense supporters for this kind of legislative battle than it was for other, more mundane issues. But intensity also entered the legislative arena another way, through the calculus that constituents apparently employ to reach voting decisions. "It is not the omniscient constituents armed with information on all of their votes that concern them," Richard Fenno observed in this travels with House members. "It is the individual or group armed with information and feeling deeply aggrieved about one vote or one cluster of votes that is most worrisome."[21] The reason for this fear, of course, is that intense individuals are more likely to vote against representatives who are insufficiently responsive to them.

Public opinion on a controversial issue like trade policy has a certain dynamic quality about it, and by 1997, public support for freer trade had clearly waned. In 1994, only 38 percent of the electorate expressed opposition to it; three years later, however, 47 percent of the people thought that NAFTA was a bad idea and a slight majority (52 percent) opposed efforts to make it easier for Congress and the President to enact "NAFTA-like" legislation.[22] No obvious event happened to cause this reversal of support. One distinct possibility, however, was that voters had not yet begun to see the effect of new employment opportunities in their own lives, while the critics of NAFTA seized the opportunity to blame every lost job on unfair competition, a posture that may have had the cumulative effect of eroding domestic support for reducing trade barriers.

Despite unfavorable public opinion and against the advice of senior staff, President Clinton chose to become deeply involved in the fight for NAFTA. He made only a few speeches in support of liberalized trade in the months preceding the September vote, and the President did not make a concerted effort to change public opinion or to rally public support behind this initiative. By the time of the September vote, however, more than 75 percent of the electorate had formed an opinion on this issue, and nearly two-thirds admitted that they did know their representative's position. Shortly after congressional approval of NAFTA, public support for this trade accord jumped from 37 percent approval in 1993 to 53 percent approval in 1994 and the positive publicity that accompanied Clinton's political success also affected his personal popularity. More than 55 percent of the voters now saw Clinton as a figure willing to stand and fight for what he believed, a category in which had fared poorly since the early days of his Administration.[23]

Fast Track: A Bipartisan Majority?

Since the end of World War II, American political leaders have attempted to conduct foreign policy on a bipartisan basis. The idea that politics stops at water's edge has an enormous appeal to the electorate as well as providing some assurance that changes in partisan control of the executive branch will not disrupt American commitment abroad. President Clinton and his allies succeeded in the passage of NAFTA because they built a sufficiently large bipartisan coalition to prevail in the House of Representatives. It was, moreover, the failure to maintain this fragile coalition that was one of the key differences between the success of NAFTA and the failure of Fast Track. Despite policy differences on a large number of issues, both President Clinton and Speaker Newt Gingrich initially voiced strong support for Fast Track legislation. In September 1998, however, Speaker Gingrich directed Bill Archer, chair of the Ways and Means Committee, to prepare this bill for floor action. All accounts agree that the floor managers still were short of the 218 votes necessary for a majority. Democrats charged that this action, approximately six weeks before the November election, was a blatant effort to embarrass them and the President. Republicans countered with the claim that if the President had demonstrated leadership and persuaded members of this own party to support this proposal, a majority would have appeared on the floor. Both sides may well be right in this dispute.

Floor business typically is leadership business in the House of Representatives and it is well within the prerogatives of the Speaker to make these decisions after consulting other party leaders. In all likelihood, Gingrich saw this as a tough issue for Democrats, one that he hoped would force them to choose between important elements of their reelection coalitions. By forcing them to choose publicly between organized labor and specific business interests, no doubt he hoped to enhance the prospects for a continued Republican majority in the Congress. Such tactics are not, it should be emphasized, an unusual feature of congressional politics. Indeed, it is frequently a minority strategy to offer embarrassing amendments with little hope of passing them. The effort, of course, is to find issues that are difficult for an incumbent to explain to constituents and that an aggressive challenger can exploit.

Democrats also charged that Republicans never seriously entertained the possibility of passing this bill because they failed to try to build support for it by modifying objectionable parts of the proposal. Congressman Robert Matsui, for example, a longtime supporter of free trade argued:

> The sensible and rational thing to do, if we want to pass it, would be to make changes to broaden the base of support on the floor of the House. But that simply has not happened. There has really been no effort to reach out to Members in other areas of this legislation. For example, there has been no discussion on labor and the environment, about language that would implement and expand the implementation if the bill is finally passed, or other bipartisan changes that could get a majority for a good fast track bill.[24]

Other than the inclusion of a provision that the Agriculture Committee had to be consulted before all proposed agreements were reached, nothing in the public record suggests that Republicans made a concerted effort to build majority support by moderating the most objectionable features of Fast Track. Ohio Democrat Marcy Kaptur even dismissed the consultation provisions with the Agriculture Committee as having no practical effect. "They mean nothing" she insisted.[25]

Democrats also criticized the Fast Track proposal for its failure to provide adequate safeguards for labor and environmental protection. In addition to organized labor, consumer groups and environmental groups coalesced in opposition to Fast Track, and Democratic members voiced many of their complaints in the debate. The United States must be, Pennsylvania Democrat William Coyne insisted, "a leader in terms of worker rights and environmental standards." Failure to promote these issues on an international basis also placed U.S. workers at a competitive disadvantage, he argued.[26] Minnesota Democrat Bruce Vento lamented that, "Trade pacts today have too often been the Trojan horse which undermines progress in these emerging areas of environmental policy, worker rights, health and safety standards." If adequate safeguards were incorporated, many Democrats claimed that they would vote for this agreement. Without these safeguards, however, Fast Track either became the "wrong track" or as Marcy

Kaptur explained, "Fast Track is not required for good trade agreements. It is required to get bad trade deals through Congress."[27]

House Republicans did not attempt to refute Democratic charges that there was no majority for this measure and that this effort was merely an attempt to gain partisan advantage before the midterm elections. Instead, they argued that foreign competitors were advantaged by the failure of the United States to enact Fast Track and that it was important to act quickly on this vital legislation. "We can no longer stand idly by," Chairman Archer explained. "Without Fast Track, our failure to participate in shaping the global trading system will allow our competitors to negotiate preferential trade agreements and form strategic relationships that exclude us."[28] Had the President exhibited greater leadership on this issue, Republicans claimed, it would have been possible to build a majority to approve for expanded trade. Republican Whip Tom Delay, for example, argued that "fast track would pass tonight if the President would honor his commitments and get his party to vote for it." This Republican leader also found it "sad that so many Democrats have relied on the politics of fear and isolation," and that "it is a scandal that the President has misled the American people about his commitment to support fast track, when negotiating trade agreements is one of his most important responsibilities."[29]

Republicans, despite the inflammatory character of their rhetoric, were correct in their assessment that the lack of presidential leadership in support of Fast Track was a key element in its defeat. Indeed, although President Clinton never formally withdrew his support from Fast Track, he did little either publicly or privately to advance its cause. By contrast, Clinton personally lobbied numerous Members of Congress to urge them to vote for NAFTA in 1993. C. Don Livingston and Kenneth Wink offered this description of extensive presidential behavior in the effort to pass NAFTA:

> One reporter covering the issue disclosed that some undecided members of the House had received as many as thirty calls a day from Clinton and members of his cabinet as they tried to win their support while another journalist noted that the Clinton White House devoted 95 percent of its time to generating support for NAFTA in the last weeks prior to the vote. In the final analysis, Clinton "won the trade battle by alienating friends, embracing enemies and working members of Congress with all the attention and care typically found in a small town's sheriff race." He pleaded, pushed, and bargained his way to victory and wooed House "with sweet reason and sweet deals."[30]

Of Clinton's effort, Speaker Thomas Foley claimed that the President worked harder "than any President I've seen, on any issue and I've been here 30 years."[31] Nearly five years later, neither the public record nor journalistic accounts suggested anything even remotely comparable to the extensive use of the President's persuasive powers in 1993.

The best explanation for Clinton's noninvolvement in the Fast Track deliberations can be summed up in two words: Monica Lewinsky. In the aftermath of the President's relationship with a White House intern, impeachment proceedings were about to begin and the president and his advisors clearly did not want to further alienate loyal Democrats whose support would be necessary to prevent his removal from office. More specifically, it was to the president's advantage if House Democrats assumed whatever position best served their own individual electoral needs. Clinton no doubt realized that he needed solid Democratic support if he were to survive the impeachment proceedings and by asking rank-and-file Democrats to cast a controversial vote in favor of Fast Track risked increasing the odds in favor of his removal from office. The election of almost any Republican was likely to add support for his removal from office. Clinton refrained from asking fellow Democrats to risk their own electoral careers and thereby helped to save his own place in office. Fast track authority ultimately became a victim of this presidential strategy.

After nearly seven hours of heated debate, a decisive majority defeated Fast Track by a vote of 180 to 243. The vote split largely along partisan lines, with only 29 Democrats and 51 Republicans supporting this measure, while 172 Democrats and 71 Republicans joined forces to seal its demise. When voting patterns on NAFTA are compared with the vote on Fast Track, party membership was an even more relevant factor in 1998

Table 4.1 Partisanship and Roll Call Votes, 1993 and 1998

	NAFTA		Fast Track	
	Republicans	*Democrats*	*Republicans*	*Democrats*
Yea	75.4%	39.5%	68.0%	14.5%
Nay	24.6%	60.5%	22.0%	85.5%
	100%	100%	100%	100%
	(175)	(258)	(222)	(200)
	epsilon = 0.36		Epsilon = 0.53	

Source: Congressional Quarterly Weekly Reports. November 20, 1993, pp. 3224–3225 and October 3, 1998, pp. 2688–2689.

than it was in 1993. In 1993, for example, the correlation between party and roll-call vote was 0.36; in 1998 it jumped to 0.53. This increase in partisan voting is part of a pattern that David Rohde has called "the striking resurgence of partisanship." Rohde attributed the changes in party unity and party support scores since the early 1970s to a realignment of electoral forces that produced greater homogeneity within the parties and greater divergence between the parties on many important issues. More important, particularly for prospects for future trade issues, he also argued that the internal reforms in the House of Representatives contributed to this heightened partisanship rather than restraining the legislative parties.[32] One important consequence of unrestrained partisanship is that it will probably be even more difficult in the future to form bipartisan coalitions on the floor of the House of Representatives on issues like liberalized trade. Parties in the House of Representatives thus appeared to be at an awkward stage of political development. They were strong enough to exert a profound influence on this decision but were not sufficiently unified to pass this measure without some votes from the other side of the aisle.

Despite increased partisanship in the resolution of this issue, perhaps the most striking feature of the data in Table 4.2 is the precipitous decline in support for liberalized trade across both parties. The failure of rank-and-file Democrats to support liberalized trade swept across traditional sectional boundaries. Southern Democrats, for example, provided 53 votes for increased trade in 1993, but only 16 votes in 1998, a decrease of 37 votes. Support from northern Democrats also slumped, dropping from 49 votes in 1993 to 18 votes in 1998. Although considerably less vocal and less visible than the Democrats, the Republican majority in the House also witnessed similar shifts away from liberalized trade. While more than 75 percent of the Republicans voted for NAFTA in 1993, only 68 percent supported Fast Track five years later. Since Republicans had increased their membership by more than 45 members when they became the majority party, this decline in support still translated into a gain of 19 votes over 1993. More than 70 Republicans voted against FTA.

Majorities in American politics usually become majorities by expanding their appeal beyond the narrow confines of a particular ideology, and after the 1996 congressional elections the Republican majority in the House of Representatives began to reveal some of the divisions associated with majority status. Republicans still formed the core of the support for free trade, but now they were joined by new Republicans who did not necessarily share this view or found themselves in constituencies that op-

Table 4.2 Comparison between Democratic and Republican Roll Call Votes on NAFTA and Fast Track, 1993 and 1998

	Democrats		Republicans	
	NAFTA	Fast Track	NAFTA	Fast Track
Yes	39.5%	14.5%	75.4%	68.0%
No	60.5%	85.5%	24.6%	32.0%
	100%	100%	100%	100%
	1.	(200)	(175)	(222)

Source: Congressional Quarterly Weekly Reports. November 20, 1993, pp. 3224–3225 and October 3, 1998, pp. 2688–2689.

posed liberalized trade. Some of the decline in Republican support occurred in districts previously represented by Democrats opposed to Fast Track. Republican gains in South Carolina, for example, came in districts that had significant numbers of textile workers. Other changes occurred in districts where a Republican protectionist replaced a Republican free trader. Members of Congress have considerable latitude in the ways that they combine primary and reelection coalitions and these coalitions may differ significantly between members with the same party label. A change in party in this instance did not necessarily mean a change in the Member's policy views. Perhaps the most apt testimony to the importance of district considerations in roll call votes is that almost 80 percent of the representatives cast identical votes (for or against free trade) to the votes cast for or against NAFTA five years earlier.

The defeat of Fast Track authority left its most ardent supporters somewhat bewildered. "We're really going to have to redefine where we're going on trade," explained California Democrat Robert Matsui the ranking minority member on the Ways and Means Subcommittee on Trade, "It's in shambles."[33] The supporters of Fast Track had designed a strategy that appeared to offer the best hope for success. By attempting to adopt a procedure that prohibited amendments and required only an up or down vote, they had hoped to capitalize on the propensity of the rules to structure the legislative choice so that a liberalized trading policy might emerge intact. They recognized that the choice of rules can have an impact on the kind of policy adopted. However, they failed to build a majority to adopt this procedure, a failure that temporarily at least appeared to reverse the nation's 50-year pursuit of global free trade.

The Battle for FTA

When the *Washington Post* columnist Marcela Sanchez asked William Perry, former Director for Latin American Affairs of the National Security Council, how active the new Bush Administration would be in seeking renewal of FTA, the former official predicted that "incoming President Bush will be as aggressive as political realities permit." For the supporters of Fast Track it is the "political realities" primarily produced by the results of the 2000 presidential and congressional elections that establish the broad parameters within which the battle to renew Fast Track will take place. And it is these same "political realities" that also will affect the strategic choices of the participants, choices that ultimately will decide the fate of Fast Track. What, then, are the specific political realities that confront the Republican President and do these realities offer much prospect for a successful effort to restore the authority?

Advocates of enhanced international trade can find considerable encouragement in the results of the 2000 presidential election. The nominees of both major political parties, Al Gore and George Bush, warmly embraced liberalized trade as part of their presidential campaigns, while two well-known third party candidates, Ralph Nader and Pat Buchanan, argued for a protectionist trade policy. Calls for a restrictive trade policy failed to resonate with most voters in 2000, and the candidates who campaigned for a protectionist trade policy fared poorly at the presidential level. Both minor party candidates finished far behind in the popular vote totals with Ralph Nader garnering approximately 3 percent and Pat Buchanan winning less than 1 percent.[34]

During the campaign, both George Bush and Al Gore advocated the renewal of FTA. Each candidate, however, adopted a distinctive position on this issue. In general, the Texas governor consistently backed liberalized trade policies without significant reservations and chose to emphasize other issues in his public appearances. The Vice President also urged the adoption of Fast Track legislation but required that any new authorization meet certain labor and environmental standards. This position, similar to Bill Clinton's winning position in 1996, was designed to appeal to the labor and environmental components of the Democratic coalition. Gore, like Bush, also emphasized issues other than Fast Track in his campaign. This agreement between the two candidates on the need to reauthorize Fast Track combined with the secondary status accorded to this issue helped to make this policy dispute a "nonissue" in the eyes of voters and journalists who covered the campaign. Under these circumstances, only the most diligent of citizens (a small portion of the electorate) could have recognized a difference between the two candidates and cast their votes accordingly.

While both candidates voiced their support for free trade, differences in the composition of their partisan coalitions most likely would have led to different priorities after the election. Corporate and business interests, for example, disproportionately supported George Bush in the election and it is likely that he would attempt to solidify his political base by attaching a greater sense of urgency to the enactment of Fast Track. Al Gore, by contrast, drew some of his most enthusiastic support from labor and environmental organizations, and to push for Fast Track legislation early in a Gore administration would have been an unusually risky proposition. In particular, it would have meant alienating his political base, ultimately threatening his entire legislative agenda. Presidents usually try to produce policies that reward their strongest supporters before they attempt to attract the support of independents and weak partisans. Although we cannot demonstrate conclusively that Gore would have acted differently than President Bush, we suspect that American voters selected the candidate most likely to pursue energetically the restoration of Fast Track authority.

The chief task for a successful presidential candidate is to use the resources available to the president to translate campaign commitments into viable public policies. Since George Bush chose to make issues other than Fast Track the core element of his campaign, he cannot legitimately claim to have a mandate from the nation's voters to restore Fast Track authority. Although many presidents have claimed policy mandates in the past, contemporary research, especially since the development of public opinion polls, suggests that claims to mandates are largely bogus.[35] The mythical quality of these mandates, however, has not stopped presidents from making these claims, especially as they try to persuade Congress to adopt specific presidential initiatives.[36] Because of the closeness of the election and Bush's unwillingness to make Fast Track a core issue in the campaign, presidential claims to a mandate lack both credibility and empirical verification. Unlike many of his predecessors, President Bush cannot argue that he and his policies best represent the will of the nation's voters.

For George Bush, the absence of an electoral mandate is compounded by the controversies over election recounts and the debates about the propriety of judicial intervention by state and federal courts that marked his ascension to office. Not only did the Texas governor enter the White House as a minority president (winning approximately 47 percent of the popular vote), but the results of the election were undermined by allegations of serious voting irregularities in Florida. It was only the timely intervention by the Supreme Court that sealed Bush's bid for the White House. No doubt historians will debate "who really won the election" for years, but the immediate significance for a Bush presidency is that the Texas Governor began his administration with a substantial portion of the American electorate questioning his right to be president. Democrats, especially African Americans, were offended by the partisan nature of the resolution of this contested election and one indirect measure of their unhappiness is that two months into his term, Bush's job approval rating stood at 55 percent, the lowest figure ever recorded for an American president at this point in his first term.[37] A high level of personal popularity does not guarantee success with Congress, but it does usually make the president's persuasive task much easier, especially with representatives whose constituents hold the president in high regard.

Presidents can engage in activities that improve their standing with the public. John F. Kennedy, for example, elected to the presidency in a close national election amid charges of widespread vote stealing, demonstrated that it is possible for a newly elected president to act in ways that encourage the electorate to evaluate his performance in favorable terms. Unless or until such reevaluations are successfully made, however, becoming president under questionable circumstances deprives the occupant of the White House of a portion of the "honeymoon period"—a time when Congress is most likely to be receptive to a newly elected president's initiatives. Congress, it should be noted, is more likely to resolve doubts about the wisdom of certain policies in favor of the president at the beginning of his term rather than at the conclusion of his administration.

Candidates for the presidency take positions on many issues and it is difficult to assess the importance that a newly elected President attaches to any particular campaign commitment. George Bush, for example, frequently criticized Bill Clinton for his failure to secure passage of Fast Track authority and his failure to pay closer attention to Latin American interests. "Should I become President, I will look south, not as an after thought but as a fundamental commitment to my presidency," he told a cheering audience at Florida International University in August 2000.[38] After the election, however, the relevant issue is not how Bush's priorities compare to Clinton's priorities but, rather, how Fast Track and liberalized trade rank in comparison to Bush's other campaign commitments such as tax cuts, educational reform, and rebuilding the nation's military. In 2001 the President placed a much higher priority on producing tax relief and educational testing than he did in securing Fast Track legislation.

Both President Bush and his closest advisers made his proposed tax cut their highest priority, a decision that certainly made sense in terms of the politics of winning reelection. However, to convince Congress to approve his tax cut proposal, the President needed to build public support for his tax cut initiative and to focus the nation's attention on how Congress responded. As a consequence, this Fast Track legislation was relegated to secondary importance and the President engaged in little visible effort to build public support for this free trade initiative until Congress has acted on the tax cut. If Bush had chosen to seek public support for both measures simultaneously, he risked the possibility that he would not develop sufficient public support to persuade Congress to enact his number one priority. For a newly elected president who hopes to have a second term in the White House, that was not a palatable result.

The implications of the congressional elections for the fate of Fast Track renewal are more difficult to discern. Democrats gained seats in both the Senate and the House of Representatives, picking up five seats in the Senate and three seats in the House. Republicans maintained a slender ten-vote majority in the House, while the Senate divided evenly with Vice President Dick Cheney ready to break ties in favor of the Bush administration. Since senators with their more heterogeneous constituencies and longer terms of office historically have been more sympathetic to efforts to promote liberalized trade than the House, our analysis shall focus on the House of Representatives. Indeed, in recent years, it is the House of Representatives that has proven to be the major stumbling block to efforts to approve Fast Track legislation and liberalized trade policies.

The most obvious conclusion about the 2000 election is that the 106th Congress looks like the 107th Congress in terms of personnel. Of the 394 incumbents who sought reelection, 385 were reelected, a reelection rate of almost 98 percent. Three of these defeats occurred in primaries and six in the November election. Of the six incumbent defeats, five of the six had supported the normalization of trade with China. (We shall use this vote as the most recent statement of a member's position on Fast Track and the liberalization of trade.) In none of these six cases does it appear that the incumbent's support for an expansion of trade with China was a decisive factor in his defeat. Members of Congress typically believe that "voting wrong" on a single issue is not apt to defeat them, and it is highly probable that factors other than "free trade" contributed to their defeat. Local journalists, at least, did not emphasize liberalized trade as a defining issue in any of the six campaigns. If only the 385 members who won reelection voted on the China trade measure, the result would have been a narrow 13-vote margin for the proponents of liberalized trade.

Changes in public policy are more likely to come about through the election of new representatives rather than the persuasion of incumbents. While incumbents were overwhelmingly reelected to the 107th congress, it is the infusion of new members that has the greatest potential for altering the outcome by shifting support from one side to another.[39] For a variety of reasons, 32 incumbents decided not to seek reelection to the House in 2000 and it is the representatives from these so-called open seats that are likely to be decisive in this controversy. Of the 32 incumbents who left the House voluntarily, nearly two-thirds had supported the normalization of trade relations with China. In other words, simply to maintain the same balance between the two sides in this contest the supporters of liberalized trade had to win 22 of the open seats. In 24 of these contests, the same party maintained control of the district, a result that suggests that the relative number of supporters and opponents did not change a great deal. However, in eight instances, party control of the district did change hands. Indeed, it is our best guess that the overall effect of the 2000 election was to produce a Congress that was only slightly less receptive to free trade arguments than its predecessor.

Standing committees perform most of the detailed work of drafting legislation in the House of Representatives and it is the Ways and Means Committee that will have jurisdiction over any Fast Track proposal. Neither the Ways and Means Committee nor its Subcommittee on Trade, it should be noted, are likely to pose serious obstacles to the enactment of Fast Track authority. In fact, representatives who are unusually supportive of free trade initiatives dominate both the Trade Subcommittee and the full Ways and Means Committee (see Appendix). All 15 members of the Trade Subcommittee, for example, voted for the normalization of trade with China. The full committee was only a little less enthusiastic in support of this proposal, voting by a 34 to 7 margin in favor of free trade. Despite intense opposition by labor and environmental groups, 12 of the 17 Committee Democrats also voted for this measure on final passage.

Members of the Ways and Means Committee are far more sympathetic to liberalized trade measures than the full House of Representatives. Republican leaders may attempt to line up a partisan majority behind Fast Track legislation in the Committee, but such a strategy seemed to be doomed to failure on the floor of the House. More than 70 Republicans

Table 4.3 The 2000 Election Results in Districts that Selected a New Representative by Party and the Former Member Vote on Normalizing Trade with the People's Republic of China

	Republican Replaces Republican	Republican Replaces Democrat	Democrat Replaces Democrat	Democrat Replaces Republican
Former member "yes" on China	18	1	1	6
Former member "no" on China	3	6	3	3
Total	21	7	4	9

Source: *Congressional Quarterly,* November 11, 2000, pp. 2652–2655 and May 27, 2000, pp. 1306–1307.

voted against Fast Track in 1998 and 57 Republicans were unwilling to support the establishment of normal trade relations with China in 2000. Indeed, the most promising approach appears to be the formation of a bipartisan coalition in the Committee, which can be sustained by a bipartisan majority on the floor. In order to produce a bare majority (218) on the floor, we estimate that about 70 Democrats and 150 Republicans will be needed to produce a small majority. Republicans in the House may be a little more willing to help out a newly elected republican president than they were willing to help Democrat Bill Clinton, but we suspect that a substantial number of Republicans will defect for constituency reasons and that a sizeable number of Democratic votes will be needed to offset these defections.

I. M. Destler suggests that the intellectual argument in the free trade versus protectionist controversy has been won by the free traders and the opponents of free trade have adopted a much more sophisticated strategy. Rather than simply arguing against free trade on its merits, he proposes that critics now insist that environmental and labor standards be maintained in any future trade agreement.[40] If Democrats are sincere in their opposition to free trade because of the possible damage to labor and environmental standards, then it may be possible for Committee members to negotiate a reasonable compromise. U.S. trading partners may find such a solution extremely distasteful and may refuse to accept any new trade agreement that contains such provisions. Indeed, the ability to find a solution that is acceptable both to the House of Representatives and to the leaders of other nations will test the political skills of George Bush and the Members of the Ways and Means Committee.

Winning Fast Track Post–September 11

The devastating attack on the Pentagon and the World Trade Center on September 11, 2001, added new complexity and uncertainty to the struggle to adopt Fast Track legislation. Some of the consequences of this terroristic attack were predictable; others are only dimly understood. For example, it required little understanding of American politics to predict accurately that public opinion would rally around the President after the attack, boosting George W. Bush's personal popularity to an all time high. Perhaps more directly related to the political viability of Fast Track, however, is whether the President can retain a significant part of this popularity as he tries "to rid the world of evil." Presidents can request that their constituents be patient, but this virtue is not apt to be practiced long, especially if the war effort goes poorly or the concrete achievements from Administration initiatives remain largely invisible to the public. No doubt George W. Bush's popular support may decline in the coming months, but the key question is: Will the President still be sufficiently popular so as to allow him to use this popularity to persuade reluctant Members of Congress to vote for liberalized trade?

Trade Representative Robert Zoellick in the last week of September called trade promotion authority "an essential tool in the war on terrorism," linking Fast Track to the war on terror. This linkage while initially appealing, is not apt to be very successful as a political strategy. Once initial reactions to this crisis begin to subside, arguments for free trade as a means to prevent terrorism will likely fail because they depend upon relationships that are not obvious to all participants. In particular, this claim rests upon a causal assumption about the relationship between economic development and the genesis of terrorist movements, a relationship that will be seriously questioned by at least some Members of Congress. Above all, however, this strategy risks undermining bipartisan cooperation on the Hill. For an American president to be viewed as pushing a partisan agenda under the guise of national security threatens to fracture national unity beyond repair. Such a short-term strategy, it should be noted, makes sense only if the President cares little about solving the problem of international terrorism.

In a televised speech on September 13, President Bush declared that winning the first war of the twenty-first century "is now the focus of my administration." If one accepts this statement of Presidential priorities at face value, then it becomes difficult to see how the President will find sufficient time to prosecute successfully the war effort and to engage in the public education and private negotiation that will be instrumental in rounding up votes. The task of keeping a large international coalition together on a sustained military and diplomatic offensive against terrorists is a daunting task. One need only recall, for example, the difficulty that the President's father had in maintaining the international coalition that backed the military effort in the Gulf War. That coalition only needed to persist for several months, not the open-ended and ill-defined period that the President envisions. Moreover, presidential leadership of an antiterrorist coalition will probably entail significant and continuous presidential involvement simply to reassure nervous coalition partners. While the cultivation of personal relationships will most likely play to George Bush's strength as a politician, it must be remembered that presidential time spent on international diplomacy cannot be devoted to building public support for Fast Track legislation.

The status of the economy will also help to determine presidential responses and presidential priorities. If the economy continues to deteriorate, the President and his advisers are apt to switch their attention to the development of a fiscal stimulus program that will help in the recovery. While all of the major participants may readily agree that deficit spending is the proper remedy for a stagnant economy, the substantive details, especially the kind of tax cuts or the targets of federal funds, historically have divided Republicans and Democrats. The sense of national unity engendered by the terrorist attack and the subsequent bipartisan cooperation that has evolved in response to this tragedy no doubt will make it easier for Congress to resolve these questions quickly. But the formulation and adoption of such a package will require significant chunks of time, time that cannot be devoted to wooing a winning coalition in support of free trade.

Proponents of liberalized international trade may call for increasing trading opportunities as a means to promote economic growth. But it is not likely that President Bush will push "trade promotion authority" as the best solution to a deteriorating economy. The difficulty is that as unemployment increases, reelection-orientated representatives become unusually resistant to policy proposals that might impose significant and immediate hardships on their constituents. Expanded international trade potentially may serve the nation well but expanded trade can also damage noncompetitive industries, ultimately weakening constituent and congressional support for these initiatives. The political problem continues to be that trade policy imposes large, concentrated costs on some districts while distributing benefits unevenly throughout the rest of the country. Moreover, even if President Bush ultimately wins congressional support for Fast Track legislation, the benefits of liberalized trade still require international agreements to be negotiated before they can be realized. If significant numbers of constituents are likely to be displaced in the near future and the improved employment opportunities develop only in the distant future, then Members of Congress, uniquely sensitive to the rhythm of the electoral cycle, typically have powerful incentives respond to the fears of their constituents.

In early December, the House of Representatives passed Fast Track legislation by a one vote margin, 215 to 214. For President Bush and the supporters of liberalized trade this win represented a significant victory in the institution that had been least receptive to this policy. However, both the narrowness of the victory and the intensity of the partisan debate that accompanied the adoption of Fast Track could be the harbinger of significant obstacles still to come. In particular, any Senate amendments to the bill will require that the House again vote on this proposal. With only a one vote margin, the danger is that one or more Senate amendment might disrupt this small House majority by adversely affecting a small number of districts, eventually resulting in the loss of support by their representatives. Some Republican supporters reluctantly voted for Fast Track only after intense pressure from party leaders and they might not require much reason to withdraw their support. Even with a popular Republican President emphasizing the need for executive leadership in a war against terrorism, 23 Republicans refused to follow their commander in chief. Republicans with either textiles or agriculture in their districts are among the likely candidates for defection from party ranks in future battles.

For the proponents of liberalized trade, the partisan nature of the debate and vote on the House floor may prove to be troublesome in the years ahead. Republicans prevailed in 2001 largely on the basis a party line vote. Despite presidential rhetoric about the need for bipartisan cooperation on this issue, rank-and-file legislators again largely followed their own party leaders in opposite direction. Even if the Senate ultimately approves Fast Track legislation, the failure to form a bipartisan coalition to bridge the deep division on labor and environmental issues is likely to surface again when the legislature is asked to approve new trade agreements. In the absence of a viable compromise on these controversial issues, a protracted battle about the merits of liberalized trade will continue to occupy a prominent place on the congressional agenda.

Latin American Skepticism

The battle for FTA in the U.S. Congress may well be the most important factor in determining how high a priority the FTAA becomes in the coming years for the Bush Administration, but it is not the only factor in determining the ultimate success of the FTAA. Even renewed leadership and pressure from the United States to move forward on the FTAA does not guarantee that it will become a reality by 2005. Enthusiasm for the agreement in Latin America has clearly waned in recent years, especially on the part of Brazil. A marker of this skepticism was the Spring 2001 meeting of the 19-nation Rio Group of foreign ministers in Santiago, Chile. The meeting focused on the recent political crisis in Argentina, Latin America's unfavorable position in the "digital revolution," and the negotiation of trade agreements with the European Union (EU). The FTAA process was discussed but not as the primary focus of the meeting.

In order to gain a better understanding of the prospects for the FTAA in Latin America, it is necessary to review the perspectives of the key players. Latin American skepticism grew during the time period of the late 1990s when U.S. leadership waned on the free trade issue. A region by region and country by country review of the perspectives on the free trade liberalization revealed that there was no single force driving the growing skepticism, but make no mistake skeptics multiplied regionwide. In a global sense, the questioning of free trade liberalization was not a full-scale retreat to protectionism or the Import Substitution Industrialization (ISI) philosophy of the 1950s and 1960s. Rather, it was an impetus for caution in the pace of change and for more regional solutions in the short term rather than a hemisphere-wide one.

Several countries are illustrative of this developing pattern.[41] For example, in 1994 Colombia was an excellent candidate along with Chile for a relatively early entry into NAFTA as part of an expansion that would eventually lead to a full-blown FTAA. This direction toward NAFTA was underscored by Colombia's commitment after 1990 to the principles of free trade liberalization and economic integration that was being pressed from Washington and was finding eager supporters throughout Latin America. Beyond rhetoric, Colombia engaged in real trade reform. Quotas were fully dismantled, while average tariffs were lowered from 40 percent in 1988 to 13 percent in 1992.[42] In the arena of economic integration, Colombia took first steps by establishing a free trade agreement with Chile in 1993 and the G-3 treaty with Mexico and Venezuela in 1994. An agreement with the Caribbean Community and Common Market (CARICOM) was also reached in 1994. The government also pursued complimentary measures such as relaxing foreign investment and foreign exchange restrictions. Traditionally state-run services such as seaports and railroads were privatized. The trade policies produced immediate benefits for Colombia. Between 1990 and 1993, total Colombian exports to

Andean countries increased by 45.5 percent per year while imports from these countries grew by 40 percent.[43] At the same time, both the United States and the European Union rewarded the country's focus on drug trafficking with unilateral tariff-reduction concessions. However, an important shift in Colombian politics occurred in August 1994 with the election of President Ernesto Samper. As early as the campaign for the presidency, it became clear that the new administration would relegate trade agreements to a low level of priority. President Samper sought to correct problems caused by what he termed sudden and unilateral trade liberalization. He also altered Colombia's approach to regional integration. The previous governments had moved quickly to pursue opportunities for negotiating access to as many new markets as possible, but under the new president the pace of negotiations slowed significantly. Integration was no longer the priority. Trade policy focused on fine-tuning previous changes with particular emphasis on protecting vulnerable sectors of the economy. Priority was given to providing subsidies to export sectors facing critical situations, occasioned by the new atmosphere of competitiveness that they faced.

Venezuela

Venezuela is another key case that demonstrated the complexity and difficulties associated with moving toward greater economic integration. Venezuela began the decade of the 1990s seemingly committed to the shift in policies that would bring them in line with the reform spirit present elsewhere in Latin America. In 1989, social democrat Carlos Andres Perez assumed office with an economic program that included currency reform and a trade policy that lifted nearly all quantitative restrictions. Tariffs were lowered from an average of 35 percent to 10 percent. Shortly after the changes were implemented, the government, in spite of some opposition from the business sector, began the process of economic integration. Over the next four years, a free trade area was created among the Andean pact countries, and Venezuela signed agreements with Chile, Central America, CARICOM, and with Mexico and Colombia in the Group of Three (G-3).

Venezuela's integration with Latin America during the Perez administration proceeded quickly, but domestic reaction to the economic results of the structural adjustment programs doomed its continued momentum. Popular resentment against the reforms was manifested by lack of support in Congress and, following two coup attempts in 1993, Perez was removed from office. New elections were held and Rafael Caldera won the presidency on a platform that rejected the economic reforms of his predecessor. In spite of the commitment to counterreform, the Caldera administration did not in reality reverse the basic trade policies that had been put in place in 1989. None of the trade pacts signed during that period were renounced, and after 1993, Venezuela's exports to its partners in the various integration schemes continued to grow. However, the growth was uneven and demonstrated misgivings about full integration. For example, within the framework of the Andean Pact, Venezuela's trade with Colombia grew rapidly, but with the other countries in the pact there was very little activity. Even between Colombia and Venezuela the integration was far from complete. Renewed demands for protectionist measures from Colombian and Venezuelan business sectors that found themselves unable to compete, together with problems of drug-trafficking and revolutionary violence, threatened to derail the integration process. The Caldera administration generally did not further the integration process, but there was an important exception. In March 1994 Caldera signed an agreement with President Itmar Franco of Brazil, which stated the two countries' intention to enlarge and strengthen their bilateral trade relations. For Venezuela, the overture was linked to gaining access to MERCOSUR (the trade pack linking Brazil with Argentina, Paraguay, and Uruguay), and foreshadowed a possible linkage of the Andean Pact with MERCOSUR. For Venezuela, Brazil is an important market for oil and oil-related exports. Brazil looks to Venezuela as a market for its manufactured goods and for foreign direct investment. However, overall the Venezuelan business sector seems to see little long-term gains in the trade relations with the MERCOSUR countries, as their exports to the other three countries, Argentina, Paraguay, and Uruguay, represent less than 1 percent of Venezuela's total exports.[44] By contrast, Venezuela's trade relationship with the United States is a solid building block for its eventual integration into NAFTA or the FTAA. Venezuela does roughly half of its trade, both imports and exports, with the United States. Venezuela is traditionally the second largest supplier of oil to the United States, lagging behind only Saudi Arabia. However, the benefits for Venezuela of being a part of a multilateral trading arrangement with the United States is not clear. Venezuela's oil enters the United States with less than 1 percent tariff under existing agreements. In the context of multilateral agreement, Venezuela could potentially face a much greater penetration of its domestic market with negative consequences for its native entrepreneurs similar to that which has befallen Mexican businesses under the NAFTA accord.

Venezuela's already shaky commitment to trade reform and integration may well have been set back even further by the election of Hugo Chavez to the presidency at the end of 1998. Chavez was elected on a populist platform that challenged the neoliberal model from which the economic integration programs follow. Chavez was critical of his predecessor for failing to follow through on his promises to reverse the direction of the country taken by the Perez administration. It is too early to tell how far Chavez may be able to go in reversing the trend of privatization and economic integration, but even if he only succeeds in preserving the status quo in Venezuela that will be a blow to those who seek greater trade liberalization and economic integration.

Brazil

Brazil's economic and political position also must be analyzed with an eye toward understanding its crucial role in the ultimate success or failure of the FTAA project. If Brazil is not a full partner in the FTAA project, it is hard to conceive how the plan could move forward in any meaningful way. Pedro da Motta Veiga argues that Brazilian regional integration strategies are shaped by beliefs widely held by its economic and political leaders that Brazil should pursue an integration strategy that acknowledges its global economic interests.[45] Brazil is a global trader—20 percent of its trade is with North America, 27 percent with the European Union, 22 percent with Latin America, and 18 percent with the Asia-Pacific region. Foreign direct investment (FDI) flows to Brazil following the same pattern—34 percent from North America, 36 percent from Western Europe, and 14 percent from Japan. As a result, Brazil's trade negotiators have a preference for improving multilateral trading systems and pursuing the agenda of the WTO. Brazilian officials are wary of trade agreements that impose stricter conditions of liberalization than current multilateral guidelines. From the Brazilian viewpoint, greater liberalization causes greater domestic dislocation and consequent protest from both workers and local entrepreneurs. The Brazilian perspective clashes with the approach preferred by the United States to incrementally expand NAFTA by bringing countries into the fold through negotiating greater trade concessions from the entering country than is mandated by current WTO guidelines.

Brazilian leaders, mindful of the U.S. approach, but secure in their own interests have adopted a defensive posture throughout the 1990s while moving away from previously strong protectionist positions. Beginning in

1990, Brazil's liberalization program removed most nontariff barriers and lowered the country's average tariff from 32 percent in 1990 to 14 percent in 1993. However, Brazil's reforms differed from the rest of Latin America: The changes were more gradual and many tariffs, such as on consumer durables, were maintained. The industrial policies of the Collor administration also limited the growth of imports. Unlike the situation in Argentina, in which many firms went under in the wake of the trade liberalization, no such pattern emerged in Brazil, the result of conscious government action to prevent it.

Within this defensive stance, the Brazilian government pursued its own integration strategies during the first half of the decade and focused on participation in the common market proposal of MERCOSUR. Narrow sectoral negotiations were replaced by a comprehensive set of tariff eliminations between Brazil and its MERCOSUR partners. This new approach modeled an "open regionalism" concept that was taking hold elsewhere in the hemisphere. Brazil embraced MERCOSUR's plans for the creation of a Foreign Common Tariff (TEC). However, Brazil's commitment even to the more cautious plan of regional integration began to wane following the Mexican peso crisis at the end of 1994. Among other policy responses to the crisis, the newly elected Cardoso administration raised tariffs on consumer durables and other items. These actions set back the MERCOSUR project, because they violated agreements that had been reached with other member countries. The trade restrictions were primarily in response to demands from domestic entrepreneurs who were experiencing the squeeze between greater foreign competition and a contracting domestic market. These actions did not signal a dramatic retreat by the Cardoso administration from the wider reform measures of his predecessors, but it marked the wariness of the Brazilian political and economic elite in the area of trade liberalization. These actions, coming in the immediate wake of the triumphal Summit of the Americas meeting in Miami, underscored that the optimistic rhetoric of that event had to be tempered by the political and economic realities in the region.

The decisions in the early days of the Cardoso administration highlighted that while Brazil continued down a path of trade liberalization its policies were not likely to contribute to an early expansion of NAFTA or quick progress on the FTAA project. It became clear in early 1995 and has remained true for the remainder of the decade that Brazil was not going to be a motor force for change. Further integration of Brazil's economy with higher income and higher productivity economies such as the United States and Canada was simply not attractive. As a result, Brazil has slowed

Table 4.4   Roll Call Vote on Motion to Make Trade Relations with the People's Republic of China by Trade Subcommittee, Ways and Means Committee, House of Representatives, and Party Affiliation, May 2000

	Subcommittee on Trade		Ways and Means Committee		House of Representatives	
	Democrat	Republican	Democrat	Republican	Democrat	Republican
Yes	100%	100%	70.5%	91.6%	34.6%	74.2%
No	0%	0%	29.5%	8.3%	65.4%	25.8%
	100%	100%	100%	100%	100%	100%
	(6)	(9)	(17)	(24)	(211)	(221)

Source: Congressional Quarterly, May 27, 2000, pp. 1306–1307.

the integration process of MERCOSUR while keeping its distance from other more ambitious schemes. Brazil has at least three primary concerns about the FTAA project. It questioned the viability of the 2005 projected start date as unrealistically early. It questioned the U.S. strategy of achieving FTAA by expanding NAFTA piecemeal rather than through combining successful regional blocs (Brazil's preference). Brazil also made clear its opposition to going beyond the current guidelines of the WTO. All of these factors together with the Brazilian elections in 2002 make the completion of an FTAA agreement by 2005 problematic. However, if President Bush does receive renewed Fast Track authority from the U.S. Congress in 2002, a very real possibility, then there will be renewed pressures on all of the Latin American countries to move the FTAA project to a successful completion.

Notes

1. www.ladb.org/exr/speeches. "Statement by Mr. Enrique V. Iglesias, President of Interamerican Development Bank to Trade Ministers, FTAA Ministerial," 1.
2. Inter-American Dialogue, *A Time for Decisions: U.S. Policy in the Western Hemisphere.* (Washington, DC: Inter-American Dialogue, 2000), 1.
3. www.alca-ftaa.org/ministerials/minis_e.asp. FTAA Declaration of Ministers, Fifth Trade Ministerial Meeting, Toronto, Canada, November 4, 1999.
4. Ibid.
5. www.aflcio.org/publ/estatements/feb2001/ftaa.htm. "Global Fairness and the Free Trade Areas of the Americas (FTAA)." Statement of the Executive Council of the AFL-CIO. Los Angeles, February, 14, 2001.

6. Ibid.

7. Ibid.

8. Ibid.

9. See, for example, Walter J. Oleszek, *Congressional Procedures and the Policy Process,* 4th ed. (Washington, DC: CQ Press, 1996). Readers desiring a more theoretical treatment of this should consult, Gerald S. Strom, *The Logic of Lawmaking: A Spatial Theory Approach* (Baltimore, MD: The Johns Hopkins University Press, 1990) and *Positive Theories of Congressional Institutions,* Kenneth A. Shepsle and Barry R. Weingast, eds. (Ann Arbor: The University of Michigan Press, 1995).

10. Cecil V. Crabb, Jr., and Pat M. Holt, *Invitation to Struggle: Congress, The President and Foreign Policy,* 4th ed. (Washington, DC: CQ Press, 1992), 2.

11. See, for example, I. M. Destler, *American Trade Politics: Systems Under Stress* (Washington, DC: Institute for International Economics; New York: Twentieth Century Fund, 1986).

12. Our approach in the first part of this chapter depends heavily on the ideas first presented by R. Douglas Arnold, *The Logic of Congressional Action* (New Haven, CT: Yale University Press, 1990).

13. See, for example, John Blydenburgh, "The Closed Rule and the Paradox of Voting" *Journal of Politics* (February 1971): 57–71.

14. R. Douglas Arnold, *The Logic of Congressional Action,* 32.

15. The action behind the scenes on this kind of issue is considerably more complex than this brief account suggests. For some of the "behind the scene" details, see Walter J. Oleszek, *Congressional Procedures and Processes,* 4th ed., 114–115.

16. David E. Rosenbalm, "House Backs Free Trade Pact In Major Victory for Clinton After a Long Hunt for Votes," *New York Times,* November 18, 1993, 1.

17. R. W. Apple, Jr., "A High Stakes Gamble that Paid Off," *New York Times,* November 19, 1993, 1.

18. Douglas Jehl, "Scramble in the Capital for Today's Pact Vote," *New York Times,* November 17, 1993, 21.

19. R. W. Apple, Jr., "A High Stakes Gamble that Paid Off," *New York Times,* November 19, 1993, 1.

20. Gwen Ifil, "Americans Split on Free Trade Pact, Survey Finds," *New York Times,* November 16, 1993, 1, 12.

21. Richard F. Femo, Jr., *Home Style: House Members in Their Districts* (Boston: Little Brown, 1978), 142.

22. George Gallup, Jr., *The Gallup Poll-Public Opinion, 1997* (Wilmington, DE: Scholarly Resources Inc. 1998), 242.

23. George Gallup, Jr., *The Gallup Poll-Public Opinion, 1994* (Wilmington, DE: Scholarly Resources Inc. 1995), 17.

24. *Congressional Record,* September 25, 1998, H8778.

25. *Congressional Record,* September 25, 1998, H8781.

26. *Congressional Record,* September 25, 1998, H9799.

27. *Congressional Record,* September 25, 1998, H8781.
28. *Congressional Record,* September 25, 1998, H8777.
29. *Congressional Record,* September 25, 1998, H8779.
30. C. Don Livingston, and Kenneth A. Wink, "The Passage of the North American Free Trade Agreement in the U.S. House of Representatives: Presidential Leadership or Presidential Luck?" *Presidential Studies Quarterly* (Winter 1997): 52–70.
31. R. W. Apple, Jr., "A High Stakes Gamble that Paid Off," *New York Times,* November 19, 1993, 1.
32. David W. Rohde, *Parties and Leaders in the Post Reform House* (Chicago: University of Chicago Press, 1991).
33. David Hosansky, "House Vote Signals a Key Reversal of U.S. Support for Free Trade," *Congressional Quarterly Weekly,* September 26, 1998, 2603.
34. Gerald M. Pomper, "The Presidential Election," in *The Election of 2000: Reports and Interpretations,* Gerald M. Pomper, ed. (New York: Chatham House, 2001), 125–153.
35. On the requirements for a mandate see Stanley Kelley, Jr., *Interpreting Election* (Princeton, NJ: Princeton University Press, 1982).
36. Robert A. Dahl, "Myth of the Presidential Mandate," *Political Science Quarterly,* vol. 105, no. 3, (1990): 355–371.
37. Dana Milbank, "Key Goals Face Early Obstacles," *Washington Post,* February 27, 2001, A06.
38. Terry M. Neal, "Bush Vows to Push for Strong Ties to Latin America," *Washington Post,* August 26, 2000, A6.
39. Ronald Keith Gaddie and Charles S. Bullock, III, *Election to Open Seats in the U.S. House: Where the Action Is* (New York: Rowman and Littlefield, 2000).
40. I. M. Destler, "Congress, Constituencies, and U.S. Trade Policy," in *Constituency Interests and U.S. Trade Policy,* Alan V. Dearhoff and Robert M. Stern, eds. (Ann Arbor, Michigan: University of Michigan Press, 1998), 93–107.
41. For an overview of how several Latin American countries have dealt with the challenges of trade liberalization and integration, see Julia Jatar and Sidney Weintraub, eds., *Integrating the Hemisphere—Perspectives from Latin America and the Caribbean* (Washington, DC: Interamerican Dialogue, 1997).
42. Mauricio Cárdenas and Catalina Crane, "Economic Integration in Colombia—Is There a Strategy" in Jatar and Weintraub, eds., *Integrating the Hemisphere—Perspectives from Latin America and the Caribbean* (Washington, DC: Interamerican Dialogue, 1997), 27.
43. Cárdenas and Crane, "Economic Integration in Colombia," 29.
44. Imelda Cisneros, "Venezuela and Integration: Is it Reversing the Process?," in Jatar and Weintraub, eds., *Integrating the Hemisphere,* 70.
45. Pedro de Motta Veiga, "Brazil's Strategy for Trade Liberalization and Economic Integration in the Western Hemisphere," in Julia Jatar and Sidney Weintraub, eds., *Integrating the Hemisphere.*

Bibliography

Apple, R. W., Jr. (1993). "A High Stakes Gamble that Paid Off," *New York Times,* November 19.

Arnold, R. Douglas. (1990). *The Logic of Congressional Action.* New Haven, CT: Yale University Press.

Blydenburgh, John. (1971). "The Closed Rule and the Paradox of Voting," *Journal of Politics,* February, 57–71.

Crabb, Cecil V., Jr., and Pat M. Holt. (1992). *Invitation to Struggle: Congress, The President and Foreign Policy,* 4th ed. Washington, DC: CQ Press, 2.

Dahl, Robert A. (1990). "Myth of the Presidential Mandate," *Political Science Quarterly,* vol. 105, no. 3: 355–371.

Destler, I. M. (1986). *American Trade Politics: Systems Under Stress.* Washington, DC: Institute for International Economics; New York: Twentieth Century Fund.

Destler, I. M. (1998). "Congress, Constituencies, and U.S. Trade Policy." In *Constituency Interests and U.S. Trade Policy.* Alan V. Dearhoff and Robert M. Stern eds. Ann Arbor, Michigan: University of Michigan Press, 93–107.

Executive Council of the AFL-CIO. (2001). "Global Fairness and the Free Trade Areas of the Americas (FTAA)," February. Retrieved from www.aflcio.org.

Femo, Richard F., Jr. (1978). *Home Style: House Members in Their Districts.* Boston: Little Brown.

FTAA Declaration of Ministers, Fifth Trade Ministerial Meeting, Toronto, Canada, November 4, 1999. Retrieved from www.alca-ftaa.org.

Gaddie, Ronald Keith and Charles S. Bullock, III. (2000). *Election to Open Seats in the U.S. House: Where the Action Is.* New York: Rowman and Littlefield.

Gallup, George, Jr. (1995). *The Gallup Poll—Public Opinion, 1994.* Wilmington, DE: Scholarly Resources Inc.

Gallup, George, Jr. (1998). *The Gallup Poll—Public Opinion, 1997.* Wilmington, DE: Scholarly Resources Inc.

Hosansky, David. (1998). "House Vote Signals a Key Reversal of U.S. Support for Free Trade," *Congressional Quarterly Weekly,* September 26.

Ifil, Gwen. (1993). "Americans Split on Free Trade Pact, Survey Finds," *New York Times,* November 16.

Inter-American Dialogue. (2000). *A Time for Decisions: U.S. Policy in the Western Hemisphere.* Washington, DC: Inter-American Dialogue, 1.

Jatar, Julia and Sidney Weintraub, eds. (1997). *Integrating the Hemisphere—Perspectives from Latin America and the Caribbean.* Washington, DC: Interamerican Dialogue.

Jehl, Douglas. (1993). "Scramble in the Capital for Today's Pact Vote," *New York Times,* November 17.

Kelley, Stanley, Jr. (1982). *Interpreting Election.* Princeton, NJ: Princeton University Press.

Livingston, C. Don and Kenneth A. Wink. (1997). "The Passage of the North American Free Trade Agreement in the U.S. House of Representatives: Presidential Leadership or Presidential Luck?" *Presidential Studies Quarterly,* Winter, 52–70.

Milbank, Dana. (2001). "Key Goals Face Early Obstacles," *Washington Post,* February 27.

Neal, Terry M. (2000). "Bush Vows to Push for Strong Ties to Latin America," *Washington Post,* August 26.

Oleszek, Walter J. (1996). *Congressional Procedures and the Policy Process* (4th ed.) Washington, DC: CQ Press.

Pomper, Gerald M. (2001). "The Presidential Election." In *The Election of 2000: Reports and Interpretations.* New York: Chatham House, 125–153.

Rohde, David W. (1991). *Parties and Leaders in the Post Reform House.* Chicago: University of Chicago Press.

Shepsle, Kenneth A. and Barry R. Weingast, Eds. (1995). *Positive Theories of Congressional Institutions.* Ann Arbor: The University of Michigan Press.

Strom, Gerald S. (1990). *The Logic of Lawmaking: A Spatial Theory Approach.* Baltimore, MD: The Johns Hopkins University Press.

Chapter 5

Latin American Armed Forces Facing the Challenges of the Twenty-First Century: Defense and Security

Hector Luis Saint-Pierre

Introduction

With the globalization process and the efforts for regional integration, the boundaries between the state's "internal" and "external" became thinner and thinner and in some cases were superfluous. In view of the serious problems that challenge Latin America today, it is difficult to decide whether they are inside the national borders and, as such, belong to the field of public security or if they are external and belong to national defense. The principle that regulates (at least theoretically) international relations of the members of the Organization of American States (OAS), that of "nonmeddling in internal affairs," makes that definition even more dramatic.

Another characteristic that increases the conceptual drama and makes operative decisions more difficult is the fact that some Latin American countries, among them Brazil, do not have Intermediate Contention Forces (ICF) between the Police Forces (PF) and the National Armed Forces (NAF). Those countries do not have a suitable resource (i.e., the gendarmery in Argentina, the carabineers in Chile, or the National Guards in the United States), which they can put to action when the PF are overcome and before deciding to call up the NAF. Lack of ICF decides that, once the PF are overcome, the use of NAF becomes the last option for the state.

To meet the purpose of this work, there will be discussion of the difference, not trivial despite being obvious, between policies internal and external to the state and between problems of public security and national defense. Without the intention of stating a solution, some aspects will be developed with emphasis on the particularities of the Brazilian case. Guidelines will be mainly the matters related to the fitness and ability of the Brazilian NAF to face the challenges created, both by its specific structure and readiness, and by the constitutional definition of its role and functioning, and by the political definition of the task. Along these lines the convenience of using NAF to solve those challenges will be questioned. Finally, there will be discussion of public security in Brazil, since it is one of the more severe social problems and appears as an incitement for the use of NAF in this matter.

Regional Situation in the International Context

We are in an international framework in permanent mutation and reconfiguration of the relationship of forces, which includes the centrality of the problem of its legitimization. In a short time we came out from a customarily and epistemologically comfortable bipolar relation of world forces into a multipolar or multifocal relation of forces. The first judgment on the Gulf War showed the indication of an orientation toward a new world order. On that occasion, forces of several countries joined together with the juridical endorsement of the United Nations, which offered a legal nature to the violence unleashed against Iraq. In view of Russia's compliance and the ambivalent international public opinion caused by the bombardment on the media, the juridical file was slowly set aside in the subsequent operations, establishing a new legitimization model ex post facto for the appliance of force, which earlier looked for legal approval from the UN. Finally against Yugoslavia, particularly in Kosovo, the mutation reached its present juridical pathological formulation: the North Atlantic Treaty Organization (NATO)—which, having lost its original purpose (that of Europe's defense from Warsaw's Pact), is no longer limited to that region nor does it obey its original purpose—puts to force its war power by sovereign decision, in an autonomous attitude and independent of the UN's juridical coverage, and with the only legitimization that provides the huge disproportion of its force. Conclusively, the fiftieth anniversary of the foundation of NATO was the consecration of the new formula intended to rule the world of relation of forces: NATO, specifically its American command, places itself, because of its self-ascribed moral reserve, as an infallible source of normalization for the world, and because of its unquestionable war power, as the necessary force for globally sanctioning it.

Within such an international state of affairs, Latin America debates its own contradictions. The case of Chile's former dictator Augusto Pinochet brings back the image of dictatorships that we thought were definitely buried, placing in a difficult situation, from a historical point of view, the desired consolidation of the democratic regimes in the region and, from an epistemological point of view, the validity and usefulness of the transition theories. The empirical proof of the inefficacy of the use of NAF in public security affairs and specifically in the battle against narcotics is in contrast with the United States's stubborn pressure for the use of those forces for such purposes. Projects of economic integration in regional markets seem to drown in the narrow margins of incompatible juridical orders. Political asylum granted to some members of the Paraguayan government accused of committing crimes in MERCOSUR countries is an indication of what we are trying to explain and is also a politically fatal wound for the future of that incipient market. The bogged-down negotiations of internal conflicts, as in Colombia and Mexico, aggravated by the employment of paramilitarism in the counter0insurgency strategies, create situations that could spread in the region. Economic recipes and the payment agenda of an endemic Latin American external debt, which forces to a concentrate the distribution of wealth, makes that possibility ever more plausible. The growth of organized crime with the resulting bankruptcy of social security mean, perhaps, the painful confirmation of the dissolution of the social pact and of civility in Latin America, as well as its inclusion in the endless list of the most important challenges of the new millennium. Finally, the generalized corruption of the governments of the region that demoralizes and splits social restriction, added to the frustration in view of the democratic electoral system's impotence to solve the urges and satisfy civic expectations, promote favorable conditions for serious political commotion and social shakings that could jeopardize public security of the countries in the subcontinent.

Strategic analysis

In the last 50 years, Latin America witnessed a series of demonstrations of the various ways of violence among men. Out of almost 40 armed conflicts taking place around the world, most are within rather than between states. With its own characteristics, Latin America has not been apart from this. Historic, territorial, sovereignty- and regional hegemony–based, are the conflicts that have marked several moments of the region's history, and some contentious of that nature are still threatening. Nevertheless, the characteristics of the conflicts that provoked lack of peace in the region were not conventionality, internationality, or regularity, but irregularity and political fights within the states.

With serious problems of distribution of wealth and growing misery, with generalized corruption that brings doubts on to the democratic elections system, with the ever more common "democratic neoauthoritarianism"—in which the state makes the legislative branch of government impotent and annuls the judiciary, restricting citizenship to the exercise of voting, limiting its voice to electoral polls of public opinion, restraining human rights to consumer's rights, shutting down spaces to the citizens' participation—Latin America is becoming a theater of unsteady and explosive social tension that puts at risk social security and peace in the hemisphere, besides threatening to export poverty toward the rich countries via migratory movements.

The clouds that keep us from being optimistic about the future in the region are not of international nature, that is, not quarrelsome motivated by boundary lines or by matters of sovereignty among the states, but they are mainly of political and social-economic nature, within the national borders. Such conflicts are aggravated by an economic project that corrodes the social conditions of cohabitation and disrupts the national economic policies; consequently the distribution of wealth is such that the poor become miserable and the middle classes are impoverished. The adjustments dictated by the neoliberal policy are creating a dangerous throng of unemployed people, disregarded by the system and the market. But perhaps the evil of that policy is its ideological wrapping, which manifests ethically in individualism, competition, social-climbing, opportunism, consumerism, and depolitization.

During the Cold War period Latin America cooperated in the system's strategic effort of defending the hemisphere from international communism. Today, free of that danger, it is considered as a potential market for selling surplus production and hiring devalued labor and providing a true and guaranteed profit for the financial capital. It is also seen as a location for human test subjects for drugs that the multinational laboratories are not allowed to test elsewhere, and as an "ecological reserve" of the biosphere and biodiversity from where to extract substances that are then patented in the First World. Finally, some see it as exotic ethnic samples for the photo albums, as a cheap destination for sexual tourism, and as a social problem that might reach them with migratory waves of poverty, but never as a region capable of making its own decisions.

From the worries of a nuclear world war new "obstacles" are looked for to justify the prerogatives and budgets of defense and to define a new role for the NAF, equipped and trained to combat against the "shared" external enemy (the armies of Warsaw's Pact) and the internal enemy (any response to the imposed order). In the new "international order," the declared strategic objectives try to be as "global" as possible.

In this manner, an agenda of subjects of "global" concern was tacitly established, which the minister of state for foreign relations of Brazil, Luis Felipe Lampreia, named in 1995 as "negative global subjects." Among these, increasing power of drug dealing, strengthening of terrorism, lack of control and proliferation of mass destruction armaments (MDA), armaments race, tension provoked by the increasing social unbalance, threat of migratory poverty waves, guarantees of democracy, overexploitation of the environment, and maltreatment of human rights are some of the motivations that lead the strategic concerns of this agenda. Terrorism clearly takes on a new priority in the wake of the events of September 11, 2001.

With these goals the axis that subordinates strategic definitions for this end of millennium consolidates: It ceases to be East/West to become North/South. The main front of strategic projection that defines political relationships separates the rich countries from the poor and the idea that continues to prevail is the NAF's guarantee of social control and the choice of force as the way to solve conflicts. The new strategic agenda with its worries points toward the relations of the rich countries with the poor ones rather than to the relations among themselves:

Poverty and Migration

The problem of poverty and of the migratory waves that it might create is not an endogenous problem for the rich countries. For them, the problem rises from the friction of the relation with the poor countries and as a result of the propaganda of their way of life, which attracts the poor from the developing world as a magnet. If poverty is not a universal problem, the way to solve it isn't either: For the north, a simple law of migration control and the reinforcement of border patrols (in boundary lines and coasts) is enough; that is, basically repressive steps. For the south, the problem of poverty is endogenous and will not be solved with laws on migration and even less by repressive steps. While there is misery and unfair distribution, it seems difficult for us to find the conditions of possibility to think of peace in the threshold of the third millennium.

Struggle Against Narcotics

Despite the fact that the largest centers of drug dealing and abusing are located in the north and that its richness encourages smuggling, production is mostly found in the south, where the north proposes to face the problem, but without any serious proposal for replacing the source of economic income offered by planting toxic plants for a large part of the population in those regions—with these, mere repression creates more unemployment, misery, and violence. Chemical products for refining the drug and the armament for exclusive use of the Army, which grants military support to drug dealing, come from the north; and the narco-dollars laundered in the south travel in that direction, thus diminishing the efforts to actually struggle against drugs. But amid the comings and goings of the interests of the chemical industries and of the financing capital, the option for violence as the way to solve conflicts left its praetorian seal through the establishment of foreign military bases in the region. Armed combat against drugs with detriment to other peaceful solutions, more creative and final, is generating, in response, the constitution of private armies that increase tension and make the understanding and solving of regional conflicts more difficult. As Willy J. Stevens admits, "Some experts acknowledge that the prohibitionist and punitive approach has a great responsibility in the drug related crimes, corruption, massive abuse of cocaine-based crack, diseases, deaths." Armed combat against narcotics increases the sophistication of armament and the fire power of the organized crime, placing the monopoly of legitimate violence in a difficult position, corrupting the bureaucratic-administrative structure of the state and sending farther away the possibilities of thinking about peace.

Protection of the Environment

The north has the intention of declaring some regions of the south as heritage of humankind or of interest for international community for their strategic value regarding the preservation of the environment. The exercise of sovereignty of these countries in which such regions are located is harmed by international meddling even in the way of punishing credits and commercial restrictions. It doesn't matter if the chimneys of the north darken the skies of the world, for them it is indispensable and strategic to preserve the tropical forests of the south, even though it is mostly the capitals of the north that encourage felling down their trees, buying and exporting their wood, often clandestinely. The forests of the south are heritage of humankind, the factories of the north have owners. But, even though the forests that give a greenish cast to poverty in the south are heritage of humankind, the imposed law of patents privatizes for the north the profits and benefits of the products from the ecological reserve and biodiversity of the South, thus kidnapping the only alternative of nonplundering production for the populations living in the forest. There is no formulation of public policies to replace the economy that impacts the environment by a sustainable development. The result is more poverty, unemployment, and increasing violence. Without a solution that harmonizes economic development with the protection of the environment, it is not possible to think about peace between man and nature.

Control and Production of Nuclear Armament

Manufacture and stock of nuclear weapons is no longer explained with the excuse of the East-West conflict, but this does not mean a decrease of its production. On the contrary, as Chomsky warned, "A researcher of the nuclear lab in Los Alamos in 1992 asked for 'real low output nuclear arms' that 'could be very efficient and reliable for counterattack against the future nuclear threats from the Third World,' with the ability to 'destroy units the size of companies' and underground command casemates and of 'neutralizing the Mafia.'" Regarding Brazil and Argentina, they ratified the Tlatelolco agreement (abandoning the development and employment of nuclear weapons) in November 1990, in the Foz Iguazú agreement, that is, almost 25 years after the first endorsement and only after both countries have sway over nuclear technology. In September 1991, with the Mendoza Commitment, Argentina, Brazil, and Chile committed themselves to not developing, receiving, or using biological, chemical, or nuclear weapons. But without a watchful culture of peace, structured with communication and denouncing networks, such commitments can be broken at any moment, starting a race for regional nuclearization with which, and given the technologic dominion of the nuclear cycle, the three countries could deploy their respective atomic bombs in the short term.

Democracy

After some decades of the epidemic of coups, Latin America experienced times of relative political calmness, now disturbed by the political trial of General Pinochet, the comings and goings of the incipient democratic institutionalization in Paraguay, and the Venezuelan paradox. With young democracies in some countries and others still consolidating, the region lives between the thrill of voting and the disappointment of the results. "Substantive democracy," which led the struggles against military dictatorships, handed over its place in the rhetoric to "formal democracy," only to finally content itself in practice with prosaic "market democracy." Curiously, the big powers are doing their best to keep the last alive, which they never did for the first. In turn, electoral campaigns—central to the formality of the democratic system—are compromised by the concentration of the media in a few hands. The high costs of these restrain the democratic game to only those parties that can afford it, often with money obtained by means of corruption, distribution of posts in the ruling machine, and promises of privileges for the "financiers" of campaigns. Rousseau's axiom meant for the English can be applied to the Latin Americans with absolute accuracy.

Briefly, with the unilateral imposition of the strategic agenda with these "negative global subjects," the axis of the original East-West conflict changed into an unveiled and unbalanced North-South conflict or, leaving aside topographic metaphors, into a confrontation between rich and poor countries. The "negative subjects" have served mainly as motivation and justification for the establishment of military bases of foreign counterinsurgency in some Latin American countries, guaranteeing their praetorian presence in the region. With that approach, tension and centers of instability have increased, thus empowering the capacity of regional destruction. Those countries that accepted "collaboration" from outside to repress the drug problem, placing their national forces in direct combat, are now facing three problems: continuation of the drug problem (better organized and armed), a corrupted and discredited NAF, and military bases staining their sovereignty. Arming the society, as counterinsurgent tactic with detriment to peaceful solutions, is leading some regions to a precontractual Hobbesian situation. As long as there isn't a definitive, unconditional prohibition and real power of punishment and surveillance on each and every sale of any type of weapons, the economic "logic" of the production of armaments will push forward encouraging and even creating conflicts, tensions, violence, and wars.

Problems limiting peace in the regional scene rise from the aggravation of social tensions. Lack of answers of the international system to solve the problems it creates itself is preoccupying. Eagerness to solve conflicts exhausts the use of repressive violence to keep tensions "under control." During the last decade the United Nations increased its peace force from 10,000 to 85,000 men, continuing to be as inefficient to reach its goals. The present economic crisis that upsets national economies, weakening the reserve of national funds and social savings, leaves no place for optimism regarding the future. It all seems to be on the way toward the aggravation of the crisis and the increase of social tensions. It should not be disregarded that in the future new centers of unsteadiness in the regional relation of forces could rise, and militaries could reappear in politics.

Until very recently, Latin America was dealing with international belligerence between Peru and Ecuador; there also were other declared and acknowledged internal wars in Colombia and Mexico. The presence of armed groups was detected in some countries while in others there were explosive conflicts for lands. By contrast, firepower of organized crime and drug-traffic, added to its internationalization, is causing an unseen and dangerous challenge for regional peace. The conflict between Peru and Ecuador was solved peacefully with the help of the Group of Rio. But the solution to the mentioned internal conflicts, despite efforts by the parties, is not yet in sight.

The path of negotiation in Chiapas was hindered by the nonfulfillment of the treaties, lack of dialogue among the parties, and offensive tactics carried out by paramilitary groups. Self-dismissal of CONAI (National Commission for Mediation) as protest in view of its impotence as mediator in the dialogue, will hinder any attempt to restart negotiations between the Mexican government and the EZLN (Zapatista Army for National Liberation). The established presence of the group Popular Revolutionary Army (EPR) operating in the state of Guerrero opens another combat front that will call for redoubling peace efforts. Uncontrolled action of armed civilian groups as an element of provocation adds a highly complicating element to the understanding of and solution to the conflict between the parties. An increase of violence and of genocide, together with xenophobic discrimination and the aggression regarding observers and defenders of human rights, draw a dark picture for Mexico.

The guerrilla phenomenon in Colombia seems to be the hardest-to-solve belligerent situation. There were several attempts on both sides, before and after the recent elections in Colombia, pointing out the possibility of dialogue, but until now contacts have been very few. The presence of several guerrilla groups operating in Colombia hampers the identification of a suitable interlocutor for the dialogue that has become a must, given the firepower of the guerrilla groups that led Colombia to a strategic balance: They cannot gain power, nor can the governmental forces wipe them out. Guerrilla forces crossing borders (or, recently, Colombian troops crossing in the north of Brazil) create international difficulties with neighbor countries by threatening to export violence.

Rearticulation of the group Shining Path and the permanence of the "emerretistas" in various regions in Peru, together with popular protests, make this country another potential force for regional instability. The violent seizure of the Japanese Embassy in Lima, when the guerrilla was negotiating and reaffirming its willingness for the dialogue as the way to end the conflict peacefully, established a very bad precedent for future attempts to solve differences peacefully.

Armed groups also have been detected in other countries and the appearance of other groups would not be surprising, if the social conditions continue to worsen, in the absence of political solutions. Other tension centers that might create confrontations, even armed ones, are the conflicts for land property. Groups of farmers without access to the land and disregarded by the cities make up well-organized groups that threaten peace in the fields and cities. Asking for agrarian reform and distribution of land for labor, the Movement of the Landless (MST) in Brazil constitutes a center of tension that could generate national and regional unrest. Similar movements could arise in other countries of the region. For instance, in Santiago del Estero, northeast Argentina, there have been confrontations between land owners and the Argentinean MST.

To find a peaceful and negotiated solution to armed conflicts in the region it is necessary to study its peculiarities. By historic contrast, we find a significant difference in the present manifestations of armed struggle in the region compared to past decades. We don't find the presence of the "third party interested" that featured in previous armed movements, nor the legitimate dispute of an ideology, nor the orientation of utopias. If earlier the political goal was socialism, today it seems to be the expansion of democracy; if the tactics were to arm guerrilla focal points, today they are to influence national and international public opinion. Everything seems to point out that the motivation that keeps these armed groups active is the development of citizenship, the acknowledgment of disregarded social and ethnic groups, demanding social justice that the traditional political parties do not seem able to achieve.

The population of the region is disappointed with its present life and has no expectations for the future. This discouragement can be ascribed to an explosive convergence of several states of crisis caused by a series of factors:

1. Economic crisis: dismantling of industrial productive capacity; unemployment, rarely occasional and mostly structural and final; squandering of public heritage by means of uncontrolled privatization; use of social savings to give way to privatization; unprotected exposure of the national treasury to financial plunder; lack of projects for sustainable economic development; and submission to a payable external debt.

2. Social crisis: transformation of the citizen into consumer; closing down the channels for participation of organized society; disassembling of the trade union movement, annulling it as negotiating subject; growing contempt for ethics as regulators of social life; promotion of values as individualism, competence, and apolitical feelings as conditions of the chances to join the labor market; collective interests subordinated to individuals; nonobservance of the fundamental rights of the man and of the citizen; consideration of promoters of human rights as foreign agents and their action as foreign meddling in internal affairs; and contempt for pacifism and for peaceful solution of conflicts.

3. Political crisis: transformation of the political sphere into market; growing distrust in the ability of the democratic system to solve social problems; generalized corruption at all levels of the administrative structure of the governments; political speech replaced by marketing; transformation of political meetings into shows; legitimacy threatened by high nonparticipation; subordination of the party's interests to personal interests for power; promiscuity between the public and the private; promiscuity between politics and show business; and lack of coherence between the electoral speech and governmental practice.

Bibliography

Chomsky, Noam. *Novas e velhas ordens mundiais,* SP, ed. Scritta, 97.

Saint-Pierre, Hector. (1991). *Max Weber: entre a paixão e a razão,* Editora da UNI-CAMP, Série Repertórios, Campinas SP.

Saint-Pierre, Hector. (2000). *A Política armanda. Fundamentos da Guerra revolucionária.* SP, Editora da UNESP.

Saint-Pierre, Hector and Suzeley Kalil Mathias, eds. (2001). *Entre votos e botas: As Forcas Armadas no labirinto latino-americano do novo milênio.* Franca-SP, UNESP.

Regional Issues

Chapter 6

Caribbean Community at the Crossroads

Armando Lopez Coll

The member states of Caribbean Community (CARICOM)—Antigua and Barbuda, The Bahamas, Barbados,[1] Belize, Dominica, Grenada, Guyana, Haiti,[2] Jamaica, Montserrat, San Cristobal and Nevis, Saint Lucia, Saint Vincent, and the Grenadines, Surinam, and Trinidad and Tobago[3]— are facing many troubles that are very typical of underdevelopment. These problems are high unemployment rate; unqualified workforce; inadequate infrastructure, specifically in areas of transportation and communications; deficits in current accounts balances; and insufficient home savings in order to reach the goals for development.

In addition, CARICOM members have nonvaried economic structure and thus they are not able to produce the capital and consumption goods required for the functioning and expansion of the economy. That is the reason why they depend on imports, including essential goods such as food. The acquisition of hard currency is a critical element for growth and even for normal economic functioning. By contrast, exports are not diversified and are concentrated on a few products, most of them being primary products and tourism, which has become the most important activity for the acquisition of currencies. These means of currency acquisition are extremely vulnerable in the face of the changes of the international economic environment, such as demands, prices, and crises. If we add to the high external economic dependence the relative market smallness and economic fragmentation as a result of the insufficient transportation and communication of the intra-CARICOM development and the enormous fragility toward natural disasters, such as hurricanes, tropical storms that cause floods and huge damage because of winds, and droughts in almost all the region, we come to the conclusion that we are facing extremely vulnerable nations.

It has been suggested that regional integration should be a catalyst to reach the needed growth for the economy, a principal way to face and overcome these problems as a whole. This will allow market expansion, the harmonization of production strategies, and development of scale economies. It is also expected that integration serves as a tool to promote industrial growth, stimulate investment and new sectors, and diversify and specialize productions and exports. In the longer term, this is expected to allow balanced economic growth, a minimum unemployment, a high standard of living, and an optimum use of human and natural available resources. These goals and expectations regarding integration appear clearly in the mandate of CARICOM, "Our mission is to provide services and dynamic leadership in association with Community Institutions and groups for the achievement of a CARICOM which becomes internationally competitive and which guarantees a better quality of life for all."[4]

Development of Regional Integration

The Caribbean Free Trade Association (CARIFTA, 1968–1973) represented the first attempt of the region's integration in which external factors or powers did not have a priority over the internal ones. The establishment of the integrating body was based, above all, on an organizational point of view, as in the example given by the European Free Trade Organization to which the United Kingdom belonged. The agreement—Article 32—established that "any territory being signatory or not can participate in this agreement . . . in the terms and condition established by the Council." This was true especially for Trinidad and Tobago, under the leadership of Williams, which agreed to openly support the entrance of new member states, including the Dominican Republic, Guadeloupe, Martinique, Haiti, and not ruling out membership for Cuba.

Commenting on this position, H. Brewster wrote, "Three reasons could be indicated—political prestige, the historical significance of Caribbean Panamericanism (a concept strongly emphasized by the First Minister Williams in his works), the building of a bridge to the transition of a

Caribbean bloc unified for insertion in Latin-American associations, and the use of the possible participation of Cuba as a symbolic isolation against American and European indiscrimination penetration."[5] Among the principal stated objectives we had the following: to promote expansion and diversification of trade among the member states, to foster balanced and progressive economy development, to guarantee an equal distribution in costs and benefits as a result of integration. At the same time other goals were stated, such as to try to reduce food imports and others. From the point of view of trade creation, the association was initially successful in the so-called easy stage; interregional commerce increased rapidly.

However, CARIFTA did not facilitate the free movement of capital and work and force, not even the coordination of agricultural and industrial policies. Thus, in its first five years of foundation, little progress was made aiming at the creation of regional integration. In 1970, the prospect of the United Kingdom's entrance to the European Economic Community warned the islands of their vulnerability in the case of a preferential trade rupture with that commercial partner. In that same year, economists from the University of the West Indies issued a report in which it was established that the creation of a free trading zone was not sufficient to give a complete and real regional integration. Together with these reasons there was an institutional and administrative crisis after five years of existence and CARIFTA started to fall apart.

CARICOM

The Caribbean Community and the Common Market (CARICOM) was established by the Treaty of Chaguaramas, and originally was subscribed to by the independent states of Barbados, Jamaica, Guyana, and Trinidad and Tobago; it started to function on August 1, 1973. Later, the eight English-speaking Caribbean countries joined in, becoming full members on May 1, 1974. From the beginning, the community has concentrated on economic integration of member states, in the coordination of external policies of the independent states, belonging to the association and in the functional cooperation in different activities such as education, culture, health, meteorology, transportation, and labor relations. The Caribbean Common Market was created on the basis of a common policy of protection, with high tax and nontax barriers in front of imports from third countries. The explicit objective of the common market was that of protecting the subregional agricultural and industrial production and at the same time supporting development of regional production that is internationally competitive, by means of the creation of a well-protected market.

After becoming signatories to CARICOM in 1981, the islands of the east Caribbean, Antigua and Barbuda, Dominique, Granada, Montserrat, San Cristobal-Nevis, Saint Lucia, and Saint Vincent and the Grenadines established the Organization of Caribbean States (OCS). The organization coordinates the strategies of development among members and facilitates economic cooperation. At the same time, it coordinates external policy and aspects of defense. It was created as a reaction to the fact that the highest benefits derived from the area's integration were polarized around the largest members, especially Jamaica and Trinidad and Tobago.

It should be mentioned that in its existence of over 25 years, CARICOM has gone through two different stages. The first one was marked by a protectionist character, in which there was a lot of ignorance by the other members of the Caribbean and by the Latin American neighbors. This period began almost with its foundation until the last years of the 1980s. The second period, which lasts up to the present, was marked by more openings and intended to insert the community into an ever more globalized world, not exempt of contradictions and inconsistencies. We believe that it is not possible to understand the second stage of CARICOM and above all its current situation, including challenges and opportunities, relative inconsistencies, and lack of definition without understanding the essential elements that characterized its first stage and that constitute the genesis of its current situation.

First Stage (1973–1989)

The State Model

For the member states of CARICOM, from its arrival to independence during the 1960s, a state-centered model was developed whose most important economic features were: state market control; closed or semiclosed economies; import substitution and a "moderate" inflation. In the framework of this model, a strong state was developed and it intended to solve economic social and political problems. In many cases it lead to a hyperpoliticized society, while people's participation in government decisions was reduced to elections. At the same time, the elite took control of decision making with little separation between party and government, where the states had a leading role over society, and where paternalism became a tradition. This state tradition has its origins during the colonial period and again in the process of decolonization. As an answer to the strong nationalist movements that started in the 1930s and 1940s, the United Kingdom started a process of gradual decolonization marked by self-government that allowed the political education of a native elite, following the organizational patterns existing in the metropolis, especially parliamentary government. By means of this process, the future English-speaking Caribbean leaders were given a political culture, based in the "Westminster" model, which has been considered a key element to understanding political stability that these countries have enjoyed for some time.

Another always present element was the ideal of gaining independence by means of the colonies' political and economic independence through a federation or other sort of union. By the end of the 1950s and during the1960s, the strengthening of state economic policy objectives were aimed at reaching development. The key elements of such policy were:

a.   industrialization
b.   import substitution and export promotion
c.   active protectionism.

The key element supporting the whole functioning of the model was foreign investment. Other conditions were also created including low or zero taxes, and abundant and cheap labor. Such a model, universally accepted in the area, was called industrialization by invitation, or "Puerto Rican model." The main promoters of such a model were W. Arthur Lewis and C. J. Burgess. This set of ideas was greatly influenced by Keynesian thoughts, and above all by the multiplier ideas, according to which a change in investment has a potential effect on economy.

Against all expectations, the industry established by foreign investment did not bring the effects foreseen, and did not help create the necessary intrasector relations or solve the problem of underdevelopment. The agricultural sector was controlled by foreign capital and not by the national one as it had been projected, and besides, with the increase of industrialization, there was an increase in migration from the countryside to the cities.

The model brought a dramatic increase in tourism that was left in the hands of transnational enterprises and did not produce an impact on the rest of the economy, due to the fact that most inputs including food were imported. The state model brought about a change in the state because it became the owner of public enterprises or the partner of transnational companies.

Alternatives for a Noncapitalist Development

During the 1970s, these state models based on the Puerto Rican industrialization model took two different paths. Some of them became involved in a capitalist orientation, whereas others searched for an alternative road to development: Jamaica, Guyana, and Granada. In these three cases, the alternative ways were attempted because it was believed that the previous model had increased social and economic differences. However, both ways increased the role of the state over the economy. In Jamaica, a so-called democratic socialism was established, in which public, private, and cooperative sectors had a huge participation. The state and cooperatives had control over the means of production. By the end of the 1970s, the increased government control directed by Michael Manley over the economy caused huge losses of capital, both national and foreign, and the almost complete stagnation of the country's economy.

In Guyana, a similar process took place, with massive nationalization in the bauxite and sugar industry between 1970 and 1976. Up to 80 percent of the economy went into state hands in the declared "Cooperative Republic." The economic situation worsened, turning the country into the second poorest in the continent.

Granada repeated in many senses the experiences of Jamaica and Guyana, creating in 1979 a very important public sector and socialism as a goal to be achieved. After four years of existence, the revolution caused concern for its neighbors in the eastern Caribbean and with other members of CARICOM and the United States. The experiment ended in 1983 with the invasion of the United States supported by the Eastern Caribbean State Organization (AECS). The implementation of this alternative economic development model led to important discrepancies in the integration process.

Evaluation of the First Stage

For CARICOM, as well as for Latin America, the decade of the 1980s was a very difficult period. There was not only a changed world economic environment, but also other factors such as varying commitments to regional integration and differing approaches to development among the member states. In the area of economic integration, the main results were the following: The intraregional trade increased between 1973 and 1981, and a part of that was manufactured products not previously traded. But this did not mean a specialization as it had been predicted by the designers of CARICOM. By contrast, duplications of products were evident. Under the combined effect of external economic crises and the lack of hard currency in the region, the countries were forced to resort to foreign borrowings that increased the foreign debt and reduced imports. The borrowing had an impact in mutual commerce, which was a 12 percent reduction in 1983, 10.9 percent in 1984, 3.3 percent in 1985, and 33 percent in 1986. What had been gained, vanished. CARICOM failed in its strategic goal of reaching great benefits from complementary use of natural and human resources in the region and of taking advantage of potential scale economies.

It couldn't even design a common policy against foreign investment—the source of many discrepancies and one of the main causes of the disappearance of the Western Indies Federation. The obstacles to commerce were removed among members and with some exceptions the free movement of merchandise was reached. However, Article 28 of Chaguaramas agreement allowed for the use of quantity restrictions if any member faced severe payment balance problems. Such a situation, which was thought to be exceptional, was invoked after 1977 by Jamaica and Guyana—because of the difficult economic situation already analyzed—and by other CARICOM members.

In this first stage, deeply protectionist, an important mechanism for the strengthening of specialization and coordination of the area's production was the Regional Industrial Program, which should have helped to avoid duplication of investments. Despite the fact that the conception of the program occurred in 1973, concrete actions did not occur until 1985. Out of 35 projects first conceived, only 23 received approval for action, and by 1986 only 16 small projects had been implemented. The most well-known regional project in the 1970s, a large aluminum refinery that would use bauxite from Guyana and Jamaica and oil from Trinidad and Tobago was never carried out.

A traditional CARICOM weakness is the lack of food imports in the region. In December 1975, the Conference of Heads of States launched the Food Plan, where it was proposed that within ten years the region would be self-sufficient and it would even have an export surplus. However, it did not reach the goals intended and even today the problem has not been solved. Transportation is a key problem in the integration process. CARICOM has given attention to it by means of the West Indies Shipping Corporation (WISCO), a small fleet inherited from the federation's times, and property of the area's governments. It received three new ships in 1973, which improved service among the islands in 1975. Caribbean Navigation Corporation, which replaced WISCO, was established and in doing so it acquired four new ships that started working between 1976 and 1977. Despite all these efforts, the problem is still unsolved. In 1987, Belize, Dominica, Saint Vincent, and the Grenadines withdrew from the corporation, claiming that they had received little benefits. Air transportation service at the end of the decade was insufficient, most of it because of lack of coordination among airlines that were then privately owned. As to economic integration, achievements at the end of the 1980s were rather small and the results far below wishes and expectations. There were still contradictions between national and regional interests.

In other main areas of CARICOM coordination of external policies among members had already reached some results at the end of the 1980s, the negotiation position of the region becoming more solid with other groups, international organizations, and other countries. Among the most important achieved objectives we can find the very favorable conditions attained at the first three Lomé Conventions, which gave free access to Caribbean goods in the European markets and to financing for exports shortfalls, other funds, and financial help for development. Since 1983, CARICOM countries participated in the Caribbean Basin Initiative, set by the United States. This gives them free access to U.S. markets for a number of goods produced in the area, as well as access to financing, investment in technical aid programs, and other opportunities. After 1986, the area's products enjoyed free entrance to the Canadian market through the Canada-Caribbean Project (CARIBCAN) program. This program was designed by Canada to facilitate commerce, investment, and industrial cooperation with the British Community in the Caribbean. However, these free-access advantages to most important markets have not been properly used. By contrast, changes, drastic in cases, in the political orientation of the region's governments endangered political coordination and polarized interests. With the end of the Cold War the Caribbean strategic importance was drastically reduced. This affected strongly the capacity of CARICOM negotiation with extraregional actors in a rapidly changing world due to globalization advances. As to functional cooperation, the organization was successful in some activities such as education, health care, and others. However, there was less success in areas like culture, transportation, and representation (e.g., the Caribbean Parliament). To summarize, the first CARICOM stage went through crisis, failures, and partial achievements, signaling the need for a revision of development styles. All of this happened immersed in a growing feeling of insecurity regarding the future and feasibility of the community.

Second Stage (1989–Present)

Since 1988, with the publication of *Caribbean Development for the Year 2000, Perspective and Policies,* the basic reasons for the deep transformations that were to be performed within CARICOM were stated with the aim of facing successfully the global challenges and for CARICOM to be integrated in the world's economy in an efficient and productive manner. At the same time, it was stated how unprepared and inadequate were the traditional CARICOM policies and existing practices to reach such objectives.

In Grand Anse, Granada, July 1989, at the time of the Tenth Conference of CARICOM Heads of State, the first minister of Trinidad and Tobago, A. N. R. Robinson, issued a declaration in which he called for a radical change in the Community that would allow the successful facing of globalization and avoidance of the total marginalization of the area. These ideas, together with those of the Bourne Report, were approved by the heads of states and are known as the Grand Anse Declaration.

The need to strengthen the integrating process was established, aiming for the creation of a single economy and market in the short term. Reaching such a result presupposed the establishment of four basic liberties: free merchandise exchange, free service exchange, free people's mobility, and free capital mobility. Also projected was the harmonization of macroeconomic policies and member states, of which general features would be: (a) the market as the main resource receiver; (b) a smaller state role in economic matters; (c) equilibrium of macroeconomic variables; and (d) economy deregulation. It was also agreed that there would be a more open policy to international trade in the form of a reduced common external tax program. Together with the need to increase their economies' international competitiveness, they also showed their concern for the negative impact that liberalization could have over state incomes and employment.

Despite the urgency of the tasks proposed and the enormous CARICOM experience regarding regional integration, the Eleventh Conference of Heads of States in Kingston in August 1990, after the corresponding revision, decided to postpone the terms of implementation of basic instruments in order to form the single market and economy. The delay was caused fundamentally by the elements associated with a paternalist state and a private entrepreneurial class used to protections and tutelage and their fear of change and the loss of their privileges. Experience seemed to show that there is a conflictive relationship between urgency and general acceptance of the required changes and the resistance to implement them. From here, we can derive a characteristic of the process; but changes occur slowly.

After the Grand Anse Declaration, a set of studies were established, such as the West Indian Commission formed by a number of personalities in the area that worked independently for more than two years (1990–1991) and presented their ideas in a document entitled "Time for Action." The works of the West Indian Committee and others were subject to consultation and has been the guide to the profound revision that is going on within CARICOM.

The Chaguaramas Agreement was changed to establish the Single Market and Economy. The process was carried out by a set of protocols:

Protocol I: Restructures the Bodies and Institutions of the Community and redefines its functional relationships aiming at strengthening participation in the integrationist movement. It offers a wider decision power to the Community's institutions and establishes voting on simple majority for all bodies.

Protocol II: Determines the right to establishment, the right to give services and the right to move capital by any nation in the region of the community.

Protocol III: Industrial Policy. Establishes that the goal of Industrial Policy of the Community will be guided by the market, internationally competitive and with a production of good and services that promotes social and economic development.

Protocol IV: Commercial Liberalization and external Commercial Policy (concluded, but not approved).

Protocol V: Agricultural Policy. Establishes that the main goal of the agricultural policy is the fundamental transformation of the agricultural sector toward a market oriented one. It should be competitive and environmentally sustainable by means of the efficient production of primary agricultural products, both traditional and untraditional ones.

Protocol VI: Transportation Policy (unconcluded).

Protocol VII: Sectors, Regions, Less Developed Countries (unconcluded).

Protocol VIII: Discrepancies solutions (unconcluded).

Protocol IX: Competence Rules (unconcluded).

Apart from the Nine Protocols, revision of the treaty was complemented with the following documents.

  a. Letter from the Civil Society.
  b. Agreement for the Establishment of the Caribbean Community Parliamentarian Assembly.
  c. Agreement on Social Security.[6]

In these documents, the respect for human rights and freedom is highlighted. They also emphasized the right to freedom and people's security; equality in the face of the law; freedom to assemble, demonstrate and request; as well as the freedom of speech. It also recognized the freedom of press and access to information. Cultural diversity is acknowledged, as well as religious freedom, the rights of women and children, the rights of the disabled, the right to education and training, and other rights. Democratic processes are strengthened as well as those of the people's representation in national frameworks. It also established the Caribbean Justice Supreme Court. It should be mentioned that according to the eighteenth Conference of Heads of Government held in July 1997, Protocols I and II were approved and become valid as of July 4, 1998.

During the nineteenth Conference of Heads of State celebrated in Saint Lucia between June 30 and July 4, 1998, marking the twenty-fifth anniversary of CARICOM, Protocol III and V were signed, but Protocol VI was not approved as it was proposed. An essential element for the consolidation of the integrating process, the formulation of a common external duty in 1993, again a new program for its establishment that was finished by the end of 1998, was defined with the exception of Belize, which had a deadline of the year 2001. The implementation program contained four stages in order to reduce the maximum duty level from 45 percent to levels ranging between 5 and 20 percent (only agricultural products keep the level to 40 percent). However, at the end of 1998, only Barbados, Saint Cristobal, and Saint Vincent and the Grenadines had already started the last stage. The majority went through the second or at least the third stage. The applied custom duties to foreign trade still constitute a strong source for fiscal incomes, especially for the smallest countries where they can reach up to half the public income. The CARICOM secretariat is working in order to seek solution to these problems so the common external duties could be implemented without additional delays. With the implementation of Protocol II, there is free mobility of capital in the region. However, it is necessary to create as soon as possible a Regional Stock Exchange and to move on with the monetary union.

As for the projected creation of a common currency, improvements have been made in monetary policies. CARICOM Central Bank Governor's Council has established the "3–12–36–15" criterion, which means that three months in import value of currency reserves must be maintained during 12 months; and that there must be 36 months of stability at the established exchange rate and the debt service must be kept under 15 percent over export incomes. The final goal of this policy is to create the Caribbean Monetary Union. The countries are more aware of the need to classify in these criteria and to be among the first to meet them.

Since 1989, CARICOM has been promoting the free mobility of the workforce. Up to the end of 1997 eight of the member states have accepted traveling documents other than passports (Barbados, Dominica, Grenada, Guyana, Jamaica, Montserrat, Saint Cristobal and Nevis, and Saint Vincent and the Grenadines). Seven countries have stated that university graduates can practice their profession inside the region without the need of a work permit (Antigua and Barbuda, Barbados, Dominica, Grenada, Guyana, Jamaica, Saint Lucia, Saint Vincent and the Grenadines, and Trinidad and Tobago). These measures may reach the other countries in the future. Later on, the free mobility of people will extend to athletes, artists, and newspaper people. Finally, there are three very important problems—related to the pending Protocols: the lack of a common policy on foreign investment, competition, and the protection of intellectual property.

The Commerce of Goods and Services and the Balance of Payment

Extraregional CARICOM exports are concentrated in a reduced number of basic products to which others have been added in the 1990s, such as products that are exported to U.S. and European markets where they have preferential access because of the Caribbean Basin Initiative (CBI) and the Lomé Convention. The products that demonstrate the insufficiently diversified economy are bananas coming from the Organization of Eastern Caribbean States (OECS), especially Dominica, Saint Lucia, Saint Cristobal and Nevis, and Saint Vincent and the Grenadines; aluminum from Jamaica; bauxite from Guyana, Jamaica, and Surinam; sugar from Guyana, Saint Cristobal and Nevis, and Trinidad and Tobago; and spices from Grenada. This concentration of basic products makes the region highly vulnerable to the changes of the external environment, crises, change in

Table 6.1 CARICOM: Main Incomes per Exports

Countries	Oil > 50% Total	Primary Non-Oil Products > 50% Total	Services, Incomes per Private Transfers > 50% Total*
Antigua and Barbuda			×
Bahamas			×
Barbados			×
Belize			×
Dominica			
Grenada			×
Guyana		×	
Haiti			×
Jamaica			×
Montserrat			×
Saint Lucia			×
Saint Cristobal and Nevis			×
Saint Vincent and the Grenadines			×
Surinam		×	
Trinidad and Tobago	×		

Source: International Monetary Fund, *World Economic Outlook,* May 1998.
Note: *Including remittances of workers abroad.

prices, and natural disasters. In addition, service exports have become the most important element that characterizes most of the CARICOM economies.

As for service exports, the first place is occupied by tourism—at present the most important economic activity—and financial service exports (extraterritorial) based above all in the Bahamas and other OECS countries. The importance of tourism for CARICOM is crucial; in 1996, the CARICOM countries had 60,499 hotel rooms and received 4.7 million tourists and 3.7 million cruise passengers with an income of $4.3 billion.

This heterogeneity in the behavior of the most important CARICOM industry creator of up to 25 percent of all jobs, underlines the vulnerability of the sector in the wake of the new millennium. In 1997, the decline of traditional exports continued. Incomes on account of banana exports[7]

Table 6.2 CARICOM: Tourism Basic Indicators, 1996

Countries	Tourists in Thousands	Cruiser Passengers in Thousands	Incomes on Tourism B. P. in Million USD	Number of Rooms
Antigua and Barbuda	220	227.4	314	3,317
Bahamas	1,598.1	1,543.5	1,378	13,421
Barbados	442.1	484.7	712	5,084
Belize	273.7	0.1*	75	3,708
Dominica	60.5	134.9	30	607
Grenada	108.0	249.9	59	1,532
Guyana	105.5	—	48	900
Haiti	145.4	—	81	850
Jamaica	1,147	605.2	1,128	20,896
Saint Lucia	232.3	193.9	297	4,202
Saint Cristobal and Nevis	79.6	120.9	63	1,563
Saint Vincent and the Grenadines	60.2	85.3	58	1,176
Surinam	20.0	—	14	N/D
Trinidad and Tobago	259.8	21.9	74	3,122
CARICOM	4,752.2	3,667.6	4,331.0	60,499.0

Source: Association of Caribbean States. Web Page, Chart 28. Retrieved from www.acs.com.
Note: *Belize suffered a decline in the arrival of cruisers, as a result of a $10 tax which led operators to choose another destination. This fact proves the strictly global character of the activity and the intense competition existing.

declined 15 percent, sugar exports lowered 7 percent, and bauxite sales were slightly reduced. By contrast, imports of goods have continued to grow, causing a growing deficit in the commercial balance, which has faced incomes coming from commercial services, mainly tourism and the net entrance of capital, which was more than one billion dollars in 1996, with continued growth in 1997 and 1998.

Intracommunity Trade

The real integration of CARICOM economies is greatly conditioned by a limited exports competition because of the small size of its market. Intracommunity trade is made up of oil and its derivatives, light manufactured goods, and food. Because of the advances in the integration process of the community market and the liberalization measures taken by all the economies, we can see a reanimation of the regional trade in the 1990s, especially after 1994. Intraregional trade went from $353 million in 1988 to $500 million in 1993 and more than $800 million in 1996. In relative terms, extraregional exports, which were 10 percent of the total exports in 1988, increased to 18 percent in 1996. We observe that a growing proportion of intracommunity exports, up to 90 percent, come from the countries qualified as those of higher relative development: Barbados, Guyana, Jamaica, Surinam, and Trinidad and Tobago. However, because of the structure of some CARICOM economies, it does not seem likely that the rate of regional trade in relation to total trade will continue to grow at this pace.

In CARICOM countries, the method used to face the deep crisis of the 1990s was the establishment of the liberalized trade plan. These processes, started in the late 1980s and early 1990s, were strongly encouraged by the groups of experts from the IMF and the World Bank. The need to use such policies led to a significant change in state participation in the economy and at the same time that of the private sector took a leading role. This meant a decreasing role of the states and, thus, their influence and capacity to advance policies. In the larger countries, especially Jamaica, Guyana, and Trinidad and Tobago, the implementation of a neoliberal adjustment brought about a defensive reaction that sought to protect the state model with its leading role. This defense was greatly influenced by a deterioration of the standard of living and the increase of unemployment following initial liberalization.

At the same time, there was a tendency to blame political parties and leaders for the difficulties caused by the changed economic policies. There were the so-called ungovernability problems while the civil society was emerging, albeit more slowly than elsewhere in Latin America. In the recent past, there also have existed a set of structural reforms in all countries. In 1997, countries were very active with fiscal policy, making the system much stronger, improving the tax acquisition, and liberating the state of those loss-attached activities by means of an acceleration of the privatization process. Budgets have behaved generally balanced. One of the main goals of economic policy has remained the stability of prices, low inflation. Other elements of monetary policy have been subjected to such a goal. Deregulation and liberalization measures have continued mainly in foreign trade, finance, and banking. Some incentives also have been instated to the attraction of foreign investment giving more information about opportunities and less about bureaucratic procedures.

The ACS countries have focused their attention on the problem of bananas. As everybody knows, the WTO has ruled against preferences given to the product by the European Union. This has greatly reduced the survival possibilities of the traditional banana production regime that is vital for Dominica, Grenada, Saint Lucia and Saint Vincent, and the Grenadines. In these countries, the main problems of economic policy have centered around measures required to face the loss of preferences, and such measures have tried to diversify crops and increase productivity and quality of the fruit in the banana sector so that it can face the new situation. Recent complications have started for all CARICOM countries with the inclusion of Barbados to ACS, which will mean a unification of currency and other revisions that affect the whole of CARICOM. This complex movement may repeat some elements of history of the West Indies Federation, but in a negative way. In the current movement the larger economies are hoping to dominate the smaller ones, leaving them little room to prosper.

CARICOM member countries have recently faced an investment liberalization process by means of revision and adjustment of national legislation with the aim of reducing costs and procedures, thus making the arrival of foreign investment possible. In this context, the laws that regulate soil property have been liberalized, as well as those related to transfers and repatriation of capital. In 1997, countries subscribed—as we have analyzed—to Protocol II for the total liberalization of investment within CARICOM.

External Relations of the Caribbean Community

Since 1989, the Caribbean Community experimented with a changed and revitalized process that saw as one of the most important moments the creation of the West Indies Commission. The closing report of the commission *Time for Action,* published in 1992, stated the need to extend and deepen CARICOM. In 1992, there was a proposal for the Greater Caribbean to Central America, including Mexico, Colombia, and Venezuela, that became reality in 1994 with the creation of the Association of Caribbean States (ACS). This had to do with a definition of the Caribbean rooted in the CARICOM region, and so belonging to it or not was just a matter of historical experience, based in the plantation economy, slavery, and the massive incorporation of ethnic minorities, especially African. According to this definition, the Caribbean will be understood as island societies of the Caribbean Sea and Guyana and Belize, which have the same identity given its ethnohistorical origin. This concept given by Trinidad and Tobago prime minister and historian Dr. Eric Williams in the 1970s served to delimit differences between the old colonial powers and the United States and the neighbors of continental Latin America. Given their identity, Caribbean countries have the capacity to regionally integrate and at the same time they strengthen their autonomy and self-determination represented by their given states.

In our opinion, the previously analyzed contractions make up a mutually related trilogy that have an influence in some way or another over all the events inside CARICOM, especially in the slowness to take decisions and implement objectives. Under the influence of economic globalization, the creation of regional blocs in the entire world, the loss of strategic importance in the area with the aim of the Cold War, and other factors such as the Venezuelan and Mexican initiative of granting preferential nonreciprocal trade agreements for CARICOM in 1992 and on the part of Colombia in 1994 brought about a quick transformation in the notion of the Caribbean to be increased into a greater Caribbean. With this new widened CARICOM notion it performs a lot of regional consultations that ended with the creation of the ACS in July 1994, open to all countries of the Caribbean region.

This creation underlined everybody's concern and especially that of the CARICOM countries over the possible undermining of the Caribbean in the new globalized reality. Beyond the ethnohistorical definition of the Caribbean, it was emphasized that the new widened one underlies the physical and geographical environment and at the same time, the challenges shared of economic globalization. This conceptual change was possible because of improved relations between the sides, and because of the wish to face the challenges as a group. According to the increased consensus, CARICOM included Surinam in July 1995 as a full member of the Community and its unique market, and it included Haiti in July 1997. In this case, it is still discussing the participation Haiti will have in the economic activities. Haiti's effective incorporation will be extremely complicated—if it were feasible, we are talking of a country whose population surpasses the combined population of the remaining states of the community, 70 percent of whom, according to more recent data, live in extreme poverty—thus, economic and social figures are far below the remaining members where instability and political crisis seem to be a constant.

In the late 1990s CARICOM made strong efforts to renegotiate the Lomé agreement. This has been very complex, since it should adjust itself to WTO requirements. A free trade agreement has been proposed between

the European Union and the Caribbean Forum (CARIFORUM—
CARICOM plus the Dominican Republic and Cuba), but it will not hinder preferences that so far they have enjoyed, since they will be part of the
European market with products and prices that will be more competitive.
CARICOM also has insisted that ACP countries (70 African Caribbean
and Pacific nations that were formerly European colonies) need support in
a period of transition, in order to improve competitiveness of their products, and thus they insist on a nonreciprocal preferential agreement. This
position, however, does not seem to have much perspective for success. Another special attention area has been the procedures with the U.S. government to try to get an even treatment like the one reached by Mexico in
NAFTA, but so far to no avail.

The joint CARICOM-Cuba Commission, established in 1993 to promote mutual cooperation and trade, has met on several occasions with
fruitful bilateral results in areas like fishing, investment promotion, meteorology education, health, and sports. During 1998, CARICOM successfully concluded the negotiation for the extension of the economic and
commercial agreement with the Dominican Republic, a free trade agreement to be implemented in 1999 and duly finished by the year 2005. For
a number of years (since 1992), CARICOM kept meetings with the Central America scheme of integration, aiming at coordinating positions, making consultations in order to find ways to strengthen reciprocal
relationships.

In the 1970s there was talk of the possibility of the establishment of a
strategic alliance between the two regions, but a number of incidents, for
example, the dispute over bananas at WTO and the election for general
secretary of OAS and other events, have cooled such relations. CARI-
COM countries are actively participating in the negotiations for the establishment of the FTAA. In all meetings, including the 1998 Chilean
Summit, they have stated their hope for their economies to be assessed as
small and vulnerable.

CARICOM efforts in the areas of external relations started in 1989,
and recently they have had varied results. At different points they have
stated free trade agreements with different countries and schemes—the
most important one being that of Central America. Up to the present they
have only finished negotiations—as stated—with Mexico and Venezuela in
1992, with Colombia in 1994, and widened with the Dominican Republic in August 1998. Neither with Central America nor other integrationist
models has this been so. This task for saving preferences (the other main
goal) has not been successful. In practice it has been spoiled, with the
United States as with Europe. The ACS, one of the main efforts of CARI-

COM, is celebrating its eighth birthday showing a remarkable distance between original expectations and what has been so far achieved.

Conclusion

Within the existence of CARICOM there have been two stages. The first stage ended up in a deep crisis. It is a simple fact that CARICOM's common market could not be implemented for the lack of an executive power with a beyond-the-nation scope. The main success inside CARICOM was that of still living despite the number of problems, difficulties, expectations, and so forth.

The second stage, which started in 1989, has involved a profound transformation of the integration, but with confirming contradictions. The main features of this period are a renovated commitment to the area's integration, including its "amplification and deepening" with a relative weakening of national states, a private sector that has a stronger role, as well as nongovernmental organizations and a growth of exportation in goods and services. However, the whole system of preferences, started 25 years ago, seems to be suffering from a serious crisis. In general, CARICOM entered into an integrationist style that CEPAL has defined as open regionalism.

This new strategy's success, implemented since 1989, will depend on CARICOM's skill and ability to fulfill efficiently what was agreed upon, and its skill in removing the system of protectionism.

Summarizing, the challenges and main problems are:

a. The need to fully implement the agreements and to establish mechanisms that guarantee validity.
b. To establish solution mechanisms for modern controversies.
c. To rationalize integrationist institutions, creating a real beyond-the-country authority.
d. To deepen macroeconomic and structural reforms. These reforms were the basis for progress as proved by intraregional trade, and by the performance of the economies in recent years.
e. To deepen education, government, and export diversification reforms.
f. To attract high technology foreign investment aimed at making the change of paradigm of development in the region.

All this is needed for the change in the process and for its insertion in the globalized economy. There are a number of signals that tell that the integrationist process carried out by CARICOM has reached limits, even taking into account the wish to increase the process through the creation of the Caribbean State Association. The future remains vague. The main route to get inside world economy and FTAA is still unknown. But it is vital in order to impede extreme poverty.

Ten years after the Grand Anse Declaration, which in fact started the process of change inside CARICOM, much still remains to be done, the terms for fulfillment are postponed. Slowness in reactions and decisions seems to be the trend. The CARICOM secretary acknowledges this. On July 21, 1998, General Secretary Edwin Carrington, at the festivities for the twenty-fifth anniversary of its creation, stated "despite recent progress we are still moving slowly."[8] But for CARICOM, time is running short and it is at the crossroads.

Notes

1. The Bahamas is a member of the community but not of the common market.
2. The eighteenth Conference of Heads of States accepted Haiti as CARICOM member and a work group has been made in order to establish terms and conditions of its ascension. Its status is that of a provisional member.
3. Barbados, Guyana, Jamaica, and Trinidad and Tobago are qualified as more underdeveloped countries; the other members except for the Bahamas are considered less developed countries. The British Virgin Isles and the Turk and Caicos islands are associate members. Anguilla, Aruba, Bermuda, Cayman Islands, Colombia, Dominican Republic, Mexico, Netherlands Antilles, Puerto Rico, and Venezuela are observers.
4. CARICOM's Mission Statement; see CARICOM Web page, http//www.CARICOM.org/.
5. Brewster, H., "Intergatión Econòmica del caribe, Problemas y Perspectivas," *Estaudios del mercado Común,* vol. IX, no. 4, 1971.
6. Protocolos Modificaudo Tratados de Chaguaramas retrieved from www.CARICOM.com.
7. A WTO panel objected to a preferential treatment of bananas and this decision has jeopardized the survival of the crop in several countries.
8. "CARICOM Region Urged to Move Faster." Retrieved from www.CARICOM.org.

Bibliography

Bourne, Compton. (1988). *Caribbean Development to the Year 2000: Prospects and Policies.* London: Commonwealth Secretariat.

Brewster, Havelok and Clive Y. Thomas. (1967). *The Dynamics of West Indian Economic Integration*. Kingston, Jamaica: UWI–ISER.

Bryan, Anthony T. (1984). "The CARICOM and Latin American Integration Experiences: Observations on Theoretical Origins, and Comparative Performance," *Ten Years of CARICOM*. Washington, DC: International Development Bank.

CARICOM. *Protocolos modifcando Tratados de Chaguaramas*. Retrieved from www.CARICOM.org.

CARICOM. *Tratados de Chaguaramas documentos modificatorios*. Retrieved from www.CARICOM.org.

"CARICOM Deepens and Widens." (1995). *CARICOM View*. March–April.

"CARICOM and NAFTA." (1995). *Caribbean Affairs*. July–August.

CARICOM Secratariat. (1984). *Ten Years of CARICOM*. Washington, DC: Inter-American Development Bank.

"CARICOM and the World." (1994). *Caribbean Affairs*. July–August.

CARIFORUM. (1995). *Documents for the 5th Ministerial Meeting of the Caribbean Forum of ACP States Secretarial (CARIFORUM)*. Trinidad y Tobago, November 21–22, 1994.

Ceara Hatton, Miguel y Pavel Isa Contreas. (1994). "La CARICOM, el Mercado Común y la Asociación de Estados del Caribe." *Informe CIECA*, Enero.

CEPAL. (1998). *Panorama de la Inserción Internacional de América Latina y el Caribe*. Edición 1997.

IMF. (1998). *World Economic Outlook*. Washington, DC: IMF.

Lestrade, Swinburne. (1981). "The Less Developed Countries Within CARICOM." Cave Hill, Barbados: Institute of Social and Economic Research (Eastern Caribbean), University of the West Indies.

Lopez Coll, Armando. (1993). "Integración y colaboración económica en el Caribe." *Revista Economía y Desarrollo* (Cuba).

———. (1994). "Proceso histórico de integración del Caribe." *Revista Economica y Dearrollo*. (Cuba).

Noruega, Mziel. (1999). *The Integration Movement in the Caribbean, a Crossroads: Towards a New Approach of Integration*. Washington, DC: World Bank.

SELA. (1998). *Dinamica de las relaciones externas de America Latina y el Caribe*. Buenos Aires: Ediciones Corregidas.

"Venezuela en la Unificación del Caribe." (1995). *Caribbean Report*. Trinidad. July–August.

World Bank. (1998). *World Development Indicators*. New York: Oxford University Press.

Chapter 7

Harmonization of Environmental Regulations: Risks and Opportunities for Developing Countries

Luciana Togeiro

The controversy between free trade and environmental protection basically resides in the subject of how to reconcile the system of multilateral trade, and its continuous liberalization, with environmental concerns. There may be some cases where free trade, without appropriate environmental policies, results in damages to the environment, or cases when environmental regulations may harm the legitimate trade. Environmentalists and defenders of free trade polarize the debate, joined by several protectionist interests.

This chapter will analyze the proposition of international harmonization of environmental regulations, identifying its theoretical and empirical foundations and verifying its repercussion in the context of the international political economy of the environment, specifically in the bargaining inside the World Trade Organization (WTO). Finally, greater access to environmental technologies is considered an issue of crucial interest for developing countries in this debate.

Theoretical and Empirical Foundations

The discussions on international trade and environment have in their origin different views concerning the effects of environmental regulations on competitiveness. The traditional point of view, the approach of environmental economics of the mainstream neoclassical school, is that environmental regulations add in additional costs for the companies and, thus, create relative loss of competitiveness compared to contestants not submitted to the same regulatory requirements. According to this approach, the environmental variable brings an additional trade-off to those already observed in the economic theory. The environmental trade-off arises out of the basic concept of externality (a negative one, that is, the microeconomic agent maximizes profits based on the choice of the alternative of minimum production cost), not taking into account the related environmental damages, the regulatory measures, that seek to induce that agent to "internalize" the environmental externalities, resulting in a cost increment.

In the 1990s, this traditional view was criticized by "Porter's hypothesis," as the approach of Michael Porter and his associates became known, affirming that the competitiveness of companies increases with the growing levels of strictness of environmental regulations and additionally fosters dynamic competitive advantages of some sectors in the United States, his native country (Porter, 1991; Porter and van der Linde, 1995a and 1995b). These authors' criticisms can be synthesized in the following comment:

> Our central message is that the environment-competitiveness debate has been framed incorrectly. The notion of inevitable struggle between ecology and the economy grows out of a static view of environment regulation, in which technology, products, processes and customer needs are all fixed. In this static world, where firms have already made their cost-minimizing choices, environmental regulation inevitably raises costs and will tend to reduce the market share of domestic companies on global markets. (Porter and van der Linde, 1995b:97)

When considering the occurrence of synergetic effects in the companies that abide to the regulations as the general case and the trade-off as a particular case, Porter totally inverts the traditional view of the mainstream environmental economics and, thus, joins the evolutionist and institutionalist schools in their criticisms of the neoclassical approach on environmental issues, achieving this stage, by the way, using concepts on the dynamics of innovation derived from the evolutionist school:

> The paradigm defining competitiveness has been shifting, particularly in the last 20 to 30 years, away from this static model. The new paradigm of international competitiveness is a dynamic one, based on innovation. . . . Competitiveness at the industry level arises from superior productivity,

either in terms of lower costs than rivals or the ability to offer products with superior value that justify a premium price. Detailed case studies of hundreds of industries, based in dozens of countries, reveal that internationally competitive companies are not those with the cheapest inputs or the largest scale, but those with the capacity to improve and innovate continually. . . . Competitive advantage, then, rests not on static efficiency nor on optimizing within fixed constraints, but on the capacity for innovation and improvement that shift the constraints. (Porter and van der Linde, 1995b:97–98)

In fact, Porter and van der Linde (1995a and 1995b) identify the challenge of sustainable development as one of the radical discontinuities verified throughout the whole history of industry, which has the effect of provoking important ruptures on the given technological paths. Porter's approach also converges to the evolutionists' one when exalting the importance of environmental regulations, which are considered indispensable to the establishment of a macrorestriction capable of guiding the company's strategic decisions on environmental improvements.

Porter's hypothesis provoked a heated debate between its supporters and representatives of the mainstream. Palmer et al. (1995) are suppliers of a replica, presenting several counterarguments, among them the lack of empirical evidence to sustain Porter's hypothesis, and reaffirming that the trade-off is the general case for the effects of environmental regulations on companies, while the occurrence of synergetic effects constitute exception to this rule: "Overall, this literature suggests that while it is possible to get results like those that Porter and van der Linde suggest are the norm from models that incorporate strategic behavior, such results are special cases" (Palmer et al., 1995:126).

The controversy regarding the effects of environmental regulation on intrafirm costs—tradeoff versus synergy—and, consequently, on their competitiveness, is broadened when the international dimension is included in the debate. Several studies went back to the effects of environmental regulations on trade and international investment, using precisely a theory derived from the trade-off vision, that associates the severity of environmental regulations to international competitiveness. By this theory, the differences on environmental regulation presented by several countries interfere in their comparative advantages, influencing trade and foreign direct-investment patterns. A country with softer environmental regulations vis-à-vis another one with more rigorous regulations incident on certain productive sectors would have, therefore, a comparative advantage in the exports of these sectors and/or they would start to attract foreign direct investments, favoring the existence of the "pollution heavens."[1]

Summing up these studies on the relationship between environmental regulations and competitiveness and their correlated effects on trade and foreign direct investment, the majority reach the following conclusion: "In any case there is little empirical evidence to suggest that raising standards stimulates innovation, just as there is little theoretical or empirical support for the notion that raising standards has a significant impact on the competitiveness of firms in industrial countries or on their decisions to invest in developing countries" (Anderson, 1997:326).

It follows that the main conclusion extracted from the whole debate briefly summarized here is that there is an insurmountable difficulty in defining a relationship of causality between the severity of environmental regulations and competitiveness. Consequently, in no way can one affirm that trade and foreign direct-investment patterns are significantly influenced by differences in environmental regulations among countries. In fact, the theoretical debate on these themes boils down to conflicting empirical evidence that is based on several methodological constructions, which hinders arrival at consensual propositions. Another conclusion, no less important, refers to the essence of the controversy on Porter's hypothesis. For the practitioners of the neoclassical school, the criticism of the trade-off hypothesis threatens their deductive theoretical logic that departs from the externality concept and ends by assuring the supremacy of cost-benefit analysis applied to environmental regulations.

Porter and his associates seem to worry less about achieving greater theoretical status by an in-depth controversy with the mainstream approach than with an essentially pragmatic objective: to defend the economic interests of some American industries and their environmental technologies and, with this, to contribute to assure the American companies' domain of the world market for these technologies in front of their strong foreign competitors—the German and Japanese rivals. That is why they defend that the environmental regulation in the United States must be established at a strictness level slightly above the one in effect in foreign countries, of course keeping a differential small enough to minimize possible competitive disadvantages in relation to foreign competitors still not subjected to the same standards, as well as for "maximizing export potential in the pollution control sector" (Porter and van der Linde, 1995b:114).

Following this brief synthesis of the theoretical and empirical foundations of the debate on the relationships among environmental regulations, competitiveness, trade, and foreign direct investments, the repercussion of this debate in the sphere of the international economic relations must be explored.

Harmonization of Environmental Regulations: Is There A Consensus?

In spite of the fact that any correlation between the severity of environmental regulations and competitiveness is under dispute because of theoretical or empirical quarrels, a consensus in favor of the harmonization of the environmental regulations is evidently established in the international political economy debate. In this level, the following elements stand out:

a. The business community is concerned with the differentials in competitiveness associated to systemic factors, whose importance is magnified by the growing economical integration associated with globalization;

b. the trade diplomacy and national interests of the United States, favoring the adoption of nontariff barriers;

c. the actions of environmental movements defending the use of trade tools to enforce environmental standards;

d. the prominent role assumed by the environmental regulatory norms in the harmonization of national regulations process in the blocks of regional economic integration; and

e. the liberal orientation of the WTO, more and more permeable to the pressures of the previous elements.

Once those several elements of pressure present themselves in the negotiations of the WTO, the debate on the harmonization of the environmental regulations inside this organization can be considered as the main reference of the international political economy surrounding this theme. For this reason, an analysis of the treatment of the environmental issues contained in the regulations of WTO is fitting here, identifying the main arguments in favor of the greening of international trade—the use of trade restrictions to assure the attainment of environmental standards—as well as those that are contrary to this orientation.

Several analyses of the international political economy tradition affirm that the WTO, from the Uruguay Round onward, becomes a privileged stage for the political dispute among national regulatory standards, much more than for technical discussions about access conditions to specific markets. The key aim that dictates a good part of the action in the WTO, present in several passages of the Uruguay Round's final text, is the harmonization of the national differences (Ostry, 1992; Tussie, 1994; Bhagwati, 1996a).[2]

Thus, if the main theme in the order of the day is the global regulation of international competition, one may guess from the following declarations of its former general secretary that the WTO intends to lead on this task:

> The multilateral system is becoming more and more a political subject. This is happening because its evolution has increasingly gone back to policies and national regulations than to frontier barriers; and that is so because the challenges the system faces are increasingly political and not technical. In this context, considering the possibility of strengthening the institutional base of the system can become very important—for instance, enlarging the political dimension of its main institution, the WTO. (Ruggiero, 1995)

This newly expressed orientation of the WTO, allied to the intense international debate on sustainable development, arouses growing attention to national environmental policies and regulations; it explains the inclusion of environmental issues in its working agenda in spite of the strong opposition of the developing countries, which oppose these issues and others, such as the regulations in the social area (labor legislation and social dumping), before completing the unfinished task of opening the markets of developed countries to their exports.[3]

Togeiro de Almeida (1999) has shown that the actual trend seems to be that the WTO, without abandoning its defense of free trade, tries to accommodate environmental concerns, betting on multilateral agreements for environmental problems of global impact, as well as on the definition of international standards as the preferred path toward the harmonization of national environmental policies.

This compromise could already be observed, for instance, on the agreements on standards that resulted from the Uruguay Round: the Agreement on Technical Barriers to Trade (TBT) and Sanitary and Phytosanitary Measures (SPS). Through these agreements, trade restrictions for environmental purposes, until then acceptable only when related to product and when the principles of most favored nation and national treatment were observed, are deemed compatible with the WTO rules even when related to productive processes, as long as they apply to the final characteristics of the products. It is worth saying that, with these agreements, the WTO explicitly enlarges its rules from traditional measures for promoting international trade (basically removing customs barriers) to reach national policies and regulations.[4]

However, many environmental groups continue to accuse the WTO of hindering the progress of the greening of international trade, emphatically defending trade restrictions as a legitimate instrument for imposing stricter environmental regulations. The positions assumed by these environmental groups are described in a precise way by Kym Anderson:

> So with adequate forums for multilateral environmental dialogue not yet fully developed and with an increasing sense of urgency about environmental problems, environmental groups—especially in industrial countries—have become interested in using trade restrictions, the one policy instrument available to their governments to influence environmental outcomes.
>
> Environmental groups see trade policy as useful in two respects: as a way of raising environmental standards at home and abroad and of inducing countries to become signatories to and abide by international environmental agreements. Imposing import restrictions on products from countries with lower environmental standards can reduce opposition by local firms to higher standards at home by offsetting the loss of competitiveness and can increase the incentive for foreign firms and their governments to adopt higher standards. (Anderson, 1997:319)

This perception is shared by Scholte et al. (1998), to whom the creation of the WTO has reflected and reinforced an important shift, as a result of large-scale globalization, from statist to postsovereign or global governance, and as a consequence regulatory activities are no longer always centered in or subordinated to national states. That is why they affirm that:

> [N]ot surprisingly, given this substantial growth in both the range and the authority of global trade law, many civic groups have developed considerable interest in the WTO. As an important influence on the distribution of resources worldwide, the institution has come to occupy a prominent place on the agenda of numerous business lobbies, labour unions, farmers organizations, environmentalist groups, women's associations, development cooperation groups, consumer unions, human rights advocates, think tanks, and other elements of civil society. Many of these nonstate actors have sought direct contact with the WTO, bypassing government authorities in order to interrogate and lobby the multilateral institution itself. (Scholte et al., 1998:3)

One of the most distinguished free-traders, Bhagwati (1996b) casts sharp criticism on the environmental groups that defend trade restrictions as a way of imposing standards under the justification of "a feeling of universal humanitarian obligation":

> The use of U.S. economic muscle and the relative efficacy of U.S.-based environmental groups in demanding compliance from the poor nations elsewhere rather than from their own country, where they must fight with powerful groups that oppose them . . . mean that the sense of obligation to humanity's survival could translate into effective demands on others and their nation-states that are unfair or unjust in relation to demands on oneself and on one's own nation-state. Indeed, it does. (Bhagwati, 1996b:15)

In fact, one can not help but notice that the international crusade for the harmonization of the environmental regulations puts together under the same roof a strange bunch: the large transnationals concerned with the transaction costs of different regulatory regimes, the NGOs advocating the environmental cause (besides those defending workers' and human rights) and the U.S. government, which insists on the need of equalizing competitive conditions (leveling the playing field) to correct America's huge and growing trade deficit.

Answering the concerns of those who point out the risk of creating a competition toward the minimum standard (race to the bottom) among countries with significant regulatory differentials, Bhagwati defends the adoption, for the developed countries, of a policy that requires their companies to implement the regulatory standards of their respective countries of origin, even when operating abroad: "That is, in Rome do, not as Romans do, but as Bostonians do. Since firms are legal persons, American firms can be treated (as indeed they are in many matters already) as American citizens, subject to U.S. laws wherever they operate" (Bhagwati, 1996b:33).

The reproduction here of quotations containing sharp criticisms of the trade restriction thesis of the environmental movement should not be misinterpreted as a full adhesion to the arguments of the free traders or a frontal opposition to many issues raised by the environmentalists. Before any such misunderstanding settles in, some explanations are needed. Of course, the international environmental groups galvanized the world population's awareness and understanding of the seriousness and urgency of the environmental trends, offering solutions and putting mounting pressure on governments to promote and accelerate the search for solutions for environmental problems. A significant number of environmental NGOs act judiciously, guided by their own deep studies on specific environmental problems, and contributing in many ways to the assembly of an international civic network, capable of leading unique global initiatives, and aimed at wider social ills that afflict the world population. In fact, it must be recognized, as Scholte et al. (1998) do, that the presence of organized civic movements in the negotiations of the WTO can lead to positive results, such as a greater democratization and transparency in those negotiations.

Why, then, do critics of the environmentalist movement take their stand? Because there is an important point of disagreement. The political strategy of the main international environmental groups, demanding that the WTO enlarges its scope of performance as well as its capacity to impose environmental obligations on its member countries, must be considered to be totally inadequate, especially for the developing countries.[5] In this sense, they are linked with the free-traders when they argue that the WTO should avoid the use of trade restrictions for fostering environmental concerns.

The main reason for this agreement is that the trade sanctions imposed by the endorsement of the WTO are imposed to whole countries and not only to companies or specific sectors. Trade sanctions can do and usually do a lot of harm before contributing to any environmental or other social improvements in developing countries. These countries already have great difficulty trying to balance their external debt in the face of trade liberalization that has opened their internal markets to foreign competition without comparable access to developed world markets.

This overriding concern—closing the gap between developed and developing countries—calls attention to the structural problem of technological dependence of the developing countries, which further burdens their external accounts with imports of goods and services, and which tends to be reinforced by the diffusion of a new technological path that incorporates the environmental variable.

Another reason to be against the greening of the international trade—under the auspices of the WTO—concerns national particularities. The principle of national sovereignty in the fixing of national political priorities, decried as old-fashioned, receives two validations in the field of environmental policies: the diagnoses of environmental problems should necessarily take into account the capacity of absorption of the medium subject; and the ecological effectiveness and economic efficiency (the costs of environmental restructuring) of a comparable standard can diverge between countries and areas. It follows that the environmental protection should be "country-specific" or "area-specific," except for the cases of environmental problems with global impact, which deserve treatment in international agreements.[6]

The claims in favor of the international harmonization of environmental regulations obviously face difficulties, and one of them comes from the fact that there is no coordination among the countless international organizations for the discussion of the environmental subjects and economic-social subjects. The WTO does not interact with the International Labor Organization (ILO) or with the Environment Program of the United Nations (UNEP). Another international organization that has dedicated a lot of attention to the environment is the Organization for Economic Cooperation and Development (OECD), which has taken an integrating initiative internally: Their trade and environment divisions have started to work together (Charnovitz, 1994). The World Bank not only has been revealing growing interest for the theme, but also has started to adopt the protection of the environment as one of their conditionals in the concession of loans and financing. Even the IMF has pronounced itself on the subject, having its own environmental staff. In short, there is an "international disorganization," which hinders a globally coordinated action to treat environmental subjects.

The Commission on Trade and Environment of the WTO is working with all these difficulties of dialogue imported from the international disorganization in the environmental area, from the North-South interest conflicts, and from the radical positioning of expressive part of the international environmental groups, so much so that the former general secretary of the WTO, a little before leaving the position, made a conciliatory proposal: the creation of an environmental multilateral organization—the World Environment Organization—with political-juridical status similar to that of the WTO (with defined rules in multilateral bases) that would work in parallel to the WTO, as its legal and institutional arm for environmental issues (WTO Proposes a World Environment Organization, 1999).[7] Without any doubt, this new institution would favor the international harmonization of environmental regulations, sidestepping the negotiation deadlock placed by the bloc of developing countries in the WTO.

With so many controversies to be settled, the debate on trade and environment should be a major theme in the agenda of the next round of the WTO (the "Round of the Millennium"), at the end of which the creation of an environmental multilateral organization may result as suggested above. At least its new general secretary, Mike Moore, already expressed deep sympathies to this proposal in a recent trip to Brazil (Gazeta Mercantil, 2000). The difficult discussion on the international harmonization of the environmental regulations can come to good results among advanced and developing countries if there could prevail a firm understanding that this goal cannot be dissociated from the much needed access to the new environmental technologies.

Environmental Technologies in the North-South Relationship

The debate between trade and environment is guided, in general terms, by the study of the reactions of the companies submitted to environmental regulations. The discussion presented in the first item does not stray from this inclination, once it is concentrated on the effects of environmental regulations on the regulated companies (trade-off or synergy) and on their strategic responses that shape the trade and international direct investment patterns, concluding that no such correlations can be established a priori.

Thus, the strong and prevailing trend in the international political economy in favor of the harmonization of the environmental regulations occurs despite the theoretical and empirical obstacles for identifying a unique relationship between environmental regulations and competitiveness. The understanding of this supposed contradiction only becomes more satisfactory when the focus of the discussion is inverted. To be more exact, when the trade and environment theme stops being thought exclusively under the view of regulated companies and starts being considered on the side of the trade of environmental technologies, which is exactly the privileged focus of Porter.

The available data on the market of the environmental technologies industries reveals its growing importance in the world economy, placing it, in size, among the markets of the pharmaceutical industry and information technologies (OECD, 1996). In 1990, the environmental industry was estimated at $200 billion, with an estimated 50 percent growth until the year 2000 (OECD, 1993; Barton, 1998). Estimates by the World Bank foresaw a much larger growth until the year 2000—of 100 percent.

The United States leads the world market of environmental technologies with a share of 39 percent of the total, followed by the European Union with 24 percent, wherein Germany leads with 36 percent of the market (Barton, 1998:134). Germany is the country that proportionally exports the largest portion of its production—40 percent—mainly equipment for water treatment and technologies to reduce air pollution

(Barton, 1998:137). Japan demonstrates an evident interest in reassuring competitiveness in that market, resorting to several consortia formed by the government and private companies with the purpose of developing new technologies destined to the commercialization of clean technologies for developing countries (Hart, 1997).[8]

The transactions in the world market of environmental technologies point out a pattern of international trade with a clear North-South dimension. This pattern elapses, first, in the pioneering of the advanced countries in the development of the industries of environmental technologies, associated with the severity and antecedence of the environmental regulations in those countries (Barton, 1998). This pattern is also explained by the difficulties of generating environmental technologies in the developing countries (Almeida, 1993; Jha and Teixeira, 1994).[9]

The difference among the stages of environmental regulatory standards of the advanced and developing countries gives margin to arguments that the technologies that become less appropriate to the regulatory systems in the North start being exported to the South, reproducing the trade pattern of technological transfers to Latin America of the 1960s and 1970s, when this area imported plants and obsolete equipment, above all pollutants, with the intention of overcoming industrialization gaps. The ecological industry acted as a reinforcement of the prevailing structural technological gaps among developed and developing countries (Barton, 1998).

Could the difficulties of the developing countries in the diffusion and generation of environmental technologies be overcome with the recent opening and liberalization of their economies? Some authors argue so, because the economic liberalization might propitiate an incentive for the adoption of more rigid environmental regulations in developing countries, that would end up stimulating the local industry of environmental technologies. Almeida (1993) argued that the economic liberalization in fact can favor the advent of environmental technologies through imports and attraction of direct foreign investments; nevertheless, the obstacles for wide access, absorption, and future local development of these technologies remain crucial issues. In the same argumentative line, Chudnovsky et al. (1998) remind that: "As technical knowledge is partly tacit and localized, to master the imported technologies firms in LDCs [Less Developed Countries] have to develop an endogenous capacity to absorb, adapt and modify new technologies" (Chudnovsky et al., 1998:6).

The actual orientation of the environmental regulations of the industrialized countries in the 1990s—with a more rigorous conception, at the same time preventive and integrated, than that prevalent in the previous decades—reveals the growing challenges faced by the world industry of environmental technologies, and it contrasts with the serious deficiencies of endogenous research and development (R&D) of the developing countries.

Thus, although the tendency to international harmonization of the environmental regulations explains the lower discrepancy in the stages of environmental control of the developing countries compared to the developed ones, this hardly represents an incentive for the overcoming of the existent technological gaps among them. On the contrary, the harmonization of environmental standards seems to raise a strong asymmetry in the distribution of the mutual gains between the developed and developing countries, which is associated to the widely different local conditions to access and develop the new technologies needed to comply with those standards. This seems to compromise the macroeconomic foundations—especially lowering the external constraint—to reach sustainable development.

Conclusion

A consensus is evidenced in favor of the international harmonization of the environmental regulations in the international political economy of trade and environment, which settled down regardless of the theoretical and empirical inadequacies to support a relationship of necessary causality between environmental regulations and competitiveness.

This article argues against those defenders of the thesis that international harmonization of environmental regulations should be made by an extension and reinforcement of the regulations at the WTO. It should be recognized that, in this specific issue, the authors that defend free trade sustain some favorable arguments on the interests of the developing countries, above all when they emphatically condemn the aggressive unilateralism of the United States.

In the most likely negotiations on the international harmonization of environmental regulations, the defense of the particular interests of the developing countries still assumes great importance to counterweight the mounting evidence of a perverse international trade pattern in environmental technologies, which expresses a deepening of the technological dependence of these countries, with negative consequences on their trade and services balance, and ultimately on their growth paths.

The developed countries, especially the United States, Germany, and Japan, are adopting aggressive policies to promote their ecoindustries to maintain their leadership in the world market, which is projected as one of the largest and most dynamic of the global economy. One of the policy instruments most thoroughly used by the governments of the OECD member-countries to raise the demand and supply of new environmental technologies are environmental and R&D subsidies, not surprisingly two of the few fields of application of subsidies made legal by the WTO.

Thus, the actual tendencies of the international political economy of the environment show that Porter's ultimate objectives are well served. Unfortunately, the final conclusion based on these tendencies is that even if the developing countries reach some competitive advantages by harmonizing their environmental regulations toward the highest patterns practiced by the developed countries, validating Porter's hypothesis, an asymmetry of gains between North and South shall prevail, because of the different access conditions and endogenous development capacity concerning environmental technologies among developed and developing countries, that is, the gains tend to remain mostly concentrated in the developed countries.

Upward harmonization may imply, in the microeconomic level, synergetic gains for the firms in the developing countries, but at systemic level the conditions of access and generation of these technologies may worsen for these countries. It must be emphasized that this likely outcome should not be considered lightly as merely a marginal reinforcement of their technological dependence: the challenge of sustainable development is one of the major discontinuities in the whole history of the industry and has the effect of provoking important ruptures on the technological paths of many industrial sectors.

Therefore, it follows that there is the urgent need to implement integrated environmental and technological policies in the developing countries, similar to those practiced by the developed countries. This would require regulations at the WTO, especially adapting the special and differential treatment clauses to establish equity and fair competition where structural conditions are so different.

Notes

1. The most evident concern behind most of those studies is with the effects of the growing costs and losses of competitive advantages due to duties im-

posed by strict environmental regulations adopted by the United States since the early 1970s, most of them before their main rivals in the international markets. These costs, according to the Environmental Protection Agency of the United States (EPA), were of approximately U.S.$190 billion per year at the end of the 1990s, which amounts closely to 2.5 percent of the American GNP in 2000 (Jaffe et al., 1995:134). For broader surveys of these studies, see also Anderson (1997) and Jayadevappa and Chaatre (2000).

2. The high controversy potential in the interpretation of the WTO's regulations as a consequence of the enlargement of its scope when disciplining national regulations could be shown by the following data: The WTO's Dispute Settlement Body received over a hundred complaints during its three years of operation, while the previous GATT faced less than a hundred cases during the preceding half-century (Scholte et al., 1998).

3. The Uruguay Round became known as the green/blue round (Anderson, 1995).

4. The environmental issues are explicitly incorporated in other agreements of the Uruguay Round, especially in the agreement on subsidies and countervailing measures.

5. There is a certain contradiction in those international social movements, because at the same time as they are positioned against the neoliberalism and the multilateral institutions that give it support, they demand a strengthening of the WTO as a way of enlarging its power to impose obligations on their members, included in these the developing countries that certainly are among the main victims of this orientation and the evils of the neoliberalism.

6. A consultant of the WTO reminds us that the economical theory of public choice teaches that the competition for regulatory marks can lead to a suboptimal result in the case of multinational externalities and of international public goods, exactly due to the particularities of countries pointed out above. That is, each country tends to present a different regulatory optimal from another. However, the author defends that those imperfections of the regulatory competition should be weighted by the risk of the "aggressive unilateralism," obviously by part of the countries with great weight in the international trade. This author's proposal is that WTO promotes "package" negotiations—containing rules of the competition, international investment, environmental and labor legislation—linked to reforms in the antidumping rules, by him considered to be an instrument of distortion of the international trade and a risk to the multilateralism of the WTO. In short, the author's proposal, interpreted under the view of the developing countries, it is that these countries should accept the environmental patterns of the developed countries, in exchange for smaller flexibility in the use of antidumping rules (Petersmann, 1996).

7. This proposal was presented on the WTO High Level Symposium on Trade and the Environment, that took place in Geneva, in March of 1999. This was

the first meeting of the official senior representatives of the WTO with non-governmental organizations. Delegations from 134 WTO member nations met with representatives from 26 intergovernment organizations and 130 nongovernmental organizations related to environment, development, agriculture, labor unions, consumers, academy, and business (WTO Proposes a World Environment Organization, 1999).

8. One of those consortia is Research Institute for Innovative Technology for the Earth (RITE), which counts on financial resources and technical personnel supplied by the Japanese government as well as by more than 40 companies, and has an ambitious plan of one hundred years to create the new generation of energy technology, which should eliminate or neutralize the emissions of gases of greenhouse effect (Hart, 1997).

9. The concept of environmental technologies in Almeida (1993) and Jha and Teixeira (1994)—environmentally sound technologies—is the same employed in the present study, while Barton (1998) concentrates on the analysis of the Ecoindustry, defined by him as the one "that embraces a wide variety of products and services related to the monitoring, treatment, control and administration of the industrial and household pollution," which is closer to the concept of cleaning technologies. However, the analysis of Barton clearly indicates that the precedence of some advanced countries in the development of the Eco-industry (of cleaning) provides them competitive advantages in the transition from this to the industry of clean technologies. Therefore, those authors' analyses, although concentrated on different concepts, present common points, which are explored here.

Bibliography

Almeida, C. (1993). "Development and transfer of environmentally sound technologies in manufacturing: a survey." *UNCTAD Discussion Papers,* no. 58.

Anderson, K. (1996). "Environmental Standards and International Trade." In: Bruno, M., Pleskovic, B., ed., (1996). *Annual World Bank Conference on Development Economics 1996.* Washington, DC: World Bank.

Barton, J. R. (1998). "La dimensión Norte-Sur de las Industrias de limpieza ambiental y la difusión de tecnologías limpias." *Revista de la Cepal,* vol. 64: 129–150.

Bhagwati, J., R. E. Hudec, ed. (1996). *Fair trade and harmonization.* 2nd vol. Cambridge, Massachusetts: The MIT Press.

Bhagwati, J. (1996). "The Demands to Reduce Domestic Diversity Among Trading Nations." In: Bhagwati, J., R. E. Hudec, ed., op. cit., 9–40.

Bhagwati, J., T. N. Srinivasan, (1996). "Trade and the Environment: Does Environmental Diversity Detract from the Case for Free Trade?" In Bhagwati, J. and R. E. Hudec, ed., op. cit., 159–223.

Charzovitz, S. (1994). "The World Trade Organization and Social Issues." *Journal of World Trade,* vol. 28, no. 5: 17–33.

Chudnovsky, D. et al. (1998). "The Diffusion of Pollution Prevention Measures in LDCs: Environmental Management in Argentine Industry." Chicago: Latin American Studies Association Meeting, mimeo, 1–20.

Hart, S. L. (1997). "Strategies for a Sustainable World." *Harvard Business Review.* January-February: 67–76.

Jaffe, A. B. et al. (1995). "Environmental Regulation and the Competitiveness of U.S. Manufacturing: What Does the Evidence Tell Us?" *Journal of Economic Literature,* vol. 33, no.1: 132–163.

Jayadevappa, R., Chaatre, S. (2000). "International Trade and Environmental Quality: A Survey." *Ecological Economics,* vol. 32, no. 2: 175–194.

Jha, V., and A. P. Teixeira. (1994). "Are Environmentally Sound Technologies the Emperor's New Clothes?" *UNCTAD Discussion Papers,* no. 89.

OECD (1993). *Pollution Abatement and Control Expenditure in OECD Countries.* Paris: OCDE and J. R. Barton (1998), op. cit.

OECD (1996). *The Global Environmental Goods and Services Industry.* Paris: OCDE.

Ostry, S. (1992). "The Domestic Domain: The New International Policy Arena." *Transnational Corporations,* vol. 1, no. 1: 7–26.

Palmer, K., W. E. Oates, and P. R. Portney. (1995). "Tightening Environmental Standards: The Benefit-Cost or the No-Cost Paradigm?" *Journal of Economic Perspectives,* vol. 9, no. 4: 119–132.

Petersmann, E. (1996). "International Competition Rules for Governments and for Private Business." *Journal of World Trade,* vol. 30, no. 3: 5–35.

Porter, M. E. (1991). "America's Green Strategy." *Scientific American,* vol. 264: 168.

Porter, M. E., van der Linde, C. (1995). "Green and Competitive: Ending the Stalemate." *Harvard Business Review,* September-October: 120–134.

Porter, M. E. and C. van der Linde. (1995). "Toward a New Conception of the Environment-Competitiveness Relationship." *Journal of Economic Perspectives,* vol. 9, no. 4, 97–118.

Ruggiero, R. (1995). World Trade Organization, Director-General. "*The global challenge:* opportunities and choices in the multilateral trading system." *The Fourteenth Paul-Henri Spaak Lecture.* Harvard University.

Scholte, J. A., R. O'Brien, and M. Williams. (1998). "The WTO and Civil Society." *CSGR Working Paper.* no. 14/98. Warwick: University of Warwick, Centre for the Study of Globalisation and Regionalisation (CSGR).

Togeiro De Almeida, L. (1999). "Comércio e meio ambiente: um novo tema para a Organização Mundial de Comércio?" *Cenários. Revista do GEICD,* no. 1: 77–101.

Tussie, D. (1994). "The Policy Harmonization Debate: What Can Developing Countries Gain From Multilateral Negotiations? *UNCTAD Review 1994,* 1–8.

"WTO Proposes a World Environmental Organization." (1999). The Gallon Environment Letter, vol. 3, no. 8.

Chapter 8

The Effects of Globalization and Neoliberalism in Central America: Nicaragua and Costa Rica

Harry E. Vanden

Central America is a region not known for strong states or independent foreign policy. Geopolitically, it is in the Caribbean Basin and has been seen as part of the U.S. backyard. The region's proximity to the United States and the enormous difference in size and power between the United States and the countries in this region suggests a very unequal relationship. An early nineteenth-century attempt to unite the Central American nations as a federation was never successful either. Thereafter, the five original Spanish-speaking nations (Guatemala, Nicaragua, Honduras, El Salvador, and Costa Rica) and the northern part of Colombia that broke off to form the nation of Panama in 1903 have been small, weak states in the Interamerican and world system (the smallest of the sardines in Juan José Arévalo's fable *El Tiberón y las Sardinas*). As such, their sovereignty has often been compromised by the hegemonic influence of the United States and other larger states.

Central American-U.S. relations were initially more fraternal, as the United States eventually decided on a policy of supporting independence for the Spanish colonies. Contacts between the United States and the Central American states were at first sparse but often influenced by the Jeffersonian concept of relations among equal, sister republics. As the United

States began to expand through the Louisiana Purchase in 1803 and the acquisition of Florida from Spain in 1819, power was projected outward from the original 13 colonies. The Monroe Doctrine aimed to exclude European powers from dominating any of the newly independent republics, but also suggested U.S. interest in the region. After 1825 the nature of international relations began to change. Growing interest in Texas eventually projected American power South and set the stage for the Mexican American war of 1846–1848. Cornelius Vanderbilt developed financial interests in Nicaragua when he set up a stagecoach and steamship line to carry passengers across the Central American isthmus after the California Gold Rush. Soon after that, the American filibuster William Walker took over Nicaragua in 1855 and even had himself declared president after he stipulated that English was to be the official language. Later, the post–Civil War industrialization and economic expansion of the United States began to redefine the economic interests of the northern state. It would no longer be primarily a producer and exporter of raw materials like its sister republics to the south. Rather, it was becoming an industrialized creditor nation that started to search out new markets for its industrial products, additional sources of raw materials, and new locations to invest its growing investment capital. By the turn of the twentieth century, relations began to reflect the hegemonic position that it was establishing in the Caribbean Basin if not Latin America more generally. From 1803 through the 1960s, Central America witnessed a diverse variety of hegemonic initiatives by the United States. The region witnessed marine occupations, gunboat diplomacy, dollar diplomacy and financial penetration, anticommunism, covert intervention, and direct occupation by U.S. troops, as most recently occurred in Panama in 1989.

However, there were challenges to U.S. hegemony like the Guatemalan revolution of 1944–1954. Later, leftist insurgents in Guatemala and El Salvador threatened to establish independent governments and the Sandinistas did so in Nicaragua from 1979 to 1990. The nationalist military populism of Omar Torrijos posed a different challenge in Panama. But, by the early 1990s, the independent, radical thrust of political movements in all of these countries had been greatly reduced and none was in control of their respective nations. Official relations were once again cordial with the United States. By the end of the 1990s, there was a turn toward nominal Western-style representative democracy and political struggle in these four nations had been channeled into less violent avenues that were more easily influenced by the United States. Traditional control was maintained in Honduras, which became a base for U.S. military and contra operations against

Nicaragua in the 1980s. Costa Rica continued its own democratic tradition, but became ever more open to American political, economic, and media influence.

More recently, these nations also have shown a great deal of vulnerability to the influence of the globalization process and the dictates of international financial institutions. Given their relative diminished sovereignty, they would thus appear much more permeable to the boundary penetrating process of globalization. Indeed, the Central American nations offer excellent case studies to examine the effects of the neoliberal changes associated with globalization. This study first focuses on Nicaragua because of the Sandinista attempt to assert national sovereignty and resist the hegemonic influences of Washington and the Washington-based international financial institutions that transpired from 1979 to 1990. It was ultimately defeated by a combination of external and internal forces. The Chamorro and Alemán regimes that ensued proved especially accommodating to the compilation of external forces advocating the globalization process. As Nicaragua became subject to neoliberal policies and ever more integrated in the globalized economy, its national economy continued to deteriorate as did its balance of payments deficit, which reached close to $12 billion in 1994. Internal economic conditions continued to deteriorate for the masses with decreases in real income, official unemployment figures in excess of 50 percent and reduced medical and educational services for the masses. Throughout the region, wealth and poverty became more concentrated and many sank even further into misery. Although economic growth increased after 1995, the persistence of poverty, unemployment, and a growing movement to reduce social services seemed to suggest that the effects of neoliberal policies on the masses were far less positive than promised and often imposed increased hardships. Indeed, the data underline the general trend that the United Nations Human Development Program (UNDP) noted in its *Human Development Report 1999,* that—in contradiction to neoliberal premises—without an active role by government to ensure equity and human services, the forces of globalization do not necessarily support human advancement at all. Nicaragua and Costa Rica provide two excellent case studies that elucidate these phenomena.

To understand the specifics of the Nicaraguan case, it is necessary to follow the development of the country since the Sandinista takeover in 1979. Under the Sandinistas, Nicaragua was one of the countries that insisted on maintaining its national sovereignty in economic and political matters and argued for a new international economic order. Its ties to the nonaligned movements and its economic relations with a variety of countries allowed it a certain amount of economic flexibility (see Vanden and Morales 1985; Vanden and Walker 1991). However, when Ronald Reagan was elected president of the United States, he brought increasing pressure to bear on Nicaragua. It included an economic embargo and low intensity warfare that utilized the contras (Vanden, 1990). In 1990, this external pressure, Sandinista errors, and the dynamics of internal Nicaraguan politics combined to cause the electoral defeat of the Sandinistas and the election of Violeta Chamorro to the Nicaraguan presidency. Yet, the electoral victory of Pedro Joaquín Chamorro's widow was in large part engineered by the United States, which in turn left the new government beholden to Washington and consequently with much less autonomy (see the last chapter of Vanden and Prevost, 1993). Based on the advice of its new conservative economic consultants and the advice from the U.S. State Department's AID, the World Bank, and the International Monetary Fund, the new regime began the process of globalization by implementing neoliberal politics in Nicaragua. This process proceeded from 1990 to 1996 under Chamorro and was continued under the even more conservative regime of Arnoldo Alemán from 1996 to 2002. A key step was taken in September of 1991 when the Nicaraguan government entered into agreements with the IMF, World Bank, and the Interamerican Bank for Development (Trevor Evans, 1995:3–4).

The Chamorro administration followed all the neoliberal prescriptions:

- Drastic reduction of public spending, including education and medical care was implemented.
- The size of the state and the number of public employees was reduced.
- External tariffs were drastically reduced and the internal market was opened to importation.
- Exports were stimulated through financial incentives.
- Restrictions on capital flow were reduced so that it became much easier to bring in capital or send it out of the country.
- Free trade zones were established.
- An attempt was made to reduce the external deficit.

Specific examples included:

- The average level for tariffs was reduced from 42 percent in 1990 to 15 percent in 1992 (Stahler-Sholk, 1997:90).
- Credit was reduced for small farmers and increased for large farmers as a way of stimulating exports.

- The government was able to reduce the salaries of rural laborers.
- A new law on external investment was passed that allowed for 100 percent remittance of investments after three years (Stahler-Sholk, 1997:93).

Neoliberalism was implemented with a great deal of enthusiasm, but the results of these policies were not always what was promised. In the early 1990s, the greatest inflow of capital did not come from investments but, rather, from aid and assistance programs from donor nations and international institutions.

Although there are many factors that influence investment, it is interesting to note that as of 1993 the total of U.S. direct investment was only $110 million, compared to $385 million in Costa Rica (Stahler-Sholk, 99). Furthermore, the value of exports actually fell by $87 million from 1990 to 1992, while the value of imports increased by $237 million during the same period. This led to a balance of payments deficit of $610 million in 1992 and $428 million in 1994 (Stahler-Sholk, 81). In 1997, it rose to $620.6 million (IMF data in *Statistical Abstract of Latin America,* 2000:785). By the mid-1990s the external debt had reached almost $12 billion, making it the highest per capita debt in the world. Nicaragua became a member of the Most Indebted Nations Club and began to ask for debt forgiveness as a way of surviving. Even so, by the end of the decade its external debt remained at $8 billion, before being further reduced to $6.65 billion in 2000 (CEPAL/ECLA online). Furthermore, the neoliberal repayments were devastating. Under the terms of the 1994 structural adjustment agreement, Nicaragua had to pay an average of $280.7 million a year in principal and interest payment. Just the debt service payments represented 60 percent of export value. Indeed, in the post-Sandinista period, better than half of government revenues (and sometimes as much as 70 percent) were designated for debt service payments (Vukelich, 1999:24). Given the dire external debt problem, it is even more amazing that Nicaragua acquiesced to pressure from Washington and withdrew a case before the World Court where the only issue left to resolve was how much of the $17 billion claimed in damages caused by the United States and U.S.-backed contras would be paid to Nicaragua. Many saw this as a clear example of Nicaragua's subordination to U.S. hegemony. The effects for the Nicaraguan people have been harsh indeed. In 1997, the government spent more than twice as much on foreign debt payments as it did on health care and education combined (Vukelich, 24).

There were, however, some successes. The end of the Sandinista period was marked by extremely high inflation—it was more than 30,000 percent in 1988. Under neoliberal policies, it was drastically reduced. Inflation fell to 13.4 percent in 1990, 3.5 percent in 1992 and 12.4 percent in 1994. It has remained in check. After negative growth in the early 1990s, the economy finally started to grow in the mid-1990s: 3.2 percent in 1994, 4.3 percent in 1995, and 4.2 percent in 1998. This represented a major turnaround.

Social Conditions

What were the effects on these policies? Unemployment in the mid-1990s was some 54 percent. Even the economic section of the American embassy estimated that 60 percent of the economically active population was suffering from unemployment or underemployment (Interview, Economic Section of American Embassy, 1995). By 1999, unemployment was officially put at 22 percent but considered much higher by most. The greatest growth in jobs had been in the informal sector, which offered no benefits. There were also problems with wealth and the distribution of income. Five percent of the population lived in misery and 19.4 percent lived in absolute poverty. The richest fifth of the population received 65 percent of the income while the poorest fifth only received 3 percent (UNDP as cited in Stahler-Sholk, 95). These same percentages continued into the next century. Medical consultations per capita fell 21 percent from 1990 to 1994 as the availability of health care was reduced. Living conditions for the masses fell to levels close to those in Haiti and the per capita gross domestic product did as well (a little more than $400 per year in the mid-1990s and some $500 per year by 2000). Misery was widespread. Indeed, Nicaragua had the lowest per capita social spending of any of the Spanish or Portuguese countries in Latin America by 1997, and was only one of two that did not increase social spending in that year (Ocampo, 1999:2).

The case of Nicaragua suggests that the incorporation of Central American nations into a globalized economy based on neoliberal principles often has created even greater suffering than before for the toiling masses and substantial sectors of the middle class. Nor does it appear that conditions will soon improve. Despite all the aid and advice from the U.S. Agency for International Development, the IMF, the World Bank, and the Interamerican Development Bank, the experiment was a failure.

The prescriptions had nearly killed the patient. The magic of the market did not work in Nicaragua and the people—beginning with women and children—suffered the consequences.

Costa Rica

Costa Rica has its unique history in Central America but also has been subject to the hegemonic influence of the United States. Often referred to as the Switzerland of Central America, it has developed a political system that is very different from that of Nicaragua. The United Fruit Company penetrated the country in the earlier part of the twentieth century and, along with other American companies, monopolized most of Costa Rica's banana production. There were strong labor actions by the banana workers from the 1930s on and the powerful banana workers union became one of the organizational bases for Vanguardia Popular, the Communist Party in Costa Rica. There was some threat of a radical restructuring of the nation that came from a combination of radical and progressive forces under President Calderón in the late 1940s. The response to this crisis was the organization of a new reformist political movement (Liberación Nacional) by an elitist political reformer, José Figueres. Don Pepe, as he came to be called, had met and married an American woman while he was studying in the United States and was sympathetic to U.S. policy. He led the revolution of 1948 that abolished the military, enacted fundamental social and economic reforms, and set up a well-run social democratic state. In the next decades, Costa Rica developed an excellent educational and health care system that rivaled those of many developed countries. Furthermore, a certain consensus on the need for the state to perform social welfare functions developed among most of the political elite and the masses as well. The state even assumed the role of insurance provider. Although Liberación Nacional became the foremost party in the 1950s, other opposition parties emerged. The last two decades of the twentieth century saw the Christian democratic Social Christian Unity Party emerge as a viable power contender and Costa Rica evolved into a consensual two-party dominant political system. In recent years, the presidency has alternated between these two parties.

The state also developed. From the late 1940s to the early 1990s, Costa Rica developed as a state apparatus that was dedicated to implementing social democratic programs that improved the standard of living of the Costa Rican masses. Among these were:

- an excellent system of free public education, crowned by the high quality and tuition-free University of Costa Rica and the National University
- one of the best Latin American infrastructures in areas such as electricity, potable water, roads, and telecommunications
- the outstanding social security, health care, and pension system that rivals those of many developed countries
- a modern state bureaucracy staffed by well-trained, educated professional public servants who are monitored and protected by Latin America's only civil service system
- progressive and enlightened labor and pension protections
- ERA-type legal and effective guaranteed equality for women
- a state-run, low-cost system of all type of insurance
- support for the arts and culture

Since the revolution of 1948, democracy has grown steadily in Costa Rica and the *Ticos* have become ever more passionate in practicing it. Elections are clean, well monitored and efficiently run; campaigns are sophisticated and fought out with public relations, political consultants, polls, and get-out-the-vote drives. Indeed, the threat to democracy comes not from coups (there is no military) or political violence, but from media and image control by some wealthy, elitist sectors and the United States. Indeed, with the Sandinista victory of 1979, the continuing revolution in Guatemala, and the outbreak of a civil war in El Salvador in 1980, the United States began to bring considerable pressure to bear on Costa Rica to become part of the counterrevolutionary project that it was constructing against Nicaragua and the revolutionary movements in El Salvador and Guatemala. Attempts were made to militarize sections of Costa Rica's National Police and to engage them in tense border confrontations with Nicaragua. John Hull and other CIA operatives were installed in a ranch in northern Costa Rica so as to provide a support and supply base for the Contras attacking the Sandinista government from the south. National press outlets—such as the well-respected newspaper *La Nación*—were employed to disseminate stories that were very damning and damaging to the Sandinistas and thus to turn public opinion against the Sandinistas and other revolutionary groups. In this way, support was also mobilized for chilling relations with Costa Rica's northern neighbor.

Diplomatic initiative by Costa Rica's Nobel Prize–winning president Oscar Arias and other Central American leaders was able to move the struggle for power toward less violent means and to assist in negotiating peace plans in Nicaragua, El Salvador, and Guatemala. This helped to diffuse the political tension in Central America and began to alleviate some of the outside pressure on Costa Rica. When the Cold War was nearing its end and the Sandinistas were voted out of office in 1990, Costa Rica's strategic importance for U.S. policy was diminished and it was easier for it to assert dimensions of national sovereignty. This was manifest in actions such as the investigation and indictment of John Hull and some of his cronies. But the development of a unipolar world in which the power of the United States was unrivaled and unbalanced facilitated the incursion of more subtle forms of influence from Washington. This came to include ever stronger advocacy for neoliberal economic reforms and the integration of the small Central American state in the globalization process. USAID and International Financial Institutions began to suggest that Costa Rica should abandon its government-directed, protectionist, social welfare state in favor of a state that would:

- be less interventionist—especially in respect to the free flow of goods and capital;
- privatize public services, including, as in Nicaragua, the lucrative telecommunications system;
- undergo fiscal reforms;
- shrink the size of the state;
- reduce social spending.

Costa Rica was to adopt these neoliberal measures and globalize—open its borders to transnational capital and transnational corporations and their products.

Although there was some discussion about the advisability of these policies, a consensus grew among local economists and many politicians that some change and restructuring in this direction was necessary to survive in the rapidly globalizing economy. The adjustments and restructuring that were begun under the presidency of Oscar Arias (1986–1990) were continued through the 1990s. Thus Costa Rica, like Nicaragua, became much more globalized during the 1990s, even during the administration of Liberación Nacional's José Figueres's son, José María Figueres (1994–1998). The administration of the neoliberal Miguel Angel Rodríguez of the Social Christian Unity Party (1998–2002) pushed these changes even more strongly. However, progressive forces within Liberación Nacional, trade unions, teachers, and other groups within society mobilized to protect hard-won social welfare, labor, and economic rights like the pension system. The general consensus on most aspects of the social democratic state as well as the mobilized political forces and social groups meant that most state services and the social safety net were generally kept in place. Furthermore, and perhaps most important, the state apparatus was maintained and the state was still seen as the primary protector of the people. Tariffs were lowered and the entrance and exit of capital was eased. Policies designed to increase exports were simultaneously enacted.

The production of nontraditional export crops like potatoes and miniature vegetables was increased. High-tech exports also were boosted as Motorola opened a silicon wafer plant to make chips for cell phones and pagers, and then INTEL opened a computer microchip plant. Some lower tech maquiladora plants also were opened. The net result was a boost in exports and the creation of new jobs—skilled and other. Other new products like computer software for hospital administration also were exported as Costa Rica was able to rely on its development in the health care sector, excellent educational system, well-trained, well-cared-for workforce and developing base in high tech to evolve new products.

The implementation of neoliberal reforms and process of globalization in Costa Rica were done very much within the Costa Rican political and social consensus. It was accomplished within a political system that not only permitted different political factions to articulate their divergent policy perspectives but also allowed and even encouraged different social groups to pressure the policy process to meet their needs and demands. This made for a rather unique example of how these changes could be made. The Costa Rican case avoided many of the worst side effects usually associated with the implementation of neoliberal reforms and globalization: radically decreased social services, fewer relatively well-paying jobs with benefits, the demise of large number of national firms that could not compete with the new, cheap imports, and the radical concentration of wealth and poverty in the national population. Relying on data collected by Dr. Justo Aguilar and a Costa Rican research team for the project "Structural Policies in Central America During the Nineties" as well as data from ECLAC/CEPAL and the UNDP, we find that the effects of these processes were quite different in Costa Rica as compared to Nicaragua and most other states.[1] There were, however, some similarities. For instance, in the beginning of the 1990s, there was a significant reduction in social spending—about 9 percent (Nowalski, 1990:4). Likewise, there was an increase in the number of jobs in the informal sectors, with concomitant loss of benefits. There was also a slight increase in salary inequity over the nineties. Although the economic growth was much better than that of Nicaragua, it did sputter in the mid-1990s, but continued to grow at the end of the decade (GDP grew 8 percent in 1999).

But unlike Nicaragua and many other countries that made these reforms, the effects in other areas were different. One of the general characteristics of the globalization process is that the gap in income between the wealthy and the poor grows within the nation. There was only the slightest change in Costa Rica. In 1990, the 10 percent of the population that was the poorest got 1.5 percent of the salary income, while in 1998 that figure declined to 1.4 percent. Meanwhile, the richest 10 percent of population got 32.8 percent of the salary income in 1990 and the same amount in 1998.[2] Furthermore, during the decade, salary income increased 7 percent in real terms, suggesting that the poor as well as the rich profited from the economic expansion. Indeed, in 1997 only 20 percent of the Costa Ricans were beneath the poverty line, as compared to 68 percent of the Nicaraguans. And per capita social expenditures in Costa Rica were $550 as compared to $49 in Nicaragua (Aguilar et al., 2000). Costa Rican urban unemployment had settled in at 5.7 percent by the end of the decade (*Statistical Abstract of Latin America,* 2000). The literacy rate never fell below 95 percent in Costa Rica whereas in Nicaragua it decreased from 85 percent in 1990 to 65 percent in 1995, and did not recover in the rest of the decade. In 1997, infant mortality was 14 per 1,000 live births in Costa Rica, but 57 per 1000 live births in Nicaragua (*Statistical Abstract for Latin America,* 2000).

Analyzing this phenomena, Juan Trejos suggests that by doing what was necessary to stabilize the economy in the earlier part of the decade, it was possible to save the levels of social investment and to target key institutions such as the Caja Costaricense de Seguridad Social (National Health Care and Pension Administration) and the National Institute for Learning (INA) for continued high levels of funding. In this way Costa Rica was able to minimize the social costs of economic adjustments (Trejos, 1999:24–25). Trejos further explains that the governmental mechanisms to insure social welfare that were built up in the 1980s to cushion the worst effects of the lost decade in economic growth (as it known in Latin America) were utilized to moderate the effects of economic adjustments and the opening up of the national economy through globalization (Trejos: 24–25). The governability that the state exercised was thus sufficient to mobilize and distribute the resources necessary to protect its people against the socioeconomic ravages usually associated with rapid implementation of neoliberal reforms and the globalization process. This was not the case in Nicaragua and has not generally been the case in those Latin American nations making such adjustments. Indeed, the executive secretary of ECLAC (the United Nation's Economic Commission for Latin America and the Caribbean) noted inadequate governability and the lack of redistributive institutions in Latin America, and the general weakness of Latin American nation-states in the face of the forces of globalization. He further noted that only 37 percent of the Latin American population were satisfied with the economic progress achieved by the political system (Ocampo, 2000).

The presidential administration of Miguel Angel Rodriguez (1998–2002) had strong support from Washington and was very favorably disposed to the advice from the international financial institutions. However, when his neoliberal Social Christian administration tried to restructure efficient, profitable institutions like the Costa Rican Institute of Electricity (ICE), he was met by a powerful political mobilization against these measures. Those opposing his proposed ICE policy included students, ICE workers, unions and many others. Indeed, there was a general consensus that ICE was an efficient organization that provided excellent service at low costs. The government was perceived as having broken the general consensus on state services (if not an unwritten social contract with the Costa Rican electorate) and the pressure was so strong that the government began to suffer a crisis of legitimacy. It relented in the face of mounting opposition. This event helped to establish the parameters of what would and would not be tolerated in Costa Rica. Such a consensus never existed in Nicaragua, where lack of consensus was more the norm. Furthermore, many felt that even the FSLN failed to act as an effective opposition to resist similar privatizations and neoliberal policies.

Costa Rica was also vulnerable to the new hegemonic project of the United States—the imposition of the Washington Consensus on the primacy of globalization and neoliberal economic reforms. However, to date, the Costa Rican consensus on the primacy of human development and the social net coupled with preexisting state mechanisms that afford a high level of governability, a well-defined political consensus, and popular political mobilizations have greatly ameliorated the worst social effects of globalization as experienced in Nicaragua and most other countries. These findings are consistent with those of the United Nations Development Program as found in documents like their *Human Development Report 1999* (1999:1–2 and 7–9). The UNDP and a growing number of scholars and governmental and nongovernmental organizations have noted the pernicious social effects of globalization and neoliberalism and are seeking viable alternatives to cushion this process.

Solely in regard to the way these processes are concentrating wealth, they note, for example, that

- the world's 200 richest people have more than doubled their income in the four years prior to 1998—to more than $1 trillion, and that
- the assets of the top three billionaires are more than the GNP of all the least developed countries and the six hundred million people who live in them.

Furthermore the *Human Development Report 1999* notes that "Social policies—and national governance—are even more relevant today to make globalization work for human development and to protect against its new threats" (1999:9). The UNDP and many others also note that globalization is creating new threats to human security in poor (and rich) countries. This is clearly the case in Nicaragua but not in Costa Rica. This preliminary study suggests that these effects are not inevitable. With popular will and stronger governance, social benefits can be preserved while the advantages of competitive markets are enjoyed, even in the transition period. But, this can only be done when clear rules and boundaries as to what will and will not be tolerated are in place and when there is a strong political will and adequate political and governmental infrastructure to take the action necessary to meet basic needs for human development.

Notes

1. Dr. Justo Aguilar Fong and his research team at the Facultad de Ciencias Economicas of the Universidad de Costa Rica supplied much of the economic data for the section on Costa Rica, and were most helpful in explaining the exact nature of the structural reforms in Costa Rica. The author is most indebted to Dr. Aguilar and his colleagues for their generous collaboration.
2. Statistics on the distribution of household income are, however, slightly different. The poorest 20 percent of households got 4.3 percent of the income, while the richest 20 percent of households got 50.6 percent of income (Human Development Report, 1999:39).

Bibliography

Aguilar, Justo et al., (2000). "Structural Policies in Central America During the Nineties." Preliminary research findings.

CEPAL/ECLAC. (2001). "America Latina y El Caribe: Deuda Externa Bruta Desembolsada," retrieved from www.ecla.org. Economico, April 27.

Economic Section, American Embassy. (1995). Interview, July, Managua.

Nowalski R., Jorge. (2000). "Los Desafíos de la Globalización en Centroamérica." Paper presented at meeting of Latin American Studies Association, Miami, March 2000.

Ocampo, José Antonio. (2001). "The Economy of Latin America in 2000." *CEPAL News,* vol. XXI, January.

Ocampo, José Antonio. (2000). "Los Retos del Dessarrollo Latinoamericano y Caribeño en los Albores del Siglo XXI." Plenary address, 50th Congress of Americanists, Warsaw, July 10–14.

Ocampo, José Antonio. (1999). "Social Spending Up Significantly in Latin America," *CEPAL News,* vol. XIX, June.

Prevost, Gary and Harry E. Vanden, eds. (1999). *The Undermining of the Sandinista Revolution.* 2nd revised printing. London and New York: Macmillan and St. Martin's Press.

Stahler-Sholk, Richard. (1999). "Structural Adjustments and Resistance: The Political Economy of Nicaragua under Chamorro." In Gary Prevost and Harry E. Vanden, eds., *The Undermining of the Sandinista Revolution.* 2nd revised printing. London: Macmillan and New York: St. Martin's Press.

Trejos, Juan Diego. (1999). "Desarrollo Social y Reforma Económica en Costa Rica." Paper presented in the International Symposium, Reforma Económica y Cambio Social En América Latina y el Caribe, Cali, Colombia, October 27–29.

United Nations Human Development Programme. (1999). *Human Development Report, 1999.* New York: Oxford University Press.

Vanden, Harry E. and Gary Prevost. (1993). *Democracy and Socialism in Sandinista Nicaragua.* Boulder: Lynne Rienner Publishers.

Vanden, Harry E. and Trudi Morales. (1985). "Nicaraguan Relations with the Nonaligned." *Journal of Inter-American Studies and World Affairs,* vol. XXVII.

Vanden, Harry E. and Thomas Walker. (1991). "U.S.-Nicaraguan Relations." In *The Central American Crisis.* Ed. Kenneth Coleman and George C. Herring, 2nd edition. Wilmington, DE: Scholarly Resources.

Vukelich, Donna. (1999). "The Devastation of Debt," *NACLA: Report on the Americas,* vol. XXXIII, September/October.

Wilkie, James, ed., (2000). *Statistical Abstract of Latin America. Volume 36.* Los Angeles: UCLA Latin American Center Publications.

Chapter 9

Globalization and Regional Integration in Latin America

Dorothea Melcher

The globalization process that occurred during the last 25 years impacts almost all aspects of human life, but it is generally accepted that the basic process is that of economic globalization. The modern industrial and financial system characterized by its enormous mass of commodities and financial instruments is invading the most remote geographic areas, influencing the cultural, social, and economic processes at the local level. It produces change in the patterns of nutrition, clothing, construction, entertainment, knowledge, religion and health care, and destroys preindustrial societies, without transforming them into modern industrial, productive societies. It occupies natural landscapes, extracts raw materials, or uses them for agriculture, roads, airports, and construction of urban spaces, without offering the inhabitants the capacity to continue enjoying what they were accustomed to or offering new possibilities for use. The social and cultural change economic globalization creates is received differently: from enthusiastic acceptance because it is considered the liberation of the individual from traditional social restraints, gaining access to all products and the capacity of social and spatial mobility, on the one hand, to cultural, social, and political movements that, with different intensity, are opposed to these results, on the other.

In this chapter, the problem is presented in historical perspective. Through knowing the historical formation of structures, it is possible to understand the forces—favorable or otherwise—that shaped it. Globalization is a new step in the intersection of human beings in one specific place, with others in a growing number of different spaces. The local is the beginning of this historical process, but it has been transformed into a complex system of visible and invisible ("virtual") relationships that connect the local with the global, without giving up the intermediate national and regional structures.

Meetings of Expansion

Discoveries were mostly local, but humankind always has been able to spread its knowledge, acquired by intelligence, creativity, and chance, to others of the human species, and has contributed to expand the common possession of knowledge and technology. In this respect we can speak of globalization since the beginnings of human history, but until the Industrial Revolution of the eighteenth century, it was the local and regional dimension that determined many of the parameters of human life.

Before Mercantilist Society (about 1500), regional unification was achieved through conquest and subordination to a political-military structure that we call the "state," generally an imperial state. Resources were extracted through a variety of methods, including intermediaries and tribute from the conquered. The resources were then distributed among the state's beneficiaries. There were internal commercial relations as well, but they had a different level of importance. In the feudal society of the Middle Ages, the tribute in specie was the main income of the nobles and the church. In the tenth century, commercial activities spread, cities were founded, and market rights and road protection were granted. Nevertheless, there were limitations on the functioning of markets and especially on the use of money. The artisan and merchants associations regulated their activities to protect their members against competition and loss of income. They considered this to be necessary to guarantee a decent level of living as the product of their honorable work and skill. The Catholic Church prohibited the lending of money at interest, because it noticed the effect of such lending, how it built up credit and debt and social instability.

Mercantilism and Colonial Expansion

The importance of large-scale trade was noticed when the Crusaders from Western Europe came in contact with the Near and Middle East and their enormous productive capacities. Taxes, tolls, and other obligations imposed on the merchants sparked a wider perspective wherein the powerful obtained high monetary incomes, and the promotion of commercial and productive activities began to determine the political and ideological system of the epoch—"mercantilism." The establishment of control over economic space, so as to promote and exploit the produced riches, caused political transformations that led to the absolutist state system and its territorial definition of sovereignty. This new organization superceded the system of personal relationships between the vassals and aristocrats, and leaders of local or regional tribes.

Small economic spaces were integrated into larger entities, creating privileges and monopolies for merchants who were nearer to centralized power. The goal was to assure access to and domination over larger markets, where it was possible to buy and sell at controlled prices and thus obtain higher revenues for the state. The absolutist state, the beginning of the modern territorial state, became the guarantor over the integrated internal space, as the basis for the access and domination over other regions farther away, and at the same time it created official policies to improve the transport infrastructure that makes trade easier (construction of channels and roads in Europe, etc.).

With these changes to the feudal system in Europe and the expansion of trade after the fifteenth century, a new step was taken to interconnect the different regions of the world. Portugal, Spain, and the Netherlands were the first to explore the globe outside the known world. They founded colonial empires whose diversity was reflected by the previous level of development among the local people. Territory was no longer the basis for the more or less complete life of the people who inhabited it; rather, it was dedicated ever more frequently to supply the needs of distant markets. The slave trade becomes logical in the context of the occupation of territories that did not have enough people willing or able to work. Such conditions induced the owners to get a workforce for the exploitation of the newly acquired lands. If workers were not available on good terms, greed and the promise of gains were sufficient to justify severe abuses of beings of the same species.

Trade was a privileged activity in these new empires. The establishment of monopolies over the European colonies was the first expression of this. Another element was the prohibition of the production of products in the colonies that were made in the "motherlands." This was to assure the market for the merchants of the colonizing countries. In this way, a "division of labor" was created between the colonies and the mother countries, and in the interior of the colonial empires we find the combination of different regional activities and their exchange, as, for example, in the Spanish colonies of America.

Industrial Revolution and Free Trade

With the introduction of machinery into the productive process at the end of the eighteenth century, the productive forces took an enormous step forward as labor productivity increased while labor was at once subordinated to domination by capital. Cheaper mass production of commodities such as textiles, and the development of new transportation facilities such as railroads and steamships, created incentives to seek out new markets by the most advanced country, England.

As support for the expansive interests of the industrial sector, David Ricardo formulated his statement on the advantages of "free trade." For Ricardo, free trade would make the cost of living cheaper through the importation of cheaper food and consumer products for the working classes, as a condition for reducing wages. Indeed, this was the only way he saw to increase capital benefits. He projected the image of an "international division of labor" that would be similar to the elevation of productivity through a greater division of labor by specialization, and that would in turn lower prices. He presented a very simple example for an exchange by "comparative advantages":

> In a system of totally free trade, every country will naturally invest its capital and its labour in those activities that would be most beneficial for both. This persual of individual benefit is admirably related to universal welfare. It distributes labour in the most efficient and economical way because it stimulates industry, favours inventions and, by more efficiently utilizing the particular capacities given by nature, increases the general mass of production, expands general benefits and unites universal society in the whole civilized world with one common interest and a common exchange between all. This is the principle which determines that wine will be produced in France and Portugal; that the grains are grown in America, and that England produce iron articles and others. (Ricardo, 1959:102)

For Ricardo, at the beginning of the nineteenth-century national frontiers were rigid limitations for the movements of capital and labor, and his analysis is, therefore, concentrated on commercial activities. He observed that the leveling of benefits was produced between regions in the nation but did not function beyond national borders:

> In general terms, the benefits of a single country are always at a certain level, or they are only different when the investment of capital is more or less secure and attractive. This does not happen between different countries. If the benefits obtained from capital invested in Yorkshire overtakes that obtained by the capital employed in London, the London capital would transfer itself rapidly to Yorkshire and the leveling of benefits will be effective. However if caused by a reduced productive rate in England, originated by an increase of capital and population, the wages increase and the benefits fall, it is not probable that the capital and the population of England move to the Netherlands, Spain or Russia where the benefits could be higher. (Ricardo, 1959:104)

Ricardo saw a corrective process for the disparities in commercial exchanges in international trade. The increase in prices and wages that resulted from the wealth of gold in a country, would cause changes in the pattern of comparative advantage. Lowering one's relative position would cause imports to be paid with transfers of gold (or silver), that is, because of the relative change of the value of national currency as compared with other currencies.

Free Trade and Protectionism—The Nineteenth Century

When England moved ahead in world trade, using its technological advantage from the Industrial Revolution and the construction of steamships and railroads, it based its ascension on its previous maritime and commercial domination, which were closely related to the activities of the British state and the large traders. The free trade ideas of Adam Smith and David Ricardo attempted to provide a theoretical vindication for this predominance.

But in England itself, and even more so in neighboring countries, the advantages of the idea were not accepted so easily. Political theories of protected development and regional integration for small countries were developed, thus excluding English hegemony. The continental blockade against Great Britain, which tried to impose Napoleon Bonaparte at the beginning of the nineteenth century (1806), led to the French war against Prussia and Russia. After the defeat of France (1815), the claim for integration and protection of the German markets and industries arose in the small German states. The theoretician was Friedrich List, who promoted the Tax League (*Zollverein*), which was established as a common market with protective external tariffs among the Northern German states in 1833 and later around Prussia in 1867 (excluding Austria). It was extended in 1868 by the unification of the Southern German states and was consolidated as a politically integrated space in the new German Empire in 1871.

In the same way, the industrialization of the United States developed after 1812:

> In the rapid development of this [the cotton textile] and other industries of the United States, not the least part corresponds to the protectionist policies of its government. The home industries received an important stimulus by the "Embargo and No-Intercourse" laws, approved after the War of 1812. These laws cut off the delivery of raw materials of England and protected temporarily the infant industries of America. . . . When the 1812 war ended, large quantities of industrial articles that had accumulated in England on cause of the continental and American blockade were sold in this latter market at very low prices. The new industries of the United States could not compete with these cheap foreign products. Protest arose that had as its result the approval, in 1816, of a protective tariff that established high tariffs on manufactured articles. Then it was believed that this measure would help not only the manufacturer interests, but, too, by stimulating the growth of towns, create the market for the agricultural products of the country. This argument constituted the basis for what Henry Clay calls "the American system." (Barnes, 457)

Friedrich List formulated the idea of free trade, in the sense that free trade supposes the unhindered circulation and selling of commodities that are produced. For him, the most important aspect is the development of the productive forces, the capacity to produce tradable goods in a competitive way. List concentrates on the location of the production site and the concomitant physical and social factors inside of the boundaries of a given country. The idea of free trade leads to the other extreme: the unlimited circulation of products worldwide. The state enters as a regulative force that intervenes politically to set or remove obstacles, according to the special needs of the moment.

The fact that the most developed European countries did not really accept the free trade proposed by the English theorists is expressed in the new colonial "imperialist" expansion of England, France, and, finally, Germany, when the competition for the domination of markets and raw materials of the world was growing. The empires had a double function: On the one hand, they were a means of guaranteed preferential access, as forms of "regional integration," and, on the other, they functioned as guarantees of the extension and penetration of the dominant capitalist economies in the colonies. These in turn suffered processes of destruction and limitation in their own productive and commercial activities (India), in the same way it had functioned with the first colonial expansion of Europe, between 1500 and 1800.

However, the enormous expansion of long distance trade was always limited by state intervention, even by Britain. The British responded to the call by a political weighty internal sector for support and protection. The expansion of the 1860s led to the Great Depression of 1870 to 1890, with its violent concentration of capital, the founding of trusts, cartels, and other instruments—often governmental—to protect powerful internal sectors against foreign competition.

An important element in the development of nineteenth-century international economic relations was the creation and functioning of a financial system that permitted the payment of merchandise and the transfer of capital, loans, and their repayments. In spite of many international financial and bank crises, the gold standard spread and reigned under the direction of the Bank of England, whose issuance of money (the pound sterling) were accepted as payments.

The growing tension of the interimperialist conflicts and their explosion in World War I shows that, in spite of the expansion of trade and financial markets and the efforts to eliminate obstacles between the different spaces where they operated, the opposite occurred. Competing forces were strengthened, tending to restrain and protect certain productive or commercial activities and to intervene in the financial mechanisms, especially in the process of change to the Gold Standard.

The Crisis and the Breakdown of the
First Round of Free Trade (1914–1944)

World War I put an end to the Gold Standard, transferred the center of the financial power from London to New York, and created heavy internal and external pressures on national and imperial economic spaces. The dismembering of three empires—the German, the Austrian-Hungarian, and the Ottoman—the creation of many new nations, and the cutting off of the political, economic, commercial, and financial spaces weakened what had been created as a network of international access. In 1919, the economist John

Maynard Keynes called the attention of the victorious countries in the Versailles Treaty to the imposition of very heavy reparations on the defeated German empire and the fact that the inevitable depression of its economy would trouble the other European countries because of the high level of economic interrelationship achieved before the war. The return to the Gold Standard and economic growth between 1925 and 1929 gave the illusion of a recreation of the process of the nineteenth century, but the disaster initiated by the breakdown of the New York Stock Exchange in 1929 in the international financial system, led to the paralization of the external markets and efforts by almost all countries to obtain higher levels of self sufficiency if not autarky. Subsequently, the 1930s, World War II, and most of the following two decades were characterized by the lack of convertible currencies, a severe downfall in the international trade, systems of international barter, and the promotion of policies of industrial development by import substitution (Raúl Prebisch). The intent of Nazi Germany to expand its economic sphere by the military conquest of industrial, mineral, and agricultural space (Belgium, France, Poland, and Russia) was repelled by the Allies—Great Britain, France, and the United States. The intent of Japan to do the same in the Pacific, and the politics of Italy to expand its possession in Africa, conquering Ethiopia (Abyssinia), were the last attempts at imposing durable political and economic control by military expansion.

During the 1930s, the governments of the United States opposed exclusive nationalism. This can be explained by the hegemonic role of the American economy. However, until the end of World War II, the United States was not eager to assume the resulting economic leadership. At the same time, there were always internal social forces that insisted on applying protective rules and interventionist policies that favored certain internal sectors. This has been shown in the process of the consolidation of Panamericanism, where the ideas of protectionism and national development, presented by Prebisch, ECLA, and, afterwards, UNCTAD, always met opposition or tactical delay by the American diplomacy (Valencia, 1997). At the same time, taxes, tolls, and a growing list of nontariff barriers on certain imports that competed with American production were erected.

The Reconstruction of an International
Financial and Economic System (1944–1970)

The most significant step to preparing the reopening of international commercial and financial relations was the 1944 Bretton Woods Conference, which established a new international financial system, coordinated by the International Monetary Fund (IMF) and supported by the World Bank as the public financing agency for investment in development. However, the creation and the politics followed by these institutions were strongly influenced by the hegemony and decisive influence of the United States, the most powerful Western nation after the war. In this way, this domination was consolidated in the new international financial system. The Bretton Woods system made the enormous economic postwar expansion possible. Lasting until the 1960s it was greatly facilitated by the monetary stability offered, which was based on gold and the U.S. dollar, rigid exchange rates and limited convertibility.

The dissolution of areas under empires between 1945 and 1970, and the incorporation into the world economy of many new sovereign nations pursuing their economic development, again brought out the contradiction between national development and the mechanisms for tying national economic areas into an international system. The 1950s and 1960s were the decades of search for economic development promoted by the state, and the protection of import substitution industrialization. The power of the national attempts at balanced, overall development was strong and found its expressions in the ideas of the UN (ECLA) and UNCTAD about a "new international economic order" (Van der Wee, 1986).

Historically, the growth of industrial production occurred in the framework of the enormous postwar economic expansion. Altvater notes that the world market expanded much more than world production, giving some sense to productive investment, and that the international monetary system made it difficult to engage in speculative movements of liquid capital on an international scale.

As a paradox, these decades of a regulated monetary system, when it was possible to speak of truly national economies, was also the period during which global market integration was produced in the most dynamic way (Altvater, 1996)

The industrial development of nonindustrial countries that only enjoyed comparative advantages in the agricultural and the mineral raw materials sector had to be achieved in spite of the market mechanism. Such national economies were generally protected and subsidized by effective governmental intervention that used external financing. This produced strong competition between exporters of raw materials and the growing of external debts. As long as the world market was expanding and the interest for credits was lower than the profit rates in the business of exporting raw materials, the system seemed to function and the IMF and the World Bank promoted this type of development.

The politics of import substitution industrialization induced the capitalist transformation of many societies, dissolving traditional forms of property and production, transforming peasants into an urban labor force, and introducing more advanced technologies into the countryside. In general, most of the developing countries continued depending on the knowledge and technologies of the industrialized countries and subsidies and/or tariff protections by the state. The labor regulations and social security systems that industrial workers had won through union struggle and political conflict in industrialized countries (as part of the industrial expansion), could not be repeated with the developing countries where in most cases only the most privileged workers had access to such benefits.

At the same time, this capitalist transformation made the societies more vulnerable to the consequences of the financial globalization of the 1970s: It was no longer possible to return to previous means of production or ways of living. Social problems—the informal sector, the exclusion of large parts of the population from access to regular paid work, and its benefits of stability and protection—were present at the national level, but the state did not have the tools to remedy them.

The End of the System of Bretton Woods and Financial Globalization

At the end of the 1960s, the expanding postwar economic development came to its end. The capital of the industrialized countries did not find lucrative investment opportunities and began to desperately look for more profitable investment opportunities. This occurred at the same time as the Oil Crisis, at the beginning of the 1970s, when the oil exporting countries, especially those of the Middle East, put their enormous incomes of foreign currency in the banks that were already overflowing with money. For the first time since the disaster of the world crisis of 1929, private banks began to give credit to everybody who applied, albeit in the context of flexible interest rates. The credit systems were deregulated everywhere; neither policies nor guarantees needed to be approved by governments or national congresses. New financial instruments were created all the time, and still the interest rates were relatively low. Many developing countries contracted those readily offered credits, often through short-term agreements, in the belief that their incomes from exports would allow for repayment.

The Bretton Woods system broke down. The U.S. dollar had been weakened in relationship to the other currencies of the industrialized countries, and its coverage in gold was fading. The pressure on the dollar led to the revaluation of the German mark and the Japanese yen, and the fixed exchange rates, which had been a central tenant of the Bretton Woods system, began to disappear.

The abandonment of the system in 1971 introduced what came to be known as financial globalization. Money in its different forms was no longer under political control by the sovereign states and became independent of the production processes and their requirements. The interest rate was transformed into central economic data, as was the case with the exchange rate for the national currency against strong currencies like the U.S. dollar, the British pound, the German mark, the Swiss franc, and the Japanese yen. The central economic goal became the short-time profit of mobile money, which could be withdrawn and reinvested again immediately, at the highest possible interest rates and best exchange rate.

For the investments in the productive process, the conditions dictated by the independent movements of money could induce sudden changes in the interest rates and other conditions, causing the bankruptcy of enterprises, which were normally considered solid because of their technology and production. The constraint to appear attractive on the stock markets induced them to lower costs to the extent they could. Key elements in this process were the cost of labor force, on the one hand, and the taxes and government charges for things like environmental protection and educational costs, on the other.

The attractiveness of the national currencies is key to attracting investment from the owners of floating capital, and consequently each country has to try to make its money as seductive as possible for this type of capital.

Far different from what was valid in the times of David Ricardo and Friedrich List, productive and money capital are now mobile around the whole world, and are a little less mobile than commodities but a bit more than the labor force. Labor moves, too, in a more rapid way, but its movements are limited by the fact that human beings are citizens of a nation-state, need passports, and have social and political rights in their state. This makes it difficult to move or exclude laborers from these rights in another state, and notwithstanding the growing migratory movements on all levels, the limitations, especially for the lower labor force, are very great.

Production still continues to be a physical process, connected to a certain place and the existence of local forms of living. That means that the conditions offered to capital to attract its investment in certain places are to be created by the official leadership of the country. The environmental, social, cultural, and political consequences that involve a productive investment will be the concern of the local administration; capital can leave and invest in another place that is more attractive or competitive.

The complexity of these relationships and the growing instability of markets, especially for productive capital, and the nation-states, has led to attempts to create regions of higher stability, to organize in larger entities to be able to manage the unforeseeableness of the process. It is a repetition, in a different form, of what happened in the Great Depression of 1870 to 1890, when the cartels and trusts were formed and imperialism expanded. Today we look at the "mergers," associations of the large transnational enterprises, and on the level of states there is a search for associations on a middle level, to form larger operation entities with more power against the forces of instability. Here we find the efforts to build regional integration, to organize groups of countries with common interests. The most successful is the European Union, and, to a lesser degree NAFTA.

The End of Development?

Financial globalization changed the framework for national economic policies. Development as it had been understood in former times—middle- or long-term processes, production and consumption increases through industrialization according to the "Fordist" model, the creation of jobs and income to create a richer and more equal society, increases of knowledge and education in general, more participation in politics by democratic mechanisms—can continue to be an ideal, but to actually achieve it seems not to be a real political option. The nations lose their social and cultural dimension and are reduced to places with strong or weak currency, which attracts capital that is currently volatile and searching for short-time profits. Monetary competition is the first problem, and a set of conditions needs to be in place so as not to lose investor confidence and in order to attract investors. Development is reduced to a secondary promise: If you are competitive, product demand will grow, currency will get stronger and attract investors, and the income level will grow and with it the general welfare.

We are before a vicious cycle: Competitivity supposes technical advance, the deepening of the division of labor, and the lowering of costs. To get to this there are needed investments in infrastructure, education, efficiency of public institutions and services, and money to pay for this—

which is generally lacking in the Lesser Developed Countries (LDCs) because the fiscal systems are weak and capital refuses to submit to taxation. The structural adjustment proposed generally by the IMF for indebted countries includes some of the above named topics, but prioritizes the payment of external debt in strong currency, forcing the production of exportable and competitive goods, diminishing protection and the opening of markets, the reduction of taxes, and the freezing of labor incomes, as well as the reduction of the costs of the social protection system.

This was a way to eliminate the option of debt cancellation, which previously was a possible measure. It was now transformed into an instrument of draining and transferring capital to the international banking system. And the conditions imposed by the IMF for refinanciation and granting new credits—necessary to survive—opened the markets of the indebted countries to the activities of such capital. This was much more the case than had been done by the stronger industrial nations. Those countries that had for some time refused to submit to those measures were blocked and saw their economies collapse, as had been the case with Peru.

Since the 1920s, there had been efforts to conclude conventions and thus form wheat, coffee, or bauxite cartels between producers and exporters of certain raw materials in order to control the prices and to obtain higher incomes. The politics of coffee valorization promoted by Brazil until the 1930s did not count on the participation of other countries. Nevertheless, the others enjoyed the "protective umbrella" of the high coffee prices Brazil could impose, since it was an almost monopolistic producer in those years. In this way, coffee growing expanded to other regions and larger spaces, undermining the bases for these politics. Later, the International Coffee Agreement also included the consumer countries (the United States accounted for 50 percent of production), and therefore could not create major benefits for the exporting countries.

After the end of the International oil cartel that had accustomed the oil exporting countries to growing tax and royalty incomes, OPEC forced up the oil prices during the 1970s and flooded the economies of Venezuela and Mexico (which is not a member of the organization but shares the benefits of its policies) with enormous incomes.

The income structure of many less-developed, less-industrialized countries is based on rents obtained by the exports of products with lower production costs and lower transportation costs to markets in the industrialized countries. These rents have a structural impact on the developing countries' economies, which had enjoyed income from international rents. Capital and labor move to the high-income sector and not to the others, which include industries and agriculture that produce for the internal market. Investments, then, do not go to those who produce for internal consumption but rather those who are dedicated to import trade. Such capital prefers to engage in financial speculation in the exterior, if the state does not intervene to limit this activity. This has been called "the Dutch disease": "The 'marriage between rent and profit' is the guarantee that the development into a modern society will be blocked" (Altvater, 1996:209).

To protect against these consequences, the governments of such countries must use a series of strict policy regulations to channel these rent incomes into productive investments and to facilitate changes in the economic and technological structure, in spite of pressures from the market. And this, again, clashes with the prevailing theories in the international financial institutions, and with the better-off national internal sectors that resist change in the distribution of income.

In the nineteenth century, the reduction of transportation costs induced a deterioration of the terms of trade, as deduced from data from England, but did not reduce rent incomes because much of the reduction of prices in England was due to a reduction of transport fees (Ellsworth, cited in Sieber, 1968:49).

In recent years, a different process has occurred: The lowering of transport costs is one of the structural conditions for globalization because it facilitates the competition from goods all over the world, and eliminates the natural protection in the economies of developing countries whose markets offered a protected space for internal industries that produced for the local market. At the same time, competition between the export products does not any longer permit high rents that are the result of advantages in geographical localization. The problem can be seen in the case of the oil prices. Since they are one of the basic ingredients for transportation costs, oil prices fell in 1998 because of the weakening of OPEC but were pushed up again significantly in 1999 and 2000. This led to heavy political protests by the transportation workers in Europe and the United States. By contrast, this same process allowed for the export of new products that previously could not be sent so far because of high transportation costs: the massive selling of Colombian flowers in Europe and the United States is an example.

Regional Integration

Since the end of World War II, the United States has pressed to reach free trade arrangements throughout the world, fighting against nationalist or autarquical systems, and against state intervention—structures that had been created under the impact of the Great Economic Crisis and the war. Nevertheless, these structures were not easy to undo.

The serious problems the European countries had to recover after the war and the influence of the Soviet Union in Eastern Europe (the expansion of the socialist system) convinced the Americans that they had to help the Western European countries in order to count on them as strong allies and a bulwark against socialism. In 1947, they created the Marshall Plan, which offered financial help for physical and economic reconstruction, with the guidance of the United States. When the USSR and the countries it controlled rejected the Marshall Plan, the U.S. tutorship began, and afterwards led to the integration of the West European countries. This was done in opposition to the socialist countries that then united in their own system, the COMINFORM, and later in COMECON.

On an international level, the United States promoted the liberalization of the international trade system, leading in 1947 to GATT (the General Agreement on Tariffs and Trade). It provided the basis for the slow reduction of tariffs and other limitations worldwide, but it provided exceptions for small neighboring countries that were trying to enlarge their market by association, as did the BENELUX states (Belgium, Netherlands, Luxembourg). For a long time, GATT only advanced in slow steps because of the predominance of economic theories that favored the intervention of the national state in the economy, and the need to protect certain branches of the economy against external competition. Its application was restricted to the area that was under the predominance of the United States, because the socialist countries remained closed to open international trade until the 1980s. When the socialist camp collapsed after 1989, the goal of open world trade could not be reached either. Instead of establishing an open world market, GATT led to the formation of three large blocks, the United States, Western Europe, and Japan, with their satellites, which protected themselves through nontariff obstacles to free trade. The fact that these blocks did form even though this challenged free trade policies suggests the need for protection against the free market mechanism.

Therefore, in spite of the intense promotion of globalization since the 1970s, we observe the formation of new political and economic blocks that increase external restrictions and reduce the internal limitations. This has been the case in the European Union, the North American Free Trade Association, and MERCOSUR.

Altvater sustains that these processes do not jive with the basic criteria promoted by the GATT, in that GATT philosophy is oriented to the establishment of free trade at the global level without the formation of regional blocks.

If the integration processes principally are oriented to unify markets, the success depends on the given scale of division of labor and on the strategies of development. The high level of industrial division of labor previously achieved determined the success of the European Union:

> While the intraindustrial division of labor is poorly developed, if for example, as in the Third World countries, foreign trade is made up to 90 percent or more by one or few raw materials, the unification into a regional block makes little sense. Inclusive, . . . if a strategy of import substitution industrialization is pursued, the formation of blocks is not a promising option because the more important aim is the mobilization of the internal market by the "developing state." . . . The regional market expansion through a free trade zone or a tariff union only produces positive results if the material conditions of a profound division of labor are guaranteed; i.e., if a minimum of intra-industrial specialization has been reached and can be further developed in perspective. It is an illusion to try to reach the goal of economic development by the creation of regional economic blocks. To achieve this it is altogether more appropriate—with historical constellation, the factor equipment and the stage of development reached before—a strategy of free trade or of national economic protection. (Altvater: 417)

In the past decade, the motive to mitigate the severe problems created by the unprotected opening to the world market, imposed by the IMF as a consequence of monetary instabilities, has become the basis of the new wave of regional block formation.

> Supranational integration can—it is hoped—create new intermediate markets between overly small national markets, closed against the innovation pressure, and the world market dominated by the industrialized countries, i.e., not open but closed, where it is possible to experience increased competitive capacity with commonly tradable industrial products. (Altvater:420)

European Integration as a Historical Model

European integration has been advancing since 1947, beginning with the Marshall Plan and its leading institutions, continuing with conferences and payment treaties and later with OECD. This was always done with some help and active interest by the United States, which actively pushed forward this process during the Cold War, as a bulwark against the socialist bloc. On the one hand, the issue was the achievement of economic recovery and the political stability of Europe as a strong ally for the United States, and, on the other, the integration of Germany—or its Western part—in this camp. We can say that the initial and the predominant intention of the European integration was political, and it counted on favorable economic elements despite difficulties and resistance. The trade exchanges, the regional division of labor, the transportation systems, and the commercial and banking enterprises had connected the different countries for centuries. As a way of transcending periods of wars for control over natural resources, the Europeans tried this new form of association, one that was based on the creation of peaceful exploitation and exchange. After the Marshall Plan, the European Coal and Steel Union was created, thus eliminating the friction provoked by the geographical and natural separation of iron ore and coal, which in the past had caused the conquest, reconquest, and occupations of regions such as Alsace, Lorraine, and the Saar. Such actions raised nationalist hatred between Germany and France, and brutally strode through small Belgium in two world wars. Another unifying step was the integration of Western Germany into the U.S.-dominated NATO military structure. The efficient Marshall Plan assisted reconstruction of Germany, and soon conducted the Federal Republic of Germany to play an important role in the Western financial and productive system. By integrating it into larger structures its power seemed less menacing to its neighbors. Political motives to reach integration seem to have dominated the European process, which was often beset by stagnation and cutbacks.

Although seemingly impelled by political motives, steps toward integration were done, in good deal, in the economic field. Economic aspects superceded social and political aspects of the integration even though these aspects were—and still are—pushed by internal social groups.

Initiatives for Integration in the 1960s: Latin America

A first wave of regional economic associations came up in Latin America during the 1960s, inspired in large part by the achievements of the European process. But the conditions and intentions were different than those for Europe, and ultimately these initiatives did not achieve the desired results. During the 1940s and 1950s, the Latin American countries had adopted strategies of economic development, promoting processes of internal industrialization to diminish dependency on the traditional exports of agricultural and mineral raw materials. Import substitution industrialization needed financing to acquire technology in the exterior, to acquire raw and intermediate materials, and was in need of larger markets for their products than those within national borders. In order to achieve national goals, the countries associated in tariff unions with privileges or in common markets. Nevertheless, the rival attitudes over where to place the new industries and which markets would need be opened to the production of a more dynamic neighbor soon developed. In the case of the Central American Common Market they developed into a military confrontation between El Salvador and Honduras, which nearly ended the integrationist experiment.

Nor was it possible to overcome complications arising from the differences of origin and levels in national incomes of the countries that were based on the exportations of raw materials. For some time, Venezuela did not participate in processes of regional integration, because of the external currency income generated from oil sales. These flowed to the government and the rest of the national economy, and facilitated the inflow of capital and goods necessary for industrialization. However, the newly created industries were not competitive, because of the overvaluation of the currency and the high labor costs, and had to be protected and subsidized, this being opposed to the regional integration. The political bureaucratic structures created around these protected industrialization processes became influential and limited the capacity for a flexible opening.

Another obstacle for regional integration was the persistence of ultra-rightist, authoritarian military dictatorships that did not allow democratic participation in negotiations and appeasement or any challenge to national sovereignty.

The dominance of the United States in its Latin American backyard—its principal area of interest after the end of World War II—its decision to help in the recovery of Europe and to promote the systems of free trade over regional integration systems, and U.S. tolerance for systems of authoritarian military dictatorships were all negative factors for the development of regional blocs in the hemisphere. The historically weak economic interconnection that existed—contrary to an intrinsic competition resulting from being producers of the same raw materials—meant that regional integration treaties in the continent did not prosper in those decades.

The New Wave of Latin American
Integration in the 1980s and 1990s

The structural changes in the economy and politics of the world during the 1970s created new conditions for sovereign national states and opened different scenarios on integration. The disappearance of the socialist bloc, as an alternative to capitalist market system, sparked a sometimes fundamentalist enthusiasm for free markets and against state intervention and state-directed development.

Regional integration, initiated during the 1980s in Latin America, was due to new political and economic motives. It became the strategy for the industrialized countries and was also implemented in the developing economies through structural adjustments imposed by the IMF and World Bank. In this way, they have opened foreign markets and reorganized governmental structures and social systems along neoliberal lines. This "new regionalism" can offer a step to integration into the world economy, but implies the adherence to a market dominated by one of the great economic and industrial powers, in our case the United States.

NAFTA and FTAA

The foundation of the North American Free Trade Agreement (NAFTA) between the United States, Canada, and Mexico is considered a first step to secure the economic and political domination of the United States over the Western hemisphere. The declared intention of integrating all the rest of the continent into one common market by 2005 in the Free Trade Area of the Americas seems to confirm this strategy. But from another perspective, NAFTA is mentioned as a bloc created by the United States to strengthen its hegemony over other blocs in the world and to recover its former strength in the world economy. As commercial exchanges with the Latin American region are only 6 percent of U.S. trade, the region has not the weight to be of primary interest as a partner in deeper economic integration. In strategic perspective, NAFTA offers investment opportunities to U.S. capital, access to raw materials, and more efficient protection for certain industries (textile, shoes, vegetables) and technological advantages (patents, software, communications) (Axline, 1999:24). The conditions to become part of NAFTA are formulated in the same spirit opening national economies to external markets and investment and the requirements for governmental and financial stability. The opening to the FTAA "represents the largest regional integration effort ever undertaken involving both developed and developing countries sharing a common objective to realize free trade and investment in goods and services, on the basis of strengthening trading rules and discipline" (FTAA Webpage: http://www.ftaa-alca.org/view_e.asp).

The different special groups are negotiating these topics, but the outcome is still not clear. Meanwhile, there are efforts to create and strengthen subregional integration projects.

Andean Community of Nations

The Pacto Andino began in the1960s. Starting in 1990, the ACN intended to pursue deeper integration, beginning with a general promotion of tariff reductions and market opening and including political and social issues similar to regulations in the European Community. However, the results were principally of a limited commercial character and different opinions and policies among the integrating states (Colombia, Venezuela, Ecuador, Bolivia, and Peru) remained fundamental. The tendency to substitute the common interest approach with bilateral conventions, especially with the United States, with NAFTA or MERCOSUR, shows the importance of a powerful economy as a gravitational center in the globalized economic process.

MERCOSUR

The formation of a new regional bloc with a large and powerful center, as a possible counterweight to the leadership of the United States through NAFTA and FTAA, is the most important element in the process of regional integration in the Americas. Initiated in 1991 and consisting of Argentina, Brazil, Paraguay, and Uruguay, in 1994 the union advanced to a tariff union that integrated 50 percent of the population and 60 percent of the GIP of the region and 40 percent of ALADI trade (Axline, 1997:43). Axline maintains that the specific form of MERCOSUR is integration on a sectorial basis, not on a simple neoliberal free trade issue. The commercial relations are "administrated," not free; and this makes MERCOSUR "a southern counterpart to NAFTA in contrary to a way to access to it" and "creates the potential for a bilateral counterweight to NAFTA" (46).

Brazil, the largest and strongest economy of the pact, has not advanced very much in the structural reforms in the neoliberal way, does not show the intent to search for admission to NAFTA, and, on the contrary, appeals to the other Latin American nations to rally with it in an Area of Free Trade of South America (ALCSA). The outcome of this proposition depends on the capacity of stabilization of Brazil and the decisions of the other Latin American nations on the issue, if they prefer to adhere to the FTAA or to a counterpart bloc—or if this block will be negotiating special conditions to enter into the FTAA (Axline).

Market and Solidarity—Economy and Politics in Regional Integration

The opposition to the neoliberal approach, which defines the free market mechanisms as the magic formula to reach economic welfare for all human beings, repeats the claim of saving human relations and social conditions, and protecting cultural values. If we observe the historical processes of opening different societies' internal markets, over all of the not yet or less-developed industrialized societies, we see that social differences are deepened by the effect of the market, and that the hegemony of the industrialized countries leads to penetration and social and cultural decomposition in the less developed countries. That is why many writers sustain in their analysis of the processes of economic opening and regional integration, the urgency of evaluation of those aspects. They believe that pure economic integration cannot be done in a stable and sustainable way without the support, the consent, of the different social actors who will be touched by the integration steps in some way. They criticize the fact that in the majority of the integration processes, the integration of the commercial and financial aspects is an extreme priority and that the commercial and banking sectors generally accept these changes, while the politically and economically powerless social groups suffer from the consequences. The decisions about how integration occurs and its range depends on the active participation of concerned sectors of civil society. Authors sustain that the only organized and, in certain way, influential sector is business, particularly those groups that benefit from integration.

Alvaro Tirado (1997) analyses the integration process of the Andean Community, the G3 (Mexico, Colombia, Venezuela), MERCOSUR, and NAFTA from the political point of view. He begins by examining the advance of democracy in Latin America, next looks on the different actors participating in the integration processes, and concludes: "unlike the integration processes of the sixties, in the nineties these processes reveal being less supported by governments and enjoy higher participation in civil society. . . . One of the principal characteristics of the integrationist models in Latin America was the excessive presence and activity of the governments" (Tirado, 1997:2).

Integration always has selective results for the different economic and social sectors, and specific decisions about an integration process always include political decisions. The advances, stagnation, and turnarounds that can be observed in the regional integration processes always are connected to political pressures from different social sectors.

Tirado maintains that the integration process needs social and political stability based on a functioning democracy, and, similarly, that political democracy does not function if the social and political stability of its participants is not guaranteed. In consequence, he compares the development of the institutions of the integration processes to democratic openings to civil society and analyses the actual participation of nongovernmental organizations in decisions about integration. In general, he affirms that there are few openings for real participation and decision making by NGOs that are generated by the institutions created by the different integration treaties. This is explained by the "disorganization of the interested sectors and the disinformation about the issues." He notes a "dispersion of the actors and diversity of the implicated interests" (Tirado, 1997:24), and a great difficulty to judge the highly complex consequences of the decisions at the summits, where a high level of information and skill is needed—one that only can be achieved by a few members of Latin American societies.

Another argument is that the importance of democratic proceedings corresponds to the latitude of the intended integration model: A Free Trade Zone touches fewer actors than a more advanced community, and permits more authoritarianism. But bureaucratization and actions by the public administration determine if the institutions that are designed to make the democratic processes function really fulfill this role.

Conclusions

The historical process of deepening and widening market mechanisms has generated multiple efforts to foster the free market process and, at the same time, the most diverse attempts to oppose or soften its effects on those societies involved. Economics and politics, represented by different social groups, are alternately set against each other and united in these processes. Their relationship is dictated by the specific circumstances of every group, the geographical space where they operate, and how they see greater market freedom. The complex interrelation of these factors depends on the level of industrial, social, and cultural development and makes it impossible to copy successful solutions from other regions. Nor can these solutions stay at one level of integration, without risking stagnation and disintegration as historical conditions change. Presently, the process of economic globalization means deepening the economic and social inequalities of sociopolitical decision-making groups in and between the nations. The process is undermining the decision-making capacity of these groups, and the search for regional or other intermediate integration schemes seems to be an option that will increase the scope of the national policies, on the one hand, and the formation of an intermediate protected space that offers elements of stability in the face of the chaotic effects to open the global market, on the other. Only careful analysis of each integration process can provide a basis to evaluate how it will affect each different group.

Bibliography

Aldcroft, Derek H. (1985). *De Versailles a Wallstreet, 1919–1929. Historia Económica Mundial Siglo XX,* vol. 3. Barcelona: Editorial Crítica.

Altvater, Elmar. (1992). *Die Zukunft des Marktes: Ein Essay über die Regulation von Geld und Natur nach dem Scheitern des real existierenden Sozialismus.* Münster: Verlag Westfälisches Dampfboot.

Altvater, Elmar, and Mahnkopf, Birgit. (1996). *Grenzen der Globalisierung: Ökonomie, Ökologie und Politik in der Weltgesellschaft.* Neuss: Westfälisches Dampfboot.

Amin, Samir. (1997). *Los Desafíos de la Mundialización.* México/Madrid: Siglo XXI Editores.

Axline, W. Andrew. (1999). "El TLCAN, el Regionalismo Estratégico y las Nuevas Direcciones de la Integración Latinoamericana." In *Escenarios de la Integración Regional.* (1999). Ed. Luis Briceño Ruiz. Mérida: Universidad de Los Andes.

Barnes, Harry Elmer. (1955). *Historia de la Economía del Mundo Occidental.* Mexico: UTEHA.

Hobsbawm, Eric. (1968). *Industria e Imperio. Una Historia Económica de Gran Bretaña desde 1750.* Barcelona/Caracas/Mexico: Editorial Ariel.

Kindleberger, Charles P. (1985). *La Crisis Económica 1929–1939. Historia Económica Mundial Siglo XX,* vol. 4. Barcelona: Editorial Crítica.

Mommer, Bernard. (1988). *La cuestión petrolera.* Caracas: Editorial Tropicos.

Ricardo, David. (1959). *Principios de Economía Política y Tributación.* Bogotá: Fondo de Cultura Económica.

Sieber, Hans. (1968). *Die realen Austauschverhältnisse zwischen Entwicklungsländern und Industriestaaten*. Doctoral Dissertation. St. Gallen, Switzerland.

Tirado Mejía, Alvaro. (1997). *Integración y Democracia en América Latina y el Caribe*. *Banco Interamericano de Desarrollo, Departamento de Integración y Programas Regionales*. Buenos Aires: INTAL (Instituto para la Integración de América Latina y el Caribe).

Valencia, Judith. (1998). "La década de los cuarenta y el sentido contemporáneo de América," In *Años de redefinición en América Latina: La década de los cuarenta*. (1998). Ed. Banko and Melcher. Caracas: Universidad Central de Venezuela.

Van der Wee, Hermann. (1986). *Prosperidad y Crisis. Reconstrucción, Crecimiento y Cambio 1945–1980. Historia Económica Mundial Siglo XX*, vol. 6. Barcelona: Editorial Crítica.

Chapter 10

Argentinean Foreign Policy: Changes and Continuities in the Relationships with the United States and MERCOSUR

Sandra Colombo

The ten years of Dr. Menem's government transformed Argentina. From flatterers to critics, this is unquestionable. From the beginning of his government, in July 1989, he put aside the nationalist politicians and populists that he had promoted during his electoral campaign, and he became preoccupied with sending an overwhelming message to the international organisms and the local enterprise economy: The economic political direction would be irreversibly determined by the opening of the economy and a larger insertion in the international system, the privatization of almost all public companies, the reduction of public employees, a rigid fiscal and monetary discipline, a partial privatization of the system of social security, and a policy of salary freezing and a flexibility of labor legislation.

In the political aspect, Menem made intense economic changes in a crisis atmosphere, excluding the participation of traditional institutional and social actors. The consequent result was the institution of a very weak democracy,[1] where many of the economic measures or more than enough foreign policies were formulated secretly, announced to the population without warning and implemented by presidential ordinances. After a decade of the Menem government, there were some positive aspects: Inflation was broken by the Plan of Convertibility, exports were increased, reserves were increased in the Central Bank, national per capita income grew, and the privatization of big state companies generated the necessary foreign currencies at the same time that they facilitated better services.

However, the other side of this success is negative. The inheritance is a deeply broken society, an economy with unprecedented concentration levels,[2] an unpublished structural unemployment,[3] a foreign debt that went from $63.4 million in 1989 to $140 billion, a fiscal deficit that is about $10 billion and a state that did not fulfill its basic functions in education, health, social welfare, and security. The state also exercised scarce rigor to defend the citizens against privatized companies, an absence that was many times directly related to corruption. The one-sided approach and methodology of Dr. Menem's government woke up in Argentinean citizens a desire for the institutions to be respected. The persistence to impose the second re-election in spite of the constitutional prohibition led to the defeat of the Justice Party by the Alliance in the October 1999 elections. The political-electoral force that triumphed in the elections of October 24, 1999, had its origin in 1997 as an alliance among the Frente País Solidario (FREPASO)[4] and the Unión Cívica Radical, which traditionally has represented middle-class society and some minority sectors linked to the agricultural sector. Proposals enunciated by the Alliance during the electoral campaign demonstrated the intention of continuing with the fundamental policies taken by Menem's government. The Alliance defended the convertibility of the dollar and the peso, and reference was made to the necessity of correcting the social effects of Menem's economic policies, to adopt political ethics, and to build an efficient and transparent state.

The type of international insertion promoted during Dr. Menem's government was strictly linked to the economic approach. The interests pursued by the foreign policy rotated around trade development and attraction of capital and foreign investments, as an indispensable condition to preserve and to assure the external goal of the program of national economic restructuring.[5] From the beginning, Menem's administration assumed as an almost single priority, the promotion of the alignment with the United States, eliminating all those topics that could negatively affect the bilateral relationship, increasing its support for U.S. positions, and in the process surpassing its own expectations.[6]

The official discourse affirmed that the special relationship with the United States would allow Argentina in the long term, to win preferential access for its exports in U.S. markets; to attract an important quota of the

U.S. direct foreign investment to obtain the support of the United States in strategic topics (e.g., Malvinas, regional democratic stability, control of ecological disasters); and to develop, with its support, a more modern and professional armed force.

In the diplomatic arena and in the context of this conception, Argentina abandoned the Movement of Nonaligned (NAM); it changed its profile of votes in intergovernmental forums[7] (i.e., United Nations and OAS); and preferred to take its distance from the Central American crisis, an issue that did not affect the national security of Argentina. The idea of a club of debtors was definitively shelved and the position of the United States, that there should be negotiations between individual countries, creditors, and financial organisms, was accepted.

The dispute with Great Britain was perceived by the Menem administration as one of the biggest obstacles for the linking with the European Community and to getting the trust of the United States. Therefore, Argentinean government ended its confrontational attitude on the Malvinas and promoted greater cooperation with the United Kingdom by means of the "diplomatic umbrella." From 1989, the government fully accepted the terms of security of the United States for the region,[8] and sought recognition as a reliable regional ally with the United States. Menem's administration viewed the new international scenario as characterized by interdependence and cooperation among democratic countries, prevalence of the democratic-liberal thought, and collective security as effective guarantee of peace. According to this, the foreign policy assumed firm commitments to the elimination of conflict hypotheses with the neighboring countries as base of its defense policies. It promoted international and regional cooperation in strategic-military matter and it joined the agreements regarding nuclear nonproliferation.

During the 1990s, an active policy of nonproliferation of weapons of massive destruction was put into practice, which facilitated the development of projects of international cooperation in the nuclear and space fields for peaceful ends, and the entrance to the international club of advanced technologies.[9] Successive agreements between Brazil and Argentina in nuclear matter since the 1980s also allowed a growing approach that includes the declaration of MERCOSUR as Area of Peace and Security and a progressive military cooperation. In this area, a significant fact of the "new foreign policy," was the dismantling of the Missile Project Condor II. The reasons announced by government to justify this decision were that "it compromised Argentina's prestige seriously" and it questioned its will to incorporate itself to the New International Order.[10] From 1992,

Argentina maintained an important contribution in missions of peace under the auspices of the United Nations.[11] This approach of cooperative security was sustained in the conviction that it positively affected the perceptions of Argentina by global actors. Equally, these policies of military participation in international security in the context of the security council helped to redefine the role of the Argentina armed forces and make them more professional.

Dr. Menem's administration was not limited to the acceptance of the security terms of the United States but, rather, accompanied and took very visible initiatives in those international conflicts in which American interests were directly affected. The Argentinean participation in the Persian Gulf War was a clear example in this sense.[12]

In not a few occasions, the tactic of following American foreign policy was sustained with negative consequences for Argentina's relations within the Southern Cone. It happened this way with the participation in the conflict of the Gulf and also when Argentina declared its support to the operations and strategies to control the drug traffic promoted in Latin America; or when it abandoned its historical posture of not interfering in internal matters of other countries of the region and it assumed an active and critical role toward the governments of Cuba[13] and Haiti.[14] In all of these cases, Menem found himself isolated within Latin America.

With President Fernando de la Rúa, the extreme positions that put at risk political relationships with the neighboring countries disappeared. The new leader affirmed that his country would have mature relationships with Washington and that automatic alignment[15] no longer existed. At the same time he requested from the Department of Treasury of the United States support of his economic plan and a guarantee to mediate a complicated agreement with the International Monetary Fund. Evidently, in the new government, conviction existed that the United States did not need "the carnal relationships" to give support in financial questions.

Like Dr. Menem's government, the de la Rúa administration received from Washington a good opportunity to negotiate with the international financial organisms and the accrediting banks.[16] This support of the big international powers has been fundamental, together to the internal electoral support, for the legitimization of the economic restructuring that has been carried out.

The guarantees offered by the American government did not prevent it from warning Argentina severely when the United States considered the economic interests of American companies to be in danger. The recurrent manifestation of concern that successive U.S. administrations have demonstrated for the lack of juridical independence and the possibility of corruption in Argentina, should be understood in the context of the limitations on business opportunity and not in a principled way.[17] Sometimes U.S. companies have been disadvantaged in the face of European competitors because U.S. law specifically prohibits U.S. companies from the payment of bribes. During Menem's period, the most serious facts of corruption involving government's high officials were the case IBM—Bank of the Argentinean Nation[18]—and the case of the illegal sale of weapons to Croatia and Ecuador.[19] When Menem's second term ended, both cases were still in the hands of the Argentina courts.

The other topic that motivated constant pressures by the United States from the beginning of Menem's government was the instrumentation of medical patents. This conflict was very difficult to solve, because of the pressure exercised by Americans, and the national strong opposition to the U.S. position by Argentina laboratories. This resistance was able to delay the approval of the bill, which was more favorable to the U.S. position, that Menem sent to Congress.

When the Alliance's government took power, American pressures resumed on the questions of the law on pharmaceutical patents,[20] and the transparency in public bids. To these sensitive topics, others were added: the agreement on commercial policies of "open skies"[21] and the radars.[22] These new divisive issues were the result of questionable agreements carried out in the last days of Menem's government and whose revision by the new government was firmly resisted by American officials.[23] The American government was also concerned about an Argentine law against the laundering of money,[24] and that its armed forces would assume an active role in the fight against drug trafficking.[25] From the Argentinean perspective, the difficulties with the United States were "normal conflicts among economically interdependent countries"[26] (e.g., the antidumping actions and the compensatory rights that paralyzed the access for some Argentinean exports to the American market (iron and steel industry, textile) and the restrictions (sanitary or quantitative) to exportation of agricultural or nutritious products[27]).

However, with the beginning of the new millennium, the Argentinean-American agenda did not contemplate any topic that could be a source of serious bilateral conflict. The economic disagreements remained (tariffs, subsidies to the exports, opening of markets) and other newer ones such as the patents could cause conflict but did not seem to threaten the good course of the bilateral relationship. The pressures of the United States on corruption, environment, drug traffic, or citizens' security, constitute a form of intervention that has been called "desirable," ignoring the risk that this pressure implies to the genuineness of a state and its democratic processes.

Many basic concepts have become entrenched in Argentine society (i.e., democracy as necessary condition for the international acceptance, acceptance of the world as an opportunity and not as a threat, the necessity to maintain a good relationship with West). However, the only policies that could be considered policies of the state are the promotion of the relationship with the European Union and the importance of MERCOSUR.[28]

Although MERCOSUR became a policy of state, the erratic search for preferential agreements with the United States during Menem's government accentuated the weakness of strategies for intraregional commercial agreements. In this sense, the Argentinean effort to obtain a unilateral entrance to NAFTA, Carlos Menem's accelerated public opposition to Brazil occupying a permanent place in the Council of Security adducing "questions of balance of power," and the acceptance of Argentina into extra-NATO activity in 1997 generated uncertainty within MERCOSUR and caused political tensions among country members.

The desire of Menem's government to reverse the negative image that the United States had of Argentina, by means of an alignment policy, subtracted his dependability to the relationship with his more important regional partner, Brazil, and the possibility of building a foreign policy of MERCOSUR was spoiled. This orientation, besides, didn't keep in mind that the commercial relationships with the United States are in deficit, while Brazil is the biggest receiver of Argentinean exports.[29]

In the last year of President Menem's government, a series of conflicts inside the environment of MERCOSUR became worse. Because of the commercial problems and the critical state of the economies, the bilateral exchange with Brazil decreased 30 percent; this fact woke up protective postures and the pressure of some industrial sectors.[30] During 1999, in a context of growing economic tensions, the Argentinean government incurred a series of measures that harmed the bilateral relationships: It promoted the dollarization of Argentinean economy; it announced the order on the entrance to NATO; it offered the border national territory with Brazil so that forces of the United States can carry out military training; and President Menem promised troops to the United States to enter Colombia.[31]

These events demonstrate the fundamental necessity to reaffirm the political commitment among the member states, and to reconstruct a common vision about the integration project. This supposed a shared understanding about the strategic direction of MERCOSUR. However, neither of the two governments had enough political support to face this task: The Brazilian government suffered a crisis of popularity, and Menem's administration suffered the characteristic weakness of the end of its term.

From the beginning the de la Rúa administration declared that MERCOSUR was the best strategic answer against globalization,[32] and it should be enlarged and consolidated by commercial policies to assure free access to markets without barriers and distortions; macroeconomic policies to impel discipline and convergence in the region; and an improvement of the institutions, in particular, the improvement of the system of solution of controversies.

The idea of the Alliance's government was to become the author of the recovery of MERCOSUR. Its strategy was to strengthen the regional bloc and to negotiate from a better position. In the first months, the Alliance's administration faced a strong political pressure from the main Peronist governors who in reality became the leaders of the opposition, and the leaders of the Argentinean Industrial Union (UIA), so measures were taken whose effects have been a hard blow to the integration project.

The situation turned more conflictive during 2001 as the result of the extremely grave Argentine economic crisis and the growing devaluation of the Brazilian real. This provoked tensions in the government and within the society.[33]

The commitment to the process of integration on the part of the governments of Brazil and Argentina was demonstrated in the Summits in Florianopolis (December 2000), Asuncion (June 2001) and Sao Paulo (October 2001). In these meetings there was progress in harmonization and coordination of macroeconomic variables and the establishment of a plan to discipline the economies in the areas of fiscal deficits, inflation, and indebtedness. All the same the ratification of the interests of Chile to join MERCOSUR, the signing of the automotive agreement by the four members, the reduction, however small, of the external common tariff, and the decision to advance the negotiations with the United States in the form of the "four plus one" completed the methods that pointed to the relaunching of MERCOSUR.

In relation to the "sensitive" themes of regional security the Argentine government cooperated with Brazil and consulted with the members of MERCOSUR. The government of Fernando de la Rúa was unable to develop alternative strategies as it was submerged in the short term by the economic emergency and the internal political crisis. It accepted the aspiration of the Brazilian leadership leaving behind all rivalry for power control that characterized the Menem years. Two events were symptomatic of this new attitude: there was no consensus to sanction the regime of Fuji-mori in Peru, de la Rúa did not accept a greater participation in the Colombian crisis in spite of pressures from North American diplomacy and the desire of Brazilian President Fernando Henrique Cardoso to move forward with political and economic integration.

In the decade of the 1990s, the governmental elite of Argentina as-cribed to a new paradigm of international involvement based on the acceptance of the hegemony of the Western alliance and global capitalism and the adoption of "universal values." The interests pursued in foreign policy revolved around the growth of commerce, investments, and the at-traction of foreign capital. The government of Dr. Menem moved to put in the past the history of confrontations in order to establish a special re-lationship with the United States with the conviction that it would pro-vide economic benefit and foster growth. MERCOSUR was the axis of the foreign policy. It created a model of regionalism for globalization that privileged the position of commercial interests over and above the active policies aimed at achieving balanced development goals that had been proposed in the 1980s.

Conclusion

The Alliance government did not change the adopted development model and did not have new strategies of foreign policy. It committed to deepen and develop MERCOSUR and proposed strong relations with the United States and continued diplomatic action that was fundamentally committed to developing the export markets of the country.

Despite the continuities from the foreign policy of Menem that were evident, it is necessary to recognize that there were differences. De la Rúa advocated the relaunching of MERCOSUR and worked to coordinate with Brazil for common positions on sensitive themes of the regional environment. Diplomacy defined itself by avoiding auto-matic alignment by developing a fine equilibrium that would not iso-late Argentina from its Southern Cone neighbors while not upsetting the United States.

President de la Rúa governed only two years. On the December 20, 2001, he resigned in the face of popular protests that multiplied through-out the country. The protests were against the effects of the government's economic policy and against a government that had been previously de-bilitated by a split in the alliance and that was no longer efficient or successful in concentrating power to solve an economic recession and gigantic fiscal deficit.

The decision to continue with the economic model of Menem and the urgency of maximizing revenues and attracting future investments obligated the government to focus its primary attention on macroeconomic requirements in the short term, regulating the government to implement the promises of the electoral campaign that evade the necessary discussion about strategies of development. It was economic management that was marked by a short-term focus and that applied the policies of deregulation, flexibility, and rigid financial discipline demanded by the multilateral credit organizations and banks that held Argentina's external debt. Without a doubt the virtuous circle of fiscal adjustment, good country credit rating, lower interest rates, and economic growth did not happen. In reality the results were more recession, record unemployment, and social unrest that provoked the most serious political and economic crisis in Argentina's history.

It is evident that the social and economic model implemented at the beginning of the 1990s failed. This project did not achieve social integration, peaceful politics, nor education, work, or health for the population. The question that emerges is whether the new Peronist government of Dr. Eduardo Dulhalde will have sufficient social force and political will to change the relationship of forces with international finance capital or the local socioeconomic sectors that were the great beneficiaries of the Menem model.

Notes

1. The Justice Party always had the control of the Senate and the second largest party in Deputies, it reformed the Supreme Court of Justice in order to dominate it, it managed most of the important districts in the country, and it amplified the President's powers through resources of doubtful legality like the Ordinances of Necessity and Urgency.
2. According to the INDEC (National Institute of Statistical and Census), the richest 10 percent of the population concentrates 36.9 percent of the wealth, while the poorest 10 percent 1.5 percent. In the 1970s, the richer 10 percent concentrated 28.2 percent while the poorer 10 percent 2.3 percent. The ECLAC has highlighted that in the 1990s, "In Argentina a marked growth of the entrance per inhabitants combined, a strong fall of the inflation at the beginnings of the decade, a high unemployment and an increase of the poverty."

3. The unemployment in October 1999, reached 14.5 percent (the maximum was reached in May 1995 with 18,4 percent). The official data point out that in the country there are 1.7 million unemployed, 1.8 million under-employed and 3 million workers with a salary average of 400 pesos, when a minimum basket of foods is valued in 480 pesos for a family of 4 people. Diario *Clarin,* June 13, 1999 (extracted data of the INDEC and of the Ministry of Economy).

4. The FREPASO is formed by dissident militants of the Justice Party and the UCR, the Christian Democracy, the Socialist Unity, sectors coming from the human rights organization, the Uncompromising Party, sectors of the Communist Party, and the Popular Socialist Party.

5. In President Menem's words: "My conception of the foreign policy is simple and clear: it is necessary to work so that the Argentina has a foreign policy that privileges the national interest, the welfare of the Argentineans. This presupposes, above all things, realism; because we know that only economic growth and the population's better welfare will give us status in the world. It is to create a climate of free trade and also for the movement of capital, for the favorable direct investments for growth and the use on the part of the national economies, of the opportunity that the world economy offers. This way, I state that foreign policy be constituted as a fundamental support for the solution of the economic and social problems of our country." MENEM, Carlos, *Estados Unidos, Argentina y Carlos Menem,* ed. CEYME (Buenos Aires, 1990), 32.

6. This conception was based in a new international context, in which the United States appeared—after the collapse of East European socialism—as the only great power of the planet in two key aspects: the military and, mainly, in the science and technology of fundamental importance in the process of "globalization." With this new reorder of the power in the world scene, the Argentinean government has the idea that "the fundamental function of a foreign policy for dependent and not very strategic countries is to remove obstacles for the economic development of the country," taking care of those who have the key to its material progress. It was mentioned in ESCUDE, Carlos: *El realismo de los Estados débiles* (Buenos Aires: GEL, 1995), 142

7. In 1990 Argentina voted with the United States 12.5 percent of the time but by 1994 voted with the United States 68 percent of the time. In the Security Council where Argentina was a non-permanent member in the period 1994 to 1995, the coincidence level with the United States was of 98.5 percent. Extracted concepts of Granillo Ocampo, R.: "Las relaciones de Argentina con Estados Unidos," in *Argentina y Estados Unidos,* F. de la Balze and E. Rocca, comp. (CARI, ABRA, 1997), 277.

8. The central demands of the United States for the region, immediately after the Cold War, seemed to be centered in the aspect of security. It claimed that the nuclear programs were placed under low international supervision, and

therefore, under its own supervision; it demanded the elimination of weapons of massive destruction or strategic missiles easy to transport; and the elimination of weapons of chemical type.

9. Among the more demonstrative events of nonproliferation policy, we can mention: the ratification of the Treaty of Tlatelolco for the prohibition of nuclear weapons in Latin America (1992); the adhesion to the Treaty of Nuclear Non-Proliferation accepting their safeguards (1994); the entrance to the technological clubs guided to the control of transfers of sensitive technologies (MTCR or Regime of Control of Missile Technology; Group of Nuclear Suppliers or Group of London; Australian Group); the signing of the Convention of Chemical Weapons (1993); the entrance to the Western Group of the Conference of the Disarmament (1995).

10. Declaration of Minister of Defense Erman Gonzalez in *Ambito Financiero,* May 29, 1991. The development of the missile Condor II had been suspended under the Chancellor Cavallo's administration, but it was in March 1991 when the decision was taken to freeze the project completely. In May, the government decided to dismantle the program although this process was slowed, by the opposition of diverse sectors, until beginnings of 1993 when it was informed that the different components of the missile had been sent to Spain and from there to the United States for its final destruction. At the same time the CONAE was created, which, under a civilian leadership, is dedicated to the design and execution of peaceful projects in space.

11. The destination places have been: Croatia, Cyprus, Macedonia, Bosnia-Herzegovina, Dominican Republic and Haiti, Angola, Mozambique, Rwanda, Western Sahara, Iraq and Kuwait, the territories occupied by Israel, Cambodia, Guatemala, El Salvador, Oriental Slovenia, Peninsula of Prevlaka. More than 10,000 officials and sub-officials of the Army have participated voluntarily in such missions, and the troops of the navy, the air force and the Argentinean border force. During 1999, more than 659 troops had service in 12 peacekeeping operations, locating our country in the eighth place among the biggest contribution of troops, with 4.45 percent of the total. In the area of participation of countries of Latin America, Argentina represents 45 percent of the total of the Latin American contribution. See Carlos Escude and Andrés Fontana, "Divergencias estratégicas en el Cono Sur: Las políticas de seguridad de Argentina frente a las de Brasil y Chile," University Torcuato di Tella, Documents of Work No. 20 (Buenos Aires, 1995); and A. Fontana, "La seguridad Internacional y la Argentina in los 90," in CISNEROS, Andrés, comp., *Política Exterior Argentina, 1989–1999. Historia de un Éxito,* (CARI, Nuevo Hacer, 1998).

12. The decision of sending two units from the Navy to the multinational force was announced hastily by President Menem, ignoring the legislative step and demonstrating some disagreements with the foreign ministers who had maintained a much more cautious attitude.

13. In the case of Cuba, Argentina was distanced by the Group of Rio once again when it voted in favor of a resolution that condemned violations of the human rights made by the Cuban regime and it demanded an investigation in charge of the Commission of Human Rights of the UN. At the same time, Menem exhorted Castro to democratize the regime and to abandon the ideology of communism. Another key moment was during the Summit of the Americas in Miami, when he affirmed that: I am willing to give my life for the freedom of Cuba! This participation was carried out in spite of apparent disagreement by the Group of Rio, and that the same Department of State would have suggested him not to discuss this topic in the context of the Summit. *La Nacion,* December 9, 1994.

14. In the case of Haiti, the Argentinean government supported the positions of the United States, condemning vigorously the military coup and participating in the international force in charge of guaranteeing the resignation of the military leaders and to promote Aristide's reinstatement. In our country, this decision led to a strong opposition of those who considered it dangerous to move away from the principles of sovereignty and of the position sustained by other nations of Latin America. Participation was justified by arguments that made reference to the defense of fundamental values and balance of power.

15. Fernando de la Rúa affirmed: "we have an excellent relationship with the United States, only it doesn't fit the words alignment or carnal relationships," La Nacion, March 18, 2000. Chancellor Rodriguez Giavarini on the other hand, affirmed that "Argentina won't support the decisions of the United States unconditionally inside the Security Council of the UN, but rather all the decisions will be consulted with the countries of the region before being taken," *Clarin,* February 2, 2000.

16. When in December 1990, Bush arrived in Buenos Aires he hailed Carlos Menem as a "world leader of privatization's," and Bill Clinton has stated repeatedly that the "bilateral relationships are excellent and they will continue improving." Of course, these statements are part of pressures on Argentina to deepen the economic reforms, reduce the fiscal deficit and fulfill the payment of the debts contracted with American banks in the eighties.

17. In this respect is the accusation of the ambassador from the United States in December 1990, T. Todman, regarding the intent of Argentinean officials of obtaining bribes from American companies—Swift-Armour, Firestone, Goodyear, Bell Atlantic and Zenith—before authorizing better conditions for certain commercial operations and of investment; again in 1992, he was truly irritated by the delay in the bid for the network of communications for which GTE was prequalified (the biggest supplier of phone services in the United States); in 1997, the Embassy of the United States in Argentina affirms that the artificial juridical insecurity and the corruption in Argentina are a danger for the business of American mining companies; in that same year, the International Transparency Organization presents a report where it

demonstrated that, in our country, the corruption levels had increased from 1995.

18. In the computerized programs of the Bank of the Argentina, important surcharges would have been paid to the American Company IBM. Up to now it is demonstrated that several high former directives of the Bank opened secret accounts in Switzerland, Luxembourg, and the United States to deposit the proceeds of the bribes. However, it seems that the investigation had clear political limits. In first term, up to now, the main leadership of IBM was not reached when denying the Justice and the American government, the extradition of the involved executives. In second place, in Argentina, neither former Minister of Economy Domingo Cavallo, nor former General Secretary of the Presidency Alberto Kohan were investigated.

19. In 1991, Menem, Di Tella and Minister of Defense Erman González signed two secret ordinances authorizing the shipment of weapons to Panama. The shipment actually went to Croatia violating the military embargo of the UN. The ordinance signed in the case of Ecuador is from 1995 and it has the signatures of Menem, di Tella, Cavallo and Minister of Defense Oscar Camilion. In this case, weapons and ammunition went from Venezuela to Ecuador when Ecuador was at war with Peru and Argentina was the mediator of peace. At the present time Oscar Camilion, former head of the Air Force Brigadier Juan Paulik and former inspector of Military Productions Luis Sarlenga have been indicted. On the other hand, former Chancellor di Tella is accused of ideological falsehood and concealment of tests, and the prosecution of former boss of the Army general lieutenant (R) Martin Balza has been requested as the organizer of the illicit sale of weapons.

20. By the end of October 2000 the Patent Law came into effect after a decade of conflicts. The discussion about medicine patents started in the 1990s. In 1995 the law was approved and gave five years to laboratories to adapt to the new system and to start to pay royalties. There were disagreements between the Congress and the Executive, which were the mirror of the hard conflict between national laboratories (most part was against the law) and the foreigners (which used their embassies to stop it). The period of validity of the law, however, will not avoid the process initiated by the United States against Argentina before the WTO. The Americans stated in this case that the Argentinean legislation is not enough, and that it does not respond to international requirements.

21. The open skies agreement would allow companies from the United States to operate domestic flights in Argentina and it would start in 2003. At the end of March, Argentinean government announced that it suspended the agreement because "it was not beneficial for most Argentineans."

22. Washington's concrete interest is that the Alliance confirms the grant of the radar plan, valued at $200 million, to the American company Northrop (associated with the Italian Alenia) whose award at the moment is in Justice.

23. It was expressed this way by the Secretary of Trade, W. Dalley, and the Under-Secretary of Economic Matters, Alan Larson, in their visits to Argentina in February 2000. *Clarin,* February 12, 2000, and *La Nacion,* February 25, 2000; March 1, 2000; March 6, 2000.

24. These pressures were mainly increased when, in Argentina, the scandals exploded because of the presence in Buenos Aires of Escobar Gaviria's widow, and the accusation carried out by the General Procurement of Mexico, that Argentina would be the final destination of a network dedicated to money obtained by the Juarez group.

25. The Alliance's government affirmed that the armed forces should not intervene in the fight against drug traffic beyond logistical tasks foreseen in the Law of Interior Security, and that they would continue with the construction of a system of regional defense with the countries of MERCOSUR, Chile and Bolivia. *Clarin,* September 19, 1999.

26. De la Balze: "La política exterior de reincorporación al primer mundo," in A. Cisneros, op. cit. (1998).

27. Argentinean products that have had difficulty accessing the American market are: sugar, peanuts, tobacco, and steel, all limited by import quotas.

28. It was by the middle of the 1990s when the priority of MERCOSUR was consolidated against more liberal postures, that defend the insertion of capitalism as absolute priority, mainly with the United States. In this option, the opposition of the U.S. Congress perhaps influenced the "fast track" decision to join NAFTA, and the growing flow of investments coming from the European Union toward the regional bloc of MERCOSUR and the signature of the Agreement of Interregional Cooperation in 1995. Malvinas seems also to be profiled as a policy of State. Although from the opposition, the Alliance questioned the policy toward the kelpers carried out by the Argentinean Chancellery and criticized the agreement of July 14, 1999, for which Argentineans must show a passport to enter the insular territory. Ten days after his electoral victory, President de la Rúa guaranteed Tony Blair the continuity of the agreement.

29. This characteristic is still being emphasized significantly from 1991. The imports to Argentina come first from European Union, next from MERCOSUR, and at last from NAFTA. The main destination of the Argentinean exports is MERCOSUR, followed by European Union and far behind by NAFTA. Regarding the Direct Foreign Investments, in Argentina from 1990 to 1996, the United States was the highest investor, concentrating 33 percent of all investors, however, the income originating from Europe was in close second at 30 percent total.

30. The tension arises because of macroeconomic problems (devaluation and recession in Brazil and recession in Argentina) and administrative problems (setbacks in the consolidation of the Customs Union and scarce advance in the deepness of integration). Starting from 1997, the operation

of the free intra-regional trade was negatively affected by the imposition of non-tariff barriers and by the use of distorted incentives. On the other hand, macroeconomic problems caused a deceleration of the intra-regional trade and a change of relative prices in favor of Brazil that contributed to an increase of commercial controversies and claims for protectionist measures.

31. Then he affirmed that when he asked to collaborate with Colombia he was thinking of the shipment of White Helmets and foods: "Some idiots began to rebut my arguments saying that I was offering troops to Colombia, because the political world is so full of stupid and clumsy people that sometimes you are upset," *Ambito Financiero,* August 16, 1999.

32. This political decision is supported in managerial sectors who believe MERCOSUR should be improved, and to advance without delays to the solution of problems that would arise. See declarations of V. Barello (President of FIAT Argentina), G. Gotelli (President of Canvas Shoes), C. Good (President of the Camera of the Industry of the Footwear), and R. Rocca (President of TECHINT), in *Pagina/12,* August 19, 1999, 2–4; *Clarin,* Economic Supplement, September 19, 1999, 4–8; and *La Nacion,* March 19, 2000.

33. The conflict became incrementally worse over several months after the devaluation of the real provoked an increase in imports from Brazil in certain manufacturing sectors and in agricultural products. It was aggravated by subsidies given by certain Brazilian state governments to enterprises for the purpose of getting them to relocate.

Bibliography

Acuña, Carlos. (1995). "Política y Economía en la Argentina de los años 90." *América Latina Hoy.* Salamanaca, Spain.

De la Balze, F., and Roca, E. (1997). *Argentina y Estados Unidos. Fundamentos de una Nueva Alianza.* Buenos Aries: CARI/ABRA.

Cisneros, A. (1998). *Política exterior Argentina (1989–1999): Historia de un Éxito.* Buenos Aires: Nuevo Hacer, CARI.

Dupas, Gilberto. (1998). "A ALCA e os interesses do Mercosul. As relaçoes entre os EUA e o continente: liderança, hegemonia ou coerçao?" In Tulio Vigevani and Jorge Lorenzetti, eds. *Globalizaçao e Integraçao Regional: Actitudes sindicais e impactos sociais.* Sao Paula: FAPESP, LTR.

Escude, Carlos. (1995). *El realismo de los estados débiles.* Buenos Aires.

———. (1992). *Realismo Periférico; Fundamentos para la nueva política exterior argentina.* Buenos Aires: Planeta.

Ferreira Rubio, D., and Goretti, M. (1996). "Cuando el Presidente gobierna solo. Menem y los Decretos de Necesidad y Urgencia hasta la Reforma Constitucional (julio de 1989–agosto 1994)." *Desarrollo Económico,* vol. 36, no. 141.

Menem, Carlos. (1990). *Estados Unidos, Argentina y Carlos Menem.* Buenos Aires: CEYME.

O'Donnell, Guillermo. (1992). "¿Democracia delegativa?" *Cuadernos del CLAEH,* no. 61, July.

Rapoport, Mario. (1994). *Globalización, integración e identidad nacional: análisis comparado Argentina-Canadá.* Buenos Aires: Centro Editor Latinoamericano.

Russell, Roberto. (1994a). "Los ejes estructurantes de la Política exterior argentina," *América Latina Internacional,* vol. 1, no. 2.

————. (1994b). *La política exterior de Bill Clinton y América Latina: de la contención a la extensión de la democracia y los mercados.* Serie de Documentos y Informes de Investigación de FLACSO, May.

Vacs, Aldo. (1995). "Vuelta a los orígenes: democracia liberal, liberalismo económico y la redefinición de la política exterior argentina." In Acuña, Carlos (ed): *La nueva matriz política argentina,* Buenos Aires: Nueva Visión.

Chapter 11

The Geopolitics of the Relationship between Mexico and the United States

Jaime Preciado Coronado,
in collaboration with Jorge Hernández

Introduction

> During the Cold War and, in fact, also during the two world wars, Mexico was considered as a vital geopolitical pivot. Located in our south flank, it was a coveted point to amuse us of other essential activities. As the later system to the Cold War has taken form, the geoeconomical importance of Mexico has taken preeminence. Sign of this is the North American Free Trade Agreement (NAFTA). The capability or inability of Mexico to incorporate to the vigorous economies of free market will be a decisive factor in the viability that has our new expansion strategy. (Dziedzic, 1997:86)

As a colonel of the American Air Force, Michael J. Dziedzic points out that the end of the Cold War didn't mean the end point of the importance of Mexico for the United States, but rather its transformation in both bilateral and geopolitical terms.

In this respect, we find that the change in the conceptual framework inside which the new geopolitics of the relationship between Mexico and the United States is bounded today is characterized by the coexistence of some of the traditional geopolitical focus[1] and the emergence of "the new realities of power" pointed out by Zbigniew Brzezinski (1997). Although it is undeniable that the geographical proximity of Mexico and the United States still determines in great measure the priorities of both states, it is also certain that the character of those priorities has to be adjusted to a new international reality. Hence we will find that the topics of the new bilateral geopolitical schedule are not completely new, but they acquire a different character.

The traditional geopolitical focus emphasizes factors like the geographical location, the territorial domain, and the access to certain strategical resources to define the status of power of a nation-state, as well as its international behavior. For this reason, it centers the realities of power strongly in the capacities and military strategies of the states.

Geographical Location (Stability— National Security and Geopolitical Pivot)

The geographical closeness of Mexico and the United States has maintained in a traditional way the importance of the stability of Mexico in the agenda of American concerns. This is comprehensible if we take into account the unavoidable interaction generated by a common frontier of around thirty-two hundred kilometers between the two countries.

Evidence of this closeness is the amount of American capital that began to flow to Mexico after World War II, in spite of the Mexican government's reticence and of the maintenance of measures that restricted the flow. "They were part of an implicit arrangement originated by the primary nexus of interdependence, which was known as the 'special relationship.' This primary nexus of interdependence was based on an exchange of vulnerabilities: Mexico provided stability, and with it, it solved a problem of 'national security' for the United States, and in exchange, Mexico received its neighbor's loans and investments, which contributed to the Mexican economic development, in spite of the nationalist rhetoric that warned of the dangers of the foreign capital" (Chabat, 1996:257–258).

This has been paradoxical in the Mexican history, because the isolation of Mexico with regard to the external world that was expressed in the import substitution policy applied by Mexico during many decades can be understood as an answer to the traumatic historical experiences that Mexico has lived in their relationship with the exterior,[2] especially with the United States.[3]

By contrast, the importance of Mexico for the United States during the Cold War was an unquestionable and broadly recognized fact. Dziedzic

(1997:85) points out that the American victory over the then Soviet Union was attributable in certain measure to a great geopolitical advantage: "While the Soviet Union was surrounded by opponents, the United States had the fortune of having kind neighbors and secure frontiers."[4] In this sense, "with its stability, Mexico contributed—in passive, but fundamental way—to the victory of the United States in the Cold War."

Nevertheless, since the American concern for the stability of Mexico didn't begin with the Cold War, neither has it ended after the end of the bipolar conflict. NAFTA is evidence of continued U.S. concern. About this issue, Jorge Chabat (1997:260) points out that "it is difficult to know for exactly what reason the American government has decided to open the doors of trade to his neighbor of the south. It has been the commercial importance that Mexico has for the United States or the threat to the American national security[5] that can be generated from Mexico." The instability of Mexico has always been one of the main American concerns, and the maintenance of its stability has been and is perceived as an objective of "American national security."[6]

Another topic derived from the geographical vicinity between Mexico and the United States is the listing of Mexico as an American geopolitical pivot.[7] In this respect, Dziedzic (1997:86) argues that the location of Mexico "has transformed it into a contention point for diverse sociogeographic or transnational problems that don't respect national frontiers. In consequence, it will play a central part in the fight to avoid the consequences of what the pessimists have called the new world disorder." The concern is that Mexico might end up succumbing to the forces of that disorder, and as a result: The "United States could not avoid the consequences of the 'future anarchy.' Therefore, Mexico is—and it will continue being—fundamental for the success of the great American strategy."

For the United States the transnational problems include terrorism, illegal migration (undocumented immigration), drug production and trafficking, and organized crime. Mexico's location makes it an important player in all of these issues.

Territorial Domain

As La Feber points out (1993), "150 years ago the predominant reason to intervene in Latin America was [an] expansionism . . . [of its] ideological base . . . [and] the methods were almost always the direct intervention of American troops." Today, the dominant interest still determines the foreign policy toward the region, but the ideological motivation has changed toward more insidious arguments on the problem of drugs, and the methods have become darker. However, the classic pattern remains. Today, "in the twilights of the twentieth century, a reconstituted version of this thought of 'free market,' well known as neoliberalism it is the one that leads to the global economy" (Agnew and Corbridge, 1995).

The economic neoliberalism that guides American policies toward Mexico is demonstrated in the North American Free Trade Agreement (NAFTA) and the privatizations, opening, and outlines of deregulation induced by the International Monetary Fund and the World Bank. In this sense, Jorge Cadena Roa (1991) points out that "in front of the challenge of its decline as the main and insurmountable economic world power of the postwar period, the United States has turned its attention toward Mexico and Latin America, seeing it as its continent, as its own space in which it can expand economically, so the United States can get itself into the competition with other blocs." This is the current version of the American territorial hegemony on Mexico and on Latin America. The main reason is that the region remains a source of raw materials and cheap labor for the American capitalists.

The Access to Strategical Resources

In November of 1996, the former Secretary of Defense of the United States, Caspar Weinberger (1981–1987) stated that the American militaries possible "scenarios of war" included "a possible armed intervention" in Mexico. In January of 1998, the American air force also revealed the consideration of Mexico as a "theater of war," because of potential Mexican threats to the national security of the United States. According to the Air Force, there are six possible threats[8] and two of them include Mexico.

These scenarios are that of a possible "migratory hurricane" caused by a recession at the beginning of the twenty-first century and that of an imminent "cartel of cartels," a product of the gathering of the Mexican drug dealers. This type of revelation is not something new, nor surprising, because from Woodrow Wilson's presidency (1913–1921) "the Department of War designed and executed the first contingency plan for an invasion of great scale against Mexico" (*Excélsior,* 1996).

According to official documents, "after Wilson carried out his political-military and naval tactics that contributed to the defeat of Victoriano Huerta, there was considerable disappointment in Washington soon after with the ascent and the institutionalization of revolutionary nationalism. It meant a change in the right of property that, as Jose Ovalle has reminded us recently, allows Mexico to retain under its domain all that is necessary for social development, including the mines, the petroleum, etc." (*Excélsior*, 1996). This gave origin to the lingering confrontation between the United States and Mexico about the jurisdiction of the Mexican state on the natural resources of the sea floor.

At the present time, the geopolitical relationships between Mexico and the United States show the importance of the strategic natural resources of Mexico for the United States. Michael Dziedzic (1997) points out the need for sure access to the petroleum of Mexico, as a crucial fact in the geoeconomical perspectives of the United States. It is a doubly significant fact that, in September of 1998, Mexico has become the main supplier of petroleum for the United States outside of OPEC, selling 38,382,000 barrels of petroleum. In the same month Mexico also consolidated itself as the second ranking commercial partner of the United States, displacing Japan. During the first three trimesters of 1998, Mexico sold the United States a total of 361,021,000 barrels of raw oil, equivalent to about 14.8 percent of the 2,443,000,000 barrels imported in this period by the powerful neighbor of the north. According to some authors, this would partly explain the American interest in the Chiapas conflict that is located in a region where some studies including the U.S. geological survey reveal the existence of important oil deposits in areas controlled by the EZLN.

The New Realities of Power

To speak of new realities of power is equal to saying that the world has changed and that the realities of the power have also. Indeed, the world changed when the bipolar order centered the realities of the power in the military capacity, and resource availability disappeared. It decreased at the same time the importance of the control of geographical-strategic pivotal areas.

The emergence of topics like economic power, technological development, and the cultural domain have displaced in importance military might as the main criterion of status and power after the Cold War, but the military remains, according to Brzezinski, one of the four decisive domains of the global power. In this sense, according to the same author, the United States would consolidate its status as global superpower shortly; because "militarily it has an insurmountable global economic power, it remains the main motor of the global growth, even if it is concerned in some aspects by Japan and Germany technologically, it conserves the leadership in the critical areas of the innovation; and culturally . . . it enjoys sympathy, especially among the youth of the world" (Brzezinski, 1997:24).

In accordance with Brzezinski, in the road toward this global supremacy, the United States has produced a new international order that institutionalizes in the exterior many of the characteristics of the American system that allows the United States to enlarge its power of global dominance. However, in spite of all this and the optimism of Brzezinski about the United States, the American global supremacy doesn't seem to be completely certain. The United States today faces competition in the economic and technological fields from Europe and Japan in this world dominated by blocs. This emergence of international economic blocs as part the new world order of post–Cold War period has modified the traditional definitions about "national security" of the United States.

As Sergio Aguayo and John Bailey point out (1997), the United States "has reconsidered the concept of national security in the light of the appearance of regional commercial blocs and of the emergence of new threats: transnational organized crime, terrorism, regional conflicts, disintegration of states and an out of control movement of refugees." Hence, the United Europe and the Asian bloc lead by Japan represent for the United States not just a serious threat to their geoeconomical pretenses, global and regional,[9] but also a new challenge to their national security.

This threat is expressed in this manner "opening the regional commercial blocs became exclusionary then, a world order could arise where European trade was made under the preponderant influence of Germany and the economic activity in Asia was centered in Japan or China. Besides negative economic consequences, the closed regional commercial blocs would cause a competition for U.S. global hegemony, which would produce a much riskier international atmosphere for the United States" (Dziedzic, 1997:99).

Here again Mexico represents a key piece for the United States. Dziedzic says (1997) because, "as a result of the current tendency toward the subregional, regional and global economical integration, geography has become an important macroeconomic aspect. As this process advances it will be vital for the United States that these regimes remain open and equitable." In this sense, "Mexico has an excellent cultural and geographical location to serve as bridge between the English-speaking America and the Spanish-speaking one. If Mexico demonstrates that economic neoliberal formula works, this will give it a strong impulse toward a global, open and equitable economic community. Otherwise it will be negative" (Dziedzic, 1997:99).

This means that for the United States, the capacity of Mexico to be integrated successfully into the world economical community via NAFTA, it is a decisive factor in its geoeconomical strategy, because the success or commercial failure of Mexico in its integration with North America could influence in an important way "the rhythm and even to the degree of advance of the other Latin American countries in the way to free trade" (Dziedzic, 1997:103).

NAFTA and the American Geoeconomical Strategy of Postwar Period

The end of the Cold War implies an important change in the guidelines of the American foreign policy in that it passes from a strongly ideological policy to a more pragmatic one, and from the confrontation with the communist threat, to the emphasis on the challenges imposed by the market. In the words of Jorge Cadena Roa (1991), "the ideological enemy was replaced by the promotion of the American economic interest in strategic markets." In the same sense, Víctor López Villafañe (1991) points out that "the confrontations of the future will take place in the markets, [and] no longer in the forests of the Third World. In this context, Japan will be the objective, and no longer 'the communism of' the USSR. [According with this] Mexico and Canada displaced Central America as key actors in the new strategic design."

This "new American strategic design" places Mexico again in first place as a necessary ally to impel the geoeconomical strategy of the United States. According to Andrés Peñaloza (1999), this agreement has meant "a change of one hundred eighty degrees in the Mexican foreign policy, abandoning the policy of diversification of commercial relationships and retreating from the process of Latin American integration."

Mexico, has committed itself to the dynamics of privatizations, deregulation, and indiscriminate trade liberalization.[10] Dynamics that have generated the signing of numerous commercial treaties and agreements of reciprocal promotion and protection of investments, as well as of agreements of economical cooperation with European and Latin American countries. Also, the government policies were added to actively impel the Multilateral Agreement on Investments (MAI), proposed by the Organization for the Economic Cooperation and Development (OECD). This agreement is reflected in chapter 11 of NAFTA and "seeks to liberalize world investments, granting maximum rights and few obligations to the multinational corporations, as well as serious restrictions on the national states to regulate their behavior" (Peñaloza, 1999). MAI did not obtain the consent of the members of the OECD, but rather it found strong resistances from civil society and has not been ratified.

In this context and in accordance with Cadena Roa (1991), "to face the current challenges of world economic power,[11] the United States has turned toward Mexico and Latin America, seeing it as its continent, as its own space within which they can expand and recover economically, and then relaunch its competition with other blocs."

In this sense, the composition of the commercial exchange between Mexico and the United States bolsters another of the macroeconomic impacts on the Mexican regional geopolitics, because the factory worker sector contributes 43 percent of the external sales while the national components used during these processes are less than 2 percent. That means that NAFTA has impelled the exploitation of the comparative advantages[12]—that in the case of Mexico is cheaper labor[13]—so that the American companies can compete under better conditions in its own market and in others like Europe and Asia.

By contrast, the greater economical integration between Mexico and the United States has been expressed in the diverse indicators, increasingly slanted[14] and more significant,[15] but strongly impelled and hurried by NAFTA. It modifies the general framework of the relationship between both countries, transforming the American policy's focus toward Mexico from a paradigm of "coercive control"—toward an outline of "associative cooperation." For example, Mexico has been an American ally in the promotion of the proposed FTAA and of the privatizing policies, trade liberalization, and deregulation instruments already mentioned.

In this sense, Mexico's success in surviving the crisis of 1994 with the strong support of the U.S. government was an important moment for the United States through its diverse institutions. As Dziedzic points out (1997), "If the United States had not acted resolutely to stop the flight of capital form Mexico and, in general, from all over the lesser developed world, the leaders of many of those countries would have been forced to question the convenience of following the U.S. model. The global economic activity could have suffered a strong blow and, in consequence, prosperity and prestige as world leader as well as our possibilities of expanding the environment for the capitalist economic systems would be threatened."

The dimension of the importance of this hemispheric commercial community is expressed in a clear way in the following lines of Dziedzic (1997): "If our own geographical region is not able to be integrated in an economic way and Europe and Asia are successful in this way, the United States will be in a clear geoeconomical disadvantage. To be protected in the worst of the cases, that is to say, the division of the world into regional commercial blocs, the United States can not be given the luxury of neglecting its neighbors."

Another point, not less important from the American geoeconomical view connected to Mexico, is their own prosperity. If Mexico is able to improve its economic capacity and maintain a sustained growth, the United States will have better market perspectives for its products, because in the first five years of NAFTA, Mexico demonstrated its potential in this sense.[16] Because at least in theory it is supposed that the increment of the bilateral trade should also be meant in the creation of employment on both sides of the frontier, according to Dziedzic (1997), "depending on the employment source—the sector of factories or that of services—$1 million of additional imports generate between 16,500 and 23,300 new jobs." With that, the increase of the bilateral trade should translate in a higher level of employment for the United States and Mexico. This way, the geoeconomical interests of the United States are closely bound with the growth of the Mexican economy and their purchasing power.

By contrast, NAFTA has not just increased bilateral trade but rather it has also contributed to increase the bilateral interest in traditional topics such as the guarantee of access to the Mexican petroleum to protect the United States from the uncertainties of the Middle East, providing in this way a sphere of energy security that guarantees the American prosperity. In this sense, it is in keeping with the opening dynamics, deregulation, and privatizations that Mexico has supported, following the economic pattern sponsored by Washington from its institutions and specialized organisms. Washington has constantly pressed that strategic sectors like petroleum be privatized.[17]

NAFTA and the Mexico-U.S. Border Area

Although we have said the primary nexus of interdependence developed with the United States around the Mexican stability, we must now add the importance of the border area. In recent years, industrial production has been increased notably in the border area between Mexico and the United

States. On the American side, this growth has been especially important in Texas, in the south and center of California and, in smaller measure, in New Mexico and Arizona. On the Mexican side a more spectacular growth has been seen, especially in cities like Tijuana, Ciudad Juárez, and Matamoros, which already have hundreds of industrial assembly plants.[18]

The establishment of assembly plants on the Mexican side along those around 3,200 kilometers of border area is a truly significant fact in the growth of Mexican exports. In this sense, "NAFTA became the motor of the quick incorporation of that industry in the international markets" (García, 1999), and it has come to displace the axis of the industrial production from the capital and the central region toward the border states, an objective outlined since 1965. This situation is reflected in the data of 1998,[19] that point out that 90 percent (around 940,674) of the jobs generated by the assembly plant industry were located in the area of the northern frontier, with the American investments being the most important.[20]

Nevertheless, the investments in the factory worker sector that generate sales to the exterior of about $10 billion, increased the differences among the big, the small, and medium companies. In this way, the "big companies"—generally those with transnational capital—have access to industrial modernization that allows them to enlarge their capacity and benefits when concentrating exports. It's enough to say that just three hundred big companies have around 80 percent of the sales to the exterior, although there are 32,592 export companies registered in Mexico.

This has been a hard blow for the small and medium companies that have not found support programs, development, and efficient capitalization that allow them to work under better conditions inside the export sector. In contrast, "for the American investors, the Mexican government has facilitated joint-ventures realization, the main line of business up to now with Mexico. That is to say, the foreign investment is arriving to acquire the 'jewels of the family' so much of the private sector as public" (Peñaloza, 1999).

Among the most important investments in this border area are the ones relating to the textile industry "that has become the number one exporter to the United States after the deterioration suffered in past decades and after overcoming the difficult negotiation of NAFTA" (García, 1999).

By contrast, the industrial growth of the border area with the United States was something that was glimpsed as logical from the same negotiations of NAFTA, and for what the North American Bank of Development (NADBANK) was instituted, to support the infrastructure projects that supported the balanced border development. Nevertheless, this institution has not been able to complete its objective, because the growth of the assembly plant industry in the border area has not been accompanied by the development of a basic infrastructure for the treatment of polluted waters and the disposition of dangerous materials.

During the debate about NAFTA, the source of the dangerous materials was discussed and the cost of establishing the systems and necessary infrastructure for the treatment of the polluted waters and dangerous materials was considered; however, the high cost of these systems, that oscillated between the $8 million and $20 million, resulted in their not being built. This outcome occurred because of the payment of few taxes by the companies. Local governments cooperate with this strategy of low taxes to attract jobs but are then left without the resources to construct necessary infrastructure.

The Mexican strategy to increase employment and exports, and relocate the industrial production has found in NAFTA the quickest way of completing these objectives, but this has meant an environmental deterioration of the border area. "The Annex III of the Agreements of La Paz, undersigned between Mexico and the United States in 1983, warn that the dangerous residuals of the assembly plants are returned to the United States, considering lack of the infrastructure for their appropriate treatment in Mexican territory" (RMALC, 1999).

To give us an idea of factory worker sector impact in the production of dangerous residuals it is enough to point out that according to the National Institute of Ecology, in 1997, industry in Mexico generated 12.7 millions of tons of these residuals, of which 10.5 million tons corresponded to the factory worker sector. The border area, contributed nearly 3 million tons (around 25 percent of the total).

The Geopolitics of the Drugs Between Mexico and the United States

The ideological justification for the American intervention in Latin America has changed from the Monroe Doctrine and the Manifesto Destiny: "The Cold War provided to the United States a new watchword in the hemisphere; to fight against the expansion of communism. It allowed the United States to justify its military presence and the repression of some regimes. Examples of this were Allende's overthrow in Chile and the American involvement in Central America in the 1980s. Today, the war against drugs represents for the United States a new ideological justification for intervention" (Castañeda, 1998).

As Edgar Hernández points out (1998), the fall of communism has left the United States without an enemy that justified their presence in the area of Latin America. As a result some members of the U.S. Congress (Jesse Helms, Diane Feinstein, Alfonse D'Amato) have exaggerated the ineffectiveness of the region in combating the drug traffic, with the purpose of pressing the executive branch to adopt a more energetic position toward Latin America.

From this point of view, the failure of the certification process[21] to reduce the consumption of drugs in the United States together with the pressure from some congress members largely explained the current antidrug policy of the Clinton administration[22] that tried to substitute the mechanism of certification for Latin America for one seemingly more stronger in the form of the Multilateral Antidrug Center. According to some analysts, the Multilateral Antidrug Center was the logical culmination of the antidrug policy that the Clinton administration started in 1996 with the appointment of General Barry McCaffrey's, former boss of the South Command, as head of the Office of Antidrug Policy of the White House.

Nevertheless, in a wider context, the Multilateral Antidrug Center was not limited to the exchange of information but, rather, was a regional project of espionage and detection based in Panama. "Hence [with the Multilateral Antidrug Center], the antidrug policy of Clinton's régime was to fulfill the objective of enlarging its maneuverability margin in the political control of the Latin American nations" (*El Financiero*, 1998).

However, the Multilateral Antidrug Center did not become an accomplished fact of American foreign policy, because of the resistance of some countries like Mexico who expressed serious doubts about this center, arguing that its operations would harm the sovereignty of the Latin American nations. However, while the new American strategy developed, Mexico continued to be a focal point of U.S. antidrug efforts.

Proof of this is the wide activity of the U.S. Drug Enforcement Agency (DEA) in Mexico, with seven headquarters located there. The point that makes evident the importance of Mexico in the antidrug strategy of Washington is the fact that these seven are compared to only two in Colombia (Barranquilla and Santa Fe) where the drug problem is far more serious. In addition, the DEA, "in fact has capacity to exercise control along the whole dividing line, since in the adjacent states to our country have offices and some of them collaborate closely with the Specialized Office in the Attention to Crimes against the Health of the General Attorney Office" (*El Financiero*, 1998). This wide border presence reflects the fact that the DEA classifies the frontier with Mexico as a "High Intensity of Drug Trafficking Area" (HIDTA).[23] By contrast, it is necessary to point out that in the United States, according to the map of the DEA, three of the six HIDTAs are strongly linked to the Mexican geopolitics: Los Angeles, California, and Houston, Texas (near the frontier with Mexico); and Miami, Florida (connected with the Mexican gulf).

This presence has been reflected in the antidrug policies of both countries. U.S. policy of "interception" seeks to use Mexico to contain sociogeographic threats, like the drug trafficking. Meanwhile, on the other side, the policy of Mexico is to be, more and more, subordinate to the designs of Washington. The interception of drugs outside of the American frontier allows Washington to diminish the social repression that it would generate in combating drug traffic inside its own territory. Instead it is passing the social costs from this repression to the producing and trafficking countries, especially Mexico and Colombia.

The fact that Mexico accepts these conditions in the fight against the drug traffic reflects the deep asymmetry of power between the two countries. A factor of this asymmetry resides in the economic capacity. For example, while the U.S. organisms in charge of this task spend about $17 billion a year in Mexico, the budget dedicated to the Mexican Special Office for the Attention to Crimes against the Health doesn't reach $9 million, less than 0.1 percent of the North American total. But "the comparison is more significant if we consider that, according to press reports, the earnings of former drug dealer Amado Carrillo ascended to more than $200 million weekly and that he dedicated just for bribes between $500 and $800 million a year" (*El Universal,* 1997). These facts reflect the enormous disadvantage amid which the antidrug fight between Mexico and the cartels can be framed and the position of Mexico in front of the United States in the same sense.

Migration and Mexico-U.S. Geopolitics

As we already have pointed out, the stability of Mexico has been a constant concern for the United States. The possible sociogeographic consequences of the instability of our country for the United States makes that careful pursuit of our internal economic, political, and social actions a topic of high priority.

In this context, we can explain that some of the scenarios of war considered by the U.S. Army include Mexico as a possible place for the emergence of new challenges to the military, political, and economic supremacy of the United States. In Mexico our pursuit of internal development allows one to see certain dangers as more than imaginary.

The possibility of a "migratory hurricane" caused by a recession at the beginning of the twenty-first century was one of the six considered by the U.S. Army during 1998. These considerations revealed that the United States initially expected positive results from the Mexican economy in NAFTA, but the events of 1994, the "peso crisis," and the subsequent economic recession in Mexico, "established the economic crisis again, adjustments, fall of revenues and shortage of opportunities in the labor market" (Alba, 1998:73).

These crises reveal the importance of the migratory phenomenon of Mexicans toward the United States as a possible sociogeographic risk to the United States. As Francisco Alba stated about the most recent crisis "it seems to be more dramatic and the consequences deeper, because it happened after the highly optimistic expectations associated to NAFTA. In this context, the 'necessity' of having the 'escape valve' that is represented by the migratory phenomenon for the traditional operation of the system is perceived with greater clarity and urgency" (Alba, 1998:74).

Although NAFTA initially was presented analytically as the most appropriate economic policy to create disincentives to the migration through the trade,[24] the reality has shown us that "although it is certain that trade is a substitute for migration, it is also true that the economic restructuring associated with trade force displaced labor to productive niches" (Alba, 1998:81).

This consideration has made clear that potential scenes of crisis in Mexico remain in spite of the recovery of macroeconomic stability achieved recently, because, in general, "the passage to macroeconomical stability over the micro-economical conditions appears full of difficulties in the long term" (Alba, 1998). Moreover, the fact that the scenario of the "migratory hurricane" is developed for the beginning of the twenty-first century, and as product of a recession, speaks to us of the association of this possible recession with an eventual political crisis emanating from the democratic transition of Mexico in the wake of the election of Vicente Fox in 2000.

From this point of view, the democratic transition of Mexico in a context of civility is a high strategic priority for the United States, because otherwise the threat of a massive wave of illegal immigrants toward that country is latent, and difficult to contain. Because, according to Dziedzic (1997), "the number of Mexicans that emigrates from their country for economical reasons would be minimal next to those that would leave if political disturbances arose." Then what is to say of a political instability that generates an economic crisis like that of 1994? The results of a crisis of this nature would be extremely disturbing to our neighbor to the north.

This explained, largely, the American position toward the presidential succession of 2000, where for the first time the United States conditioned its traditional support to the candidate of the Institutional Revolutionary Party and showed an openness and even support for a victory by Vicente Fox. In accordance with Guadalupe González (1997), this posture of Washington had a strategic objective that is the "transformation of the basis of the internal stability and peace, that is to say, the substitution of the fragile balance of 'authoritarian stability' for a transitory one 'democratic uncertainty.'"

González continues, " the time when Mexican stability rested in a 'social corporativism' managed by the official party are now just a memory. The economic transformation that has followed the change in the development pattern has been deep and quick, but the political transformation has been too slow and gradual, with an official political system that has not been able to adjust to the new social realities. The 'unstable balance between state power and society' has been corroded" (González, 1997).

In this context, the political transformation was clearly necessary and imminent: "Mexico of the 1990s is a divided society and broken into fragments by deep regional, cultural, ethnical and economical distances, with serious problems of social and political integration that can end up being translated in threats to the stability and internal peace" (González, 1997:132–133). For that reason, it is urgent to assist the demands of political modernization impelled from civil society; inattention to the demands could cause, and in fact is causing, the emergence of violent ways of political and social change.

These violent forms of political and social change imply a high potential of uncertainty, because they threaten to transform the order of what Guadalupe González (1997) has called the "basic elements of the national security:" territorial integrity, social peace, self-government, and rule of law. From the perspective of Washington, this uncertainty in Mexico means scenarios of risk that could be translated in an economic, political, and social crisis with all that this bears:

- recession and deterioration of their second most important commercial partner's economic capacity;
- political vacuums and the deterioration of the rule of law that could be exploited by drug traffickers and international organized crime to penetrate and to even corrupt more the spheres of the power; and

- a possible increase of the influence of some extremist groups that promote radical changes in the economic, political, and social order through subversive ways.

This means that several U.S. interests could be affected by Mexico, as the bilateral trade (that reaches $19.6 billion): its geopolitical and geoeconomical policies (consolidation of the FTAA and its economic plan of global trade promotion); the combating of some transnational threats like the drug trafficking; the interest of their investors in Mexico, and accessibility to the vital resources of Mexico. Of this group of threats, the most disturbing for Washington could be the drug trafficking and the migration that were considered as possible scenarios of war by the U.S. Army.

Because the problem of the drug traffic was already described in one of the sections, now we can turn to analyze in detail why migration is a topic of national security for the United States. According to data of the Immigration and Naturalization Service (INS), at this moment there are a little more than five million "illegal immigrants" in the United States, and accepting that figure, the following conclusions are highlighted:

- Almost three million "illegals" are immigrants that entered without inspection by the United States. Another group of migrants belongs to the category of immigrants that legally entered the country, but lengthened the period of stay granted in its entrance visa.
- Two million "illegal immigrants" reside in the state of California alone.
- 2.7 million "illegal immigrants" are Mexican.
- 275,000 people is the annual flow of illegal immigrants to the United States.

These figures reveal in a partial way the Mexican migratory scene, which should be supplemented by other data including the fact that approximately 13.5 million American citizens are of Mexican origin; that every year arrive to the border area more than 450,000 people with the intention of entering the United States, and that annually the flow of apprehended undocumented migrants and returned by the Border Patrol of the INS, is near 670,000 Mexicans.

"The annual net flow (the difference between entrances and exits) has been multiplied—in absolute terms—by more than 10 times in the last three decades, from an annual average of between 26,000 to 29,000 people in the decade of the 1960s, to near 300,000 migrants per year in the first five year period of the 1990s. As a consequence of this dynamic, the population born in Mexico that inhabits the United States reached in March 1996 a volume of between 7 and 7.3 million, of which between 4.7 and 4.9 million are documented residents and between 2.3 and 2.4 millions, are illegal aliens" (Tuiran, 1997:166).

The Current Population Survey of the United States allows us to identify some of the characteristics of these people born in Mexico that reside in the United States:

- The predominance of men (of the Mexican residents 55 percent are men and 45 percent women).
- The majority proportion represented by the youth and adults between 15 and 44 years of age (around 70 percent).
- The concentration of the Mexican residents in some states (California, Texas, Illinois, and Arizona) and counties of the United States. Around 90 percent of this population is in these few places (Tuiran, 1997).

The consequences of the magnitude of these figures for both sides of the frontier are ambivalent. In the case of the United States, certain political sectors try to use these figures to promote xenophobic attitudes, looking to discourage the migration and to attribute to these population flows diverse internal economic and social problems. "The dominant tendency has been the one of stereotyping the immigrants: they are defined as transgressors of the migratory legislation, as usurpers that take the jobs that belong by law to the American citizens and as directly responsible for many social problems" (Tuiran, 1997:158).

Nevertheless, those statements underrate the stabilizing role of migration as a safety valve for social conflicts and economic problems that could put in danger Mexico's internal order, with all the implications that this bears for the United States. Another detail that it is also ignored, or it is generally underrated in the American vision, is the economic importance of the Mexican migrants for some regions. For example, in the Tijuana-San Diego area—the most important for the migratory phenomenon—the Mexican community spends more than $2 billion annually. Paradoxically, in this same area, the repression of the migration is especially strong. The Border Patrol has more than twenty-four hundred agents and seven detection positions, plus five of the INS whose main task is to stop and to deport Mexican citizens who seek to enter the United States without authorization.

From Mexico's point of view, the economic importance of the migration is maybe even more visible. Besides being an escape valve of labor that cannot be used in Mexico, the remittances sent by the migrants to their relatives in their communities of origin have been of great importance for the development of some regions. "To give an idea of the importance of the productive use of the remittances in some local and regional contexts, we point out that at the beginning of the 1980s it was considered that around 16 percent of the small industrial companies in Jalisco,[25] they had been founded by migrants" (Tuiran, 1997:170).

Conclusions

Although the world has changed, and with it the form in which states are related to each other, and there are new realities of power, it is an undeniable fact that the traditional geopolitical factors have not lost all importance and they continue influencing in great measure the behavior of the states, and even many times, they still determine their priorities.

Among the most characteristic transformations in the world of post–Cold War period is the loss of influence of the developing countries that, when with the conclusion of the East-West conflict lose their attractive and/or their strategic character in the bipolar alignment and they become an economic burden and a threat of transmission of sociogeographic problems to the developed countries. Mainly, when the axis of confrontation for hegemony moves from the military field toward the economic one, the new alignments imply the search of commercial partners before military allies.

The relationship between Mexico and the United States has not escaped the remake of post-bipolar international order and its implications, but their geographical vicinity modifies the content of the transformation by the new order substantially. In this way, Mexico, as a member of the developing world that loses influence with the new order, consolidates its economic integration with the United States via NAFTA, when other similar countries as Brazil or Chile suffer the American protectionism. The Mexican case is different largely thanks to the unavoidable development of their primary nexus of interdependence with the American power on a shared and extensive frontier.

NAFTA has become prominent in the geoeconomic strategy of the post–Cold War period with the emergence of the economic blocs that compete with American hegemony. NAFTA has allowed the United States to compete in their own market, having in Mexico a much cheaper labor force and reexportation through intrafirm trade. But also, the power of the North has transformed Mexico into an export pattern toward the Latin American economies, in the context of the search of a continental agreement of free trade (FTAA).

In this sense, the current context of the geographical vicinity between both countries has allowed both to develop a policy of "associative cooperation," where the United States has collaborated in Mexico's insertion into the world networks of interdependence and, in return, Mexico promotes the idea of the Washington Consensus[26] intensely and its model of the promotion of the free trade with the United States for the rest of Latin America, in order to achieve the consolidation of the continental bloc that maintains American hegemony through the use of the advantages of the international division of labor.

The importance of the geographical vicinity can not only be observed in the commercial field, but, rather, it is evident in transcendental topics of the bilateral relationship like migration and drug trafficking, that affect the United States. For that reason Mexican history has as many American military interventions in internal matters, as financial rescues like the one that supposed financial crisis of 1995 after the "error of December of 1994"; and for that reason Mexico achieves the certification, year after year, in spite of the heated debate in the American Congress about the Mexican antidrug efforts.

An economic crisis in Mexico also effects the United States; not only in terms of fewer exports to our country, but in the massive migration of Mexicans toward the United States with all the economic and social conflicts that this implies. Also, a decertification of Mexico in the antidrug matter would have very similar effects, since it would not only mean the suspension of help to combat to the drug dealers, but also voting in the IMF against international lending that Mexico requests. There would be an enormous risk if the political transition—as is traditional—creates crisis, crisis impossible to overcome, even with the alternative credit lines that could arrive from the Asian Pacific or Europe.

Notes

1. It emphasizes the geographical location, the territorial domain, and the control of some strategical resources as principal factors of the status of power of a nation state and international behavior.

2. According to some authors, the attachment of Mexico to principles like nonintervention that have characterized to the Mexican foreign policy can also be explained in the same context.

3. The American territorial expansion during the nineteenth century was at the expense of a big part of the Mexican territory. In the twentieth century there were constant American incursions in the internal matters of Mexico and the latent or real invasions of the U.S. Army in Mexico like the occupation of Veracruz in 1914.

4. As Dziedzic points out (1997:85), the stability in the south frontier of the United States "was derived mainly of Mexico's one-party and pseudo-democratic order. Coincidentally, just when the Mexico's corporatist regime began to show serious signs of weakening, the Soviet empire succumbed to its lingering deterioration at the same time that it liberated to its satellite states and abandoned its neo-imperialist pretenses."

5. Jorge Chabat proposes the revision of some papers to document the consideration of NAFTA in the perspective of American national security by some of the American government's sectors, and the arguments about considering NAFTA as a topic of national security, among those Chabat highlights: "EU: el TLC sería de seguridad nacional," in *La Jornada*, August 8 1993, and, Paul Krugman, "The Uncomfortable Truth about NAFTA. Its Foreign Policy Stupid," in *Foreign Affairs*, vol. 72, no. 5, (November-December 1993).

6. The consideration of NAFTA inside the context of national security is reflective of the redefinition of the topic on both sides of the frontier that can be traced from the late 1980s. Since then the Mexican government is shown more open to discuss topics of national security and a schedule of bilateral security as part of the fundamental reformulation of its development project; it identifies new threats to their security, like drug production and trafficking; and it recognizes the existence of topics of security that concern both countries. By contrast, Washington reconsiders the concept of national security in the light of the appearance of commercial regional blocs and the emergence of new threats: transnational organized crime, terrorism, regional conflicts, disintegration of states, and uncontrolled movements of refugees.

7. According to Brzezinski, "The geopolitical pivots are the states whose importance is derived not from their power and motivation but rather from their sensitive location and from the consequences of their potentially vulnerable condition for the behavior of geostrategic players. Most often, geopolitical pivots are determined by their geography, which in some cases gives them a special role either in defining access to important areas or in denying resources to a significant player. In some cases, a geopolitical pivot may act as a defensive shield for a vital state or even a region. Sometimes, the very existence of a geopolitical pivot can be said to have very significant political and cultural consequences for a more active neighboring geostrategic player."

8. These possible scenarios are: (1) Gulliver's problems: the United States ends up exercising, at levels never seen, the function of world police and it begins to appear as overflowed by the terrorism and the local conflicts; (2) Zaibatsu, (the Japanese word to define a family corporation): in 2025 it will be the term to describe a world controlled by mega-corporations with enough capacity to move governments according to its necessities and, even, to buy the presidency of the United States in 2020; (3) digital cacophony: nearer to the usual visions about the future, it outlines a world dominated absolutely by the technology "it can be the best thing given to the individual and State, but it can also be the worst thing;" (4) crossroads 2015: it establishes an intermediate point to arrive at any one of the previous crossroads; (5) migratory hurricane: caused by a recession at the beginning of the XXI century; and (6) cartel of cartels, the product of the gathering of the Mexican drug dealers (*El Financiero,* January 18, 1998).

9. This is mainly because although the American influence on Bretton Woods's institutions or the WTO is imposed with relative ease on the underdeveloped economies of the planet. Generally, the developed countries are less susceptible to accepting this type of influence on the conduct of their economic and commercial policies.

10. Dynamics that increase their vulnerability vis-à-vis the big investors and the multinational companies, are already evident from the end of 1994 when the most recent Mexican crisis occurred.

11. Obviously this is in contrast with Brzezinski's point of view.

12. This is largely as strategic answer to the growing of globalized production.

13. For example, it is enough to point out that the automotive industry (a clear example of the globalized production and the most important item of NAFTA, due to the greatest speed that characterizes its integration) in spite of having the better paid workers inside the manufacturing field, receive salaries that represent just a tenth of the part of what is paid in the United States.

14. The Mexican figures related to trade and investment, principally in assembly plants, show a high degree of concentration toward the United States.

15. The United States figures show the growing importance of Mexico, especially after its consolidation as their second ranking commercial partner just after Canada and displacing Japan.

16. Let us remember that in these six years, Mexico has been constituted as the second ranking commercial partner of the United States, just after Canada and displacing Japan.

17. They have already opened up partially some sectors like the petrochemical one, and the dynamics seems to aim to a bigger privatization.

18. There are also important traditional sectors as the oil exploration and refinement, mining and aluminum manufacturing.

19. Data taken from the newspaper *Público,* January 28, 1999.

20. According to data of the SELA, in Mexico there are around 8,326 companies registered with American investment and 63.2 percent of these societies register with American majority capital. Hence the American capital in Mexico reaches an average of 85 percent.

21. Evident failure if we consider that the American government spends around $1.7 billion annually in its anti-drug plan (16 times higher than in 1980), while the purchase of narcotics constantly stays in ascent (it is calculated that 70 million North Americans have ingested, at least once in its life, some type of illegal drug).

22. Another explaining element of the antidrug current policy is that to keep the certification process could affect the support that the countries to the south of its frontiers—including Colombia and, mainly Mexico—to achieve the Americas' plans for the FTAA.

23. A High Intensity Drug Trafficking Area, according to the DEA is "that which fulfills three characteristics: it is a center of illegal production, manufacture, import or distribution of narcotics; it has a harmful impact in other areas of the country; and it may demand federal resources to combat the trade of enervating."

24. This because international trade and the economic opening are considered substitutes for migration when propitiating, both, the convergence of prices of productive factors.

25. It is necessary to point out that a significant proportion of the revenues of many communities located in states like Guanajuato, Jalisco, Michoacán, and Zacatecas also come from this source.

26. In spite of the considerations made by some international institutions, the post-Washington Consensus tries to overcome the big contradictions that the politics of structural adjustment created. Cf. Stiglitz, 1999.

Bibliography

Agnew, J., and S. Corbridge. (1995). *Mastering Space: Hegemony, Territory and International Political Economy.* London: Routledge.

Aguayo, S., and J. Bailey. (1997). "Estrategia y seguridad en las relaciones México-Estados Unidos." In S. Aguayo and J. Bailey, coords. *La Seguridad de México y Estados Unidos en un momento de Transición.* México City: Siglo XXI editores.

Alba, F. (1998). "Dialogo y Cooperación México-Estados Unidos en Materia Migratoria." In O. Pellicer & R. Fernández, coords. *México y Estados unidos; las rutas de la cooperación.* México City: Instituto Matías Romero (SRE) e Instituto Tecnológico Autónomo de México.

Barreda, Andrés, and R. Espinosa. "Los mapas el oro negro chiapaneco: el petróleo que no existía." *La Jornada,* retrieved from www.jornada.unam.mx.

Brzezinski, Z. (1997). *The Grand Chessboard: American Primacy and its Geostrategic Imperatives.* New York: Basic Books.

Cadena, J. (1991). "El Tratado de Libre Comercio México-Estados Unidos-Canadá y su impacto en América Latina, ponencia presentada en el Seminario," "Quinto encuentro de Ciencias Sociales. 1492–1992 Integración de América Latina," celebrada en Guadalajara, Jalisco, November 23–29.

Castañeda, J. (1993). *Utopia Unarmed.* New York: Vintage.

Chabat, J. (1996). "La integración de México al mundo de la posguerra fría: del nacionalismo a la interdependencia imperfecta." In A. Borja, G. González, and B. J. R. Stevenson, coords. *Regionalismo y Poder en América: los límites del neorrealismo.* México City: CIDE y Grupo Editorial Miguel Angel Porrua.

Dziedzic, M. J. (1997). "México y la gran estrategia de Estados Unidos: eje geoestratégico para la seguridad y prosperidad." In S. Aguayo and J. Bailey, coords. *La seguridad de México y Estados Unidos en un momento de transición.* México City: Siglo XXI Editores.

García, R. (1999). Representante de la Cámara Nacional de la Industria del vestido, durante su intervención en los Foros de Consulta realizados por la Comisión de Comercio del Senado dentro del proceso de evaluación del TLCAN a cinco años de su entrada en vigor. Cited in RMALC. *Boletín Alternativas, núm. 25,* May–June.

Garza, H. (1984). "Desequilibrios y contradicciones en la política exterior de México." *Foro Internacional,* vol. XXIV, no. 4, April.

González, G. (1997). "Los desafíos de la modernización inconclusa: estabilidad, democracia y seguridad nacional." In S. Aguayo and J. Bailey, coords. *Las seguridades de México y Estados unidos en un momento de transición.* México City: Siglo XXI Editores.

Hernández, E. (1998). "Estrategia antidrogas descertificada: reconfiguración de la hegemonía estadounidense." *El Financiero,* March 8.

La Feber, W. (1993). *Inevitable Revolutions: The United States in Central America.* 2nd ed. New York: W. W. Norton & Company.

López, V. (1991). "Los inicios de la posthegemonía norteamericana. La declinación en la Cuenca del Pacifico y la política de nuevas alianzas: el caso del Tratado de Libre Comercio con México," ponencia presentada en el "XVIII Congreso ALAS," celebrado en La Habana, Cuba, May 28–31.

Peñaloza, A. (1999). "La crisis sigue y los empleos no alcanzan: el TLCAN ha acentuado la vulnerabilidad de la economía mexicana y no ha cumplido su promesa de mejorar la calidad de vida." In RMALC. *Boletín Alternativas, núm. 25,* May–June.

Stiglitz, J. (1998). "Más instrumentos y metas más amplias para el desarrollo. Hacia el Consenso Post-Washington," *Revista Instituciones y Desarrollo, No. 1,* (Barcelona) October.

Tuiran, R. (1997). "La migración mexicana a Estados Unidos; tendencias presentes y desafíos futuros." In O. Pellicer and R. Fernández, coords. *México y Estados*

Unidos, las rutas de la cooperación, México City: Instituto Matías Romero (SRE) e Instituto Tecnológico Autónomo de México.

Villalba, A. (1999). Representante del Frente Autentico del Trabajo y la RMALC, durante su intervención en los Foros de Consulta realizados por la Comisión de Comercio del Senado dentro del proceso de evaluación del TLCAN a cinco años de su entrada en vigor. Cited in *Boletín Alternativas, núm. 25,* May–June.

Chapter 12

MERCOSUR: Democracy and Political Actors

Tullo Vigevani, Karina Pasquariello Mariano, Marcelo Fernandes de Oliveira, and Marilia Campus

There would be a variety of motives for international cooperation—thus also for regional integration—according to several authors. In a classic study, Aron (1962) suggests different forms or levels whereby states build up their relationships, among which temporary alliances, and permanent coalitions are often determined by geographic conditions.

From the late decades of the nineteenth to the early twentieth century, relationships between states have often taken the form of two-front alliances. Until the end of the Cold War prevailing issues were those of power distribution and of keeping global or regional equilibrium. In South America, such issues have also been at stake mainly around the Plata Basin and, particularly, within the relations between Brazil and Argentina—of which the history from the nineteenth century on is not the object of the present chapter.

Aron (1962:125) also points out that "states' behavior toward others is not driven uniquely by power relations; rather, decisions made by international actors are influenced by ideas and feelings," which, by the way, is an issue intensely debated upon by contemporary constructivists (Wendt, 1994; Adler, 1997; Checkel, 1998). In other words, the issue on the nature of political regime and institutions, much dealt with at the end of the twentieth century, has not been irrelevant to international relations through previous decades, particularly to the various forms of cooperation among states. The distinction made by Aron (1962) between homogeneous and heterogeneous systems may enlighten this. According to him, a system is heterogeneous when states involved are organized under different principles, whereas an homogeneous system assembles similarly organized states.

In the case of MERCOSUR, it may be said that, among Argentina, Brazil, Paraguay, and Uruguay, as well as the free-trading associates Bolivia and Chile, one of the important factors that has driven the integration process in the 1980s, particularly between Argentina and Brazil, was the perception of common values shared in their respective societies, especially that of democracy. A starting point for the discussion on democracy and MERCOSUR political actors may thus be the acknowledgement that some of the necessary conditions are present, though not sufficient, for successful integration.

It is worth remarking that the democratic issue in MERCOSUR has been considered, from the beginning, a vital one for regional integration. Governments have always been concerned with assuring legitimacy to negotiations therein, seeking to incorporate various society representatives along the process. In fact, the concern with the democratic regime in countries taking part in MERCOSUR has acquired increasing importance within regional integration for, in as much as this progresses, impacts upon society become more conspicuous and bring about a mobilization of the interests involved therein. Provided that the integration process does not suffer serious interruptions—and on the contrary, if it gets deeper—it is likely to generate new demands and a need for improving society's lobbying channels, including the creation of new mechanisms for influence or intervention.

Ever since its beginning in 1991, there has been room for legislative participation by means of the MERCOSUR Joint Parliamentary Commission. In the Brazilian case, and that can be generalized for the other countries involved, participating in this institutional forum has brought about little influence on the integration process and scarce representation of political and social interests. In the medium and long run, we believe, it is likely that such pressures and interests will be sufficiently organized so as to become determinant factors in shaping MERCOSUR. For the time being, and after almost ten years of existence, the evolution of this regional bloc is still basically defined and controlled by government agencies in charge of its operation: in the Brazilian case, the ministers for foreign affairs, economy, and planning.

This chapter discusses a few issues currently under analysis by CEDEC (Centro de Estudos de Cultura Contemporânea) in the scope of the pro-

ject titled "MERCOSUR: The Emergence of a New Society." The starting point of such analysis is the belief that the integration process will
likely give rise to issues beyond current trade matters, requiring increased
participation of political actors. Furthermore, results obtained so far tend
to increasingly affect the everyday life of populations involved, thus creating more favorable conditions for higher interest and mobilization around
the issue of regional integration. Such interest, in turn, also may lead to the
incorporation of this theme into the negotiation agenda of political parties, attracting attention and even votes, and eventually making both politicians and voters rank for and against the integration. Nevertheless, as will
be seen ahead, neither such process directions, deepening, stagnation, or
crisis may be previously determined.

Within this framework, the present text analyzes the intersection between MERCOSUR integration process and current political interests,
seeking to ponder to what degree integration will be included among national political parties' interests. The themes of democracy and political actors are dealt with in their interrelations by addressing four aspects: (a) the
formal evolution of the issue of democracy in MERCOSUR creation and
development; (b) structural motives for the bloc countries to adhere to the
value of democracy; (c) the participation of Brazilian political parties and
other agencies that express representative democracy, particularly the Joint
Parliamentary Commission, its role and activity; and (d) a case study of the
sugar trade, exemplary of concrete forms of political actors' mobilization
in their relations with society at large.

Democracy in Constituting Treaties

The understanding of much of recent problems involving MERCOSUR
is linked to an appraisal on how democracy is understood and how so-
called universal values are shared among its various members. At the outset of integration between Brazil and Argentina in the mid-1980s, during
the administrations Alfonsín and Sarney, planners believed that the redemocratization process taking place in both countries would lever and make
possible the necessary social consensus to strengthen their countries' capacity of international negotiation. Furthermore, the very alliance between
them would be an important factor to the same aim. In other words, both
democracy and the onset—for the first time in the region—of important
forms of cooperation between the two countries should strengthen them
and provide protection against the risks already at sight then, brought

about by international economy new phases—U.S. Trade Acts of 1984 and 1988, the Uruguay GATT rounds as of 1986, the globalization of production systems.

That was a time to seek to understand the changes operating at the international level, to recognize the fall of CEPAL developmentism prevailing through the 1950s and 1960s, and to accept that relatively protectionist forms would no longer be tolerated. By contrast, economic space broadening from national to regional might induce economic growth, requiring increasing competitiveness in order to adapt countries to the new times.

The democracy issue was an important theme for integration, even though it was not explicit on the Asunción Treaty. In fact, on this founding document of MERCOSUR, signed on March 26, 1991, by presidents Menem from Argentina, Collor de Mello from Brazil, Rodríguez from Paraguay, and Lacalle from Uruguay, issues addressed are mostly economic, related to the constitution of a common market—commodities, services, production factors, common tariffs toward third countries—laying down the grounds for the articulation of sector and macroeconomic policies. Although implicit, the democracy issue was no doubt underlying the regional agreement; a clear indication of this is the fact that Paraguay was only accepted into the negotiations after the end of the Stroessner era.

The historical reasons for such assembling, as analyzed elsewhere, are remote. A clear starting point was the agreement signed by military regimes of Videla (Argentina) and Figueiredo (Brazil) in October 1979 as a result of tripartite negotiations around the waterpower potential of Parana River, from which derived the construction of hydroelectric Corpus (between Argentina and Paraguay) and Itaipu (between Brazil and Paraguay) plants. The following negotiations as of 1985, between Alfonsín and Sarney, aimed at strengthening national economies. Apparently these countries' aims were then to reach technical economic progress within an environment of democracy consolidation, besides that of improving their competing capabilities in the world market (Peña, 1992).

In this new disposition for cooperation in the Southern Cone it is worth underlining the shift from a situation of noncooperative competition, originating from the nineteenth century but prevailing through most of the twentieth, to a situation where part of the national elites in both countries start to recognize advantages deriving from regional integration policies. Within this perspective, on November 30, 1985, was signed the Iguaçu Declaration, emphasizing the consolidation of the democratic process, the assembling of efforts for joint defense of both countries' interests in international fora, and the shared usage of common resources. The full economic dimension of this new political relationship was reached on July 29, 1986, when the Argentine-Brazilian Integration Act created the Program for Integration and Economic Cooperation (PICE); 24 protocols were signed.

Central to the understanding of present difficulties involving MERCOSUR is the assessment of the two countries' basic motivations for the integration process: Brazilian policymakers, mostly at the Ministry for Foreign Affairs, were concerned with international insertion, whereas their Argentine counterparts wagered on modernization and the possibility of reaching a market almost thrice the size of theirs (Caputo and Sabato, 1991).

With such motivations, on November 29, 1988, both countries signed the Treaty for Integration, Cooperation, and Development, establishing a ten-year term for setting a common economic area, with no tariff or other barriers for commodities and service trade, and aiming at the convergence of their macroeconomic policies. With the exception of the latter, those goals were reached within a much shorter time span—the coordination of macroeconomic policies has certainly not been achieved until the end of the 1990s, being one among relevant factors for the 1999 to 2000 crisis in these countries relations. Following 1989 elections, new presidents (in Argentina, Menem, and in Brazil, Collor de Mello) openly supporting liberal ideas such as free trade and economic liberalization, regional integration was then seen as a means to put them in force. The two presidents signed the Buenos Aires Act in July 1990, setting December 31, 1994, as the deadline for the setting of a common market between both countries, thus anticipating by five years the onset of "common customs" foreseen for 1998 (Barbosa, 1991; Almeida, 1998).

As to Uruguay, already linked to Argentina and Brazil by means of the Agreements for Economic Complementation within ALADI (Latin America Association for Integration), its joining in was consolidated during that phase. In August, 1990 Paraguay was also invited to take part in the negotiations that would lead to formalization of the regional bloc in the following year, as described above.

Reading through MERCOSUR documents from the Asunción Treaty on shows clearly that economic themes prevail. The Treaty foreword deals with democracy only at its last paragraph, where it is stated that "political will must lay the bases for ever tightening links between their peoples." Besides, another statement has gained political meaning—which was to become a matter of controversy between Argentina and Brazil at the end of the 1990s—by pointing to the role of the "evolution of international affairs, specially the consolidation of huge economic spaces, and [to] the importance of member countries' achieving an adequate international insertion" (*apud* Almeida 1998:95). Along the Treaty, all six chapters with its 24 articles deal only with economics and trade issues, or with administrative matters, the same happening to its five appendices.

Likewise, on the Ouro Preto Protocol, signed on December 17, 1994, to formally install the incomplete "common customs," thus closing the transition period to the common market, all 12 chapters and 53 articles concentrate on organizational and economic issues. This document determines that the Common Market Council—made up by ministers of foreign affairs and economy, and counting on the biannual presence of member state presidents—is responsible for the political conduction of the integration process; however, council assignments do not include those related to maintaining democracy or democratic stipulations.

The Joint Parliamentary Commission, in operation since 1991 following the Asunción Treaty, became a full part of MERCOSUR institutional structure in 1995, being assigned some new functions. Its role has not been widened though: according to article 26 of Ouro Preto Protocol, all it must do is to refer recommendations to the Council through the Common Market Group. Nevertheless, it is worth noting that the commission has discussed its own possibilities of contribution to integration, as will be seen ahead, such as to accelerate internal processes, to act as a consultant agency to the council, or to cooperate in seeking legislation compatibility, but, on the formal level, has not had any role in fostering democratic debate on integration, nor any control on enacting democratic principles within the four member-countries.

The other agency created by the Ouro Preto Protocol was the Economic-Social Consulting Forum, which might have played a role in condensing social and democratic interests, since its function is to act as speaker for the economic and social sectors. Besides its merely consulting character, limited to issuing recommendations to the Council, it suffers from lack of precision of its functions and of operational difficulties.

In spite of the omission from legal documents, though, and of the controversy on the definition of relations between democracy and integration in the case of MERCOSUR, this regional bloc has indeed had a role in reinforcing democratic values and, we believe, in consolidating them. In order to discuss this perspective, we must first take an overview on the debate on democracy and its meaning, so as to examine how these values interacted in MERCOSUR political evolution.

Democratic Motivations within Integration

In order to examine the issue of democracy, or better, the effectiveness of the informal democratic clause in the case of MERCOSUR, one must address a question that concerns the international system at large: whether this bloc should be considered an association based on shared goals or a practical one. This question will probably gain relevance in the coming years. The answer to it will show whether the regional bloc, by surviving apparently conjunctured albeit deep crises, will consolidate itself on the basis of common interests shared by the societies, or will vanish as a meaningful proposal, even if it survives as a free-trading agreement.

So far, judging from the autonomous manifestations of its member governments (on matters such as the United Nations Security Council, the proposal to integrate NATO, the FTAA negotiations, or currency devaluation), MERCOSUR has shown that it can not be considered a shared-goals association. This kind of association implies—using an extreme metaphor—a shared *weltanschauung,* even if not thoroughly, whereas shared values in a practical association are only those necessary to maintain relations with no reference to common goals, in a situation where states are forced to interact, led by concrete needs, but sharing no common perspective (Nardin, 1987). In the post–Cold War era, a rising debate might be placed within the field of shared-goals association, that brings themes like democracy to the center of international relations; according to Nardin (1987:27), "It is common practices, rather than shared goals, that offer conditions for international association." Thus, the incorporation of democratic values would be one of the elements to assess the success of regional integration. In other words, such success may be foreseen by verifying whether its process consolidates shared values, or comes down to a convenient practical association, though solid, where there could be shared goals, but not a strong common perspective.

Ever since Westphalia (1648), the international system has not shown common norms in its basic conceptual structure—at least until the end of the twentieth century. One of regional bloc's roles, among others, would be that of introducing mutually accepted common rules that might be politically and juridically accepted, even through coercion. In the analysis of the democratic issue within MERCOSUR, that which matters is to understand the meaning of norms and the fact that, even if in most cases they are put forward by the strongest, they do not exclude the possibility of serving the weakest. Recent MERCOSUR events expose this rationale, such as the institutional crises in Paraguay in early 1996 and 1999, both linked to the role of the armed forces, particularly to General Oviedo.

As it is well known, MERCOSUR as a process of regional integration relies on the principle of intergovernability, the idea of supranationality having been rejected mainly by Argentina and Brazil. Bull (1995) supports the idea that through history the interstate system has allowed for rendering norms compatible to anarchy, leading to the prevalence of some common norms. We believe that, in spite of intergovernability, democratic principles have in fact been reaffirmed in the regional bloc. Such standing is not spontaneous and is linked to current changes in the international system. It is a theoretical, as well as a practical, issue.

In April 1996, when General Oviedo threatened Paraguay's constitutional president Wasmosy, a response centered on ambassadors from the United States (Service), Brazil (Oliveira Dias), and Argentina (Auad) rapidly led to the failure of the attempt against formal legality. Their arguments included threats to political and economic isolation, including the risk of freezing Paraguay participation in MERCOSUR, and eventually brought about an agreement that basically secured constitutional order (Mariano and Oliveira, 1999).

The trend to universal consolidation of democracy as a value is due to different factors. The matrix of this phenomenon is closely linked to liberal-democratic values that have become hegemonic through the past 50 years. Side by side with, and complementing power relations, soft-power has been gaining relevance (Nye, 1992), with the double advantage of absorbing the idea of hegemony and of effectively meeting peoples' interests. Forces other than the states strengthen some trends, mostly those linked to so-called universal values. More actors perform international roles and bring new interests into the international scene. According to Bonanate (1989), if such interests resulted in international regimes, the latter would thus be in position of dictating behavior rules. In an extreme interpretation, the political behavior of each national state and each society would be guided by universal values rather than by national logic, those values being transferred to the sphere of regional blocs and into every state.

In the interpretation of major sectors of the Brazilian state, international regimes capacity of imposing their rules onto states and societies is linked to the existence of a compact. Meaningful for the understanding of MERCOSUR interjection of democratic values is that, for these Brazilian sectors—but the same applies to part of national elites in Argentina, Paraguay, and Uruguay, though to variable degrees, and even to those in Chile and Bolivia—the fact that these values result from a compact does not imply its rejection. They may be in accordance to those prevailing in each country, which implies positive attitudes to support regimes, even though these are backed by an international consensus with the explicit support of powerful countries (Fonseca Jr., 1999). Thus, the convergence of interests between such concert and countries like Brazil, concerning some but not all values, would be signaling a potential to increasing stability rules, including those related to regional policies, and specially to MERCOSUR. Attachment to democratic values would be one of those cases of coincidence of interests, thus favoring the stability of the integration process.

Inquiring into the reasons for Brazil's low profile and faint performance in matters related to softpower, Hurrel (1999) suggests this could result in weakening the country's position in the international system, and it might interfere in the very process of regional integration. In as much as other MERCOSUR countries would comply more easily to the logic of concert, this might weaken regional cohesion. This is a valid questioning, of which the answer lies in that to the elites—its larger part, in the Brazilian case—some, but not all, hegemonic values coincide with Brazilian interests.

Within MERCOSUR, the issue of adherence to democracy has become an apparently homogeneous subject, there being a consensus about it among governments and decisive sectors of their respective societies. But the same cannot be said concerning other issues, on which rich countries' positions are differently interpreted by every MERCOSUR government. An empirical example of this is the issue of the Pinochet Spanish trial and his extradition from the United Kingdom: Paradoxically, a certain homogeneity in region countries' positions also may be interpreted as a concern for Chile's democratic stability; there are certainly other interpretations, specially those linked to the ways the concept of national sovereignty is valued.

Another factor must be taken into account when studying democracy in MERCOSUR: in the current historical phase, besides state actors, nonstate ones gain importance, as mentioned. There is certainly an increasing concern on the subject by public opinion and nongovernment organizations. Opinion trends, organized movements, the media, all express powerful forces favoring not only democracy but also human rights, national rights, social rights, and minorities' rights. The direction of such pressure is not fully disconnected from hegemonic, concert interests. But, in most cases, these same pressures coincide with the wishes of large social layers and classes.

Furthermore, within the regional level an apparently universal movement also takes place, dislodging themes that had been historically functional to the logic of difference and competition—traditional in Argentina-Brazil relationships—making room for others that require cooperative forms. For instance, the very fact that Task Force 10 of the Common Market Group, devoted to labor and social issues, is discussing legislation compatibility—so far with scarce results—strengthens social actors involved, who notice that their participation in MERCOSUR is a valuable tool to heighten their bargaining capacity at home (Vigevani, 1998). Such perception is certainly not new: intergovernment liberals have analyzed this in the beginning of the 1980s, when studying the European Economic Community, showing that actors see in regional cooperation an advantageous tool for their own interests. Another issue to take into consideration, when examining the basis for democratic motivations within MERCOSUR, is linked to the debate on the so-called crisis of the state that, in addition to the phenomenon generically known as globalization, fosters the rising role of non-government actors who, in turn, influence national, regional, and international agendas.

All processes of regional integration have had to deal with, and welcome, democratic aspirations of participation. Even though the European Union is the most developed experience, democratic and participatory pressures have also been exerted within MERCOSUR and NAFTA, and are already visible in the negotiation processes of FTAA and the free-trading area between the European Union and MERCOSUR. Such participation consists in a facet of democracy other than that of liberal political representation. It is clear that, in the past ten years, the articulation of civil society, lobbies, and public opinion, even if often intertwining to state interests, has indeed interfered with the position of powerful states. In the case of MERCOSUR, relatively new and less systematically studied, it may be said that democracy benefits the integration process—which is not an obvious trend. Some studies show that, in general, the capacity of mobilization of groups negatively affected is bigger than that of those who are benefited. In a moment of crisis, fairly intense social sectors' mobilization in favor of the integration process continuity is a clear sign of the positive weight of democracy toward consolidation of the regional bloc.

The crisis experienced in 1999 has shown governments that there is a broad social basis to whom MERCOSUR is a conspicuous reality and in whose view a setback in the process would be negative to at least a part of national and class interests. An example of this is the fact that, during 1999 presidential election campaign in Argentina, both candidates—Duhalde, *justicialista,* and Radical-FREPASO De la Rúa—were led, probably by electoral motives, to declare themselves in favor of deepening the integration process. To a certain degree, that is the same position taken by Brazilian government. In other words—and this seems a relevant, although optimistic, conclusion—a virtuous circle would arise between the integration process and consolidation of a democratic perspective, concerning both Schumpeter's (1979) democracy rules and the heightening of participation expectations, which in turn reminds us of Dahl's analysis (1985) on the forms of mass integration into democracy.

Anchored on a certain notion of globalization, the rising debate on the concept of public cosmopolitan sphere (Archibugi, Held, and Kohler, 1998) would partially apply to MERCOSUR. Integration encourages debate on the idea of association based on shared goals, rather than that of practical association. The concept of a public cosmopolitan sphere, even if applied only to the regional level, implies increasing homogeneity on normative questions that would make up the collective will of regional bloc states. The weakening or failure of democracy in one state, for instance, would encourage the debate on the formalization of the democratic clause, already discussed by heads of state in their biannual meeting in December 1998 in Rio de Janeiro. Thus it might be thought that if a member state broke the rules of democratic play, it would be excluding itself from MERCOSUR.

Although nothing has been formally written about it, this theme can be read between the lines at every semester's presidential declarations. Concerning the concept of public cosmopolitan sphere, part of the powerful political and social actors feel that democratic conditions within states are determined by three converging parameters: the international hegemonic regimes; the four countries' historically recent democratic evolution; and the regional public sphere, which would encourage exclusion of a nondemocratic state. Thus the joining three parameters, among which that of the public sphere, would definitely favor defense of democracy.

Once again the 1996 and 1999 Paraguay experiences may be taken as an example. The three parameters have been effective during the crises. In terms of international relations, the relevant actors were the American, Argentine, and Brazilian embassies, as well as European Union governments. In June 1996, the Brazilian president Cardoso traveled to Asunción with the explicit aim to "reaffirm both Brazil and MERCOSUR interest in keeping up democratic institutionality in Paraguay" (Mariano and Oliveira, 1999:267). In 1998, while the election campaign was taking place in Paraguay, during a meeting of the World Economic Forum in Davos both presidents Menem and Cardoso issued statements where it was clear, though not explicit, that an interruption in Paraguayan democratic process would lead to the cessation of the country's benefits from MERCOSUR. In the crisis at the beginning of 1999, the intervention by MERCOSUR countries, as well as the United States and the European Union, was again crucial to avoid institutional discontinuity.

In this search to understand the relevance of democracy for integration, one final factor must be underlined: Among the reasons for regional cooperation, one of the motives is the need, felt by each member state, to reduce the degree of uncertainty toward the others' behavior; through time, this leads to the creation of various structures within which mutually advantageous agreements may be negotiated. Such structures, in turn, influence states' behaviors, who then consider or expect the other actors' actions to follow the rules, norms, and conventions previously established by all. This means acknowledging and accepting a certain institutionality, even in the case of intergovernability-based processes such as MERCOSUR. Of course, the mere existence of a democratic regime by itself is no guarantee of rule continuity; but compliance to constitution, to laws and institutions allow for enduring stability.

In MERCOSUR moments of crises (like the one in 1999 and 2000), some leading actors have pleaded for a higher degree of institutionality (Lampreia, 1999), like the creation of a Permanent Arbitration Court; this reveals a trend to higher cohesion and to widening common structures. In fact, crises have been generated precisely by those unforeseen, or disagreed on, actions such as the Brazilian currency devaluation in January 1999, or by Argentina quota imposing on Brazilian imports like shoes, textiles, and steel in June 1999. Such crisis could be prevented by the creation of structures that might help prevent or at least manage them. Although these are measures of administrative nature, the perspective underlying such proposals is that integration is of common interest. Coming back to the discussion on the relevance of democracy, it must be stressed that creating transparency tools in the relations between states also strengthens integration.

According to Lafer (1997:253), "From the moment Argentine and Brazilian policy makers became aware that ambiguities of any nature did not serve their real interests, a change took place in the nature of their relations, so that all that previously appeared as a tie-ending game could now be seen as convergence and joint effort." Still following this author, MERCOSUR would be a means for the four countries to show the world "they have the shared interest to promote themselves to the condition of centers of a stable and peaceful subregion that does not threaten international peace and security; of poles of a dynamic and open integration process; and of partners, as far as values are concerned, in the building of an international order based on democracy and the human rights" (Lafer, 1997:260). In this perspective, democracy is not only intrinsic to the possibility of anticipating each other's next step, but also to integration itself and its unfolding, concerning both institutions and the compatibility of political and moral values.

Political Participation in MERCOSUR

We have so far discussed the ways by which the idea of democracy is incorporated to the MERCOSUR constituting process, by trying to understand how this value is viewed by states and how it is absorbed in interstate relations within the bloc. In this section, we examine the bloc internal mechanisms of democratic control, seeking to understand which instruments are used in the building of MERCOSUR and how the actors assert their interests. We have chosen to examine the position of Brazilian political parties and the role of the Joint Parliamentary Commission, since legislative processes are at the basis of the democratic system.

Building a legislative body within an integration process is almost a constant along known processes that aim beyond a free-trading area; it is the case of the European Union, of the Andean Pact, and also of MERCOSUR. There are possibly two reasons for this: the need to create channels for the expression of society's demands; and advocacy for democracy as a fundamental value for integration. In the case of MERCOSUR, as seen, it may be said that since the Iguaçu Declaration (1985) through Asunción Treaty (1991) to the Ouro Preto Protocol (1994), integration has been seen as basically economic, the main actors being government top-ranking officials and business managers, the latter considered as the most dynamic agents. By contrast, a forum joining representatives from national congresses was created; and, recognizing that even a body of representatives of the whole population—such as direct-vote elected European Parliament—would not be able to represent all interests, the Economic-Social Consulting Forum was installed.

From the beginning of the process, congressmen of the four countries have not been a part of the integration movement, possibly for two reasons. At the beginning it was not clear how the cooperation would take place and the internal processes of redemocratization in Brazil and Argentina gave way to demands that have greatly mobilized parties, congressmen, politicians. The intensity of the internal agenda implied scarce concern, by society and its representatives, with the issue of institutionally organizing the integration process, thus leaving a relative autonomy for negotiators from both countries to direct it following their own points of view. Besides, this lack of concern is not exclusive of MERCOSUR. According to Schmitter (1998) and to functionalist theory in general, the adherence of parties and politicians to integration is linked to the degree to which debate on integration would yield prestige and votes; thus actors in general, and particularly politicians, act according to integration impacts. The present analysis is grounded on the idea that the higher the actors' sensibility to MERCOSUR decisions and effects, the greater their will and mobilization to influence the process. In as much as MERCOSUR is incorporated into everyday life of societies it will gain importance in national political party agendas.

Brazilian Political Parties and Regional Integration

Brazilian political parties seem to follow what may be called a reactive logic, as if waiting for impacts to be felt, and adopting the traditional attitude along which regional integration is a matter of foreign policy, hence should be dealt with by the federal government and diplomats. So far MERCOSUR has not been incorporated as a relevant subject into their political action strategy and is practically only dealt with at the moment of Congressional approval of international agreements to be signed by the federal government. Unconcern for the issue of integration is thus linked both to the broadness of national agenda and to the idea that foreign policy is not Congress's affair.

Traditionally Brazilian political parties assign priority to what is usually called "the great national themes." These are, in brief: in the economic sphere, stabilization, growth, reduction of unemployment, and so on; in the political sphere, the reform of political and party systems, the federation; and in the social sphere, education, health, violence. Democracy and its consolidation underlies these debates. With such an agenda, foreign policy is understandably neglected by Congress, all the more so that there is a federal office exclusively devoted to it, the Ministry of Foreign Affairs. Beyond an office, this ministry is rather a school of thought where strategies for international insertion are planned, relying on its large tradition and experience on Brazilian foreign policy.

Although there is some logic in the parties' neglect of foreign affairs, in many cases foreign and home policies interact. According to Lima (1994), in spite of a generalized belief in continuity and consensus, there have been significant changes in Brazil's international position brought about by changes in internal political relations. Besides, MERCOSUR does not fit that clear distribution of assignments. If, on the one hand, it is a subject duly dealt with and coordinated by the Foreign Affairs, on the other hand, its effects are closely linked to national issues. As integration deepens, MERCOSUR increasingly influences societies' everyday life, thus requiring their representatives clear standing. Since Brazil is the largest among member countries, such influence, yet significant, is proportionally less felt.

In such context, political parties in general are scarcely prepared to face new the challenges, having no established position as to the various dimensions of the process of regional integration. The Brazilian Section of the MERCOSUR Joint Parliamentary Commission, during the Brazilian Congress' fiftieth term (1994–1998), was made up by representatives from the biggest national parties (Table 12.1).

It is interesting to note that, save two, all representatives come from southern (and a southwestern) states sharing borders with other MERCOSUR countries; to these must be added the representative from São Paulo who, because of this state's top ranking in industry and trade, is strongly interested in the matter. The same distribution repeats itself in the

Table 12.1 Brazilian Representatives and Respective Parties at the MERCOSUR Joint Parliamentary Commission, 1994–1998

Party	Representative	Position	State of the Federation, Region
PMDB	José Fogaça	Senator	Rio Grande do Sul, South
PMDB	Casildo Maldaner	Senator	Paraná, South
PMDB	Paulo Ritzel	Deputy	Rio Grande do Sul, South
PMDB	Valdir Colatto	Deputy	Santa Catarina, South
PFL	Wilson Kleinubing	Senator	Santa Catarina, South
PFL	Romero Jucá	Senator	Roraima, North
PFL	Paulo Bornhausen	Deputy	Santa Catarina, South
FPL	Luciano Pizzato	Deputy	Paraná, South
PPB	Osmar Dias	Senator	Paraná, South
PPB	Epiridião Amin	Senator	Santa Catarina, South
PPB	Júlio Redecker	Deputy	Rio Grande do Sul, South
PPB	Dilceu Sperafiro	Deputy	Paraná, South
PSDB	Lúdio Coelho	Senator	Mato Grosso do Sul, Center-West
PSDB	Franco Montoro	Deputy	São Paulo, South-East
PTB	Emília Fernandes	Senator	Rio Grande do Sul, South
PT	Miguel Rosseto	Deputy	Rio Grande do Sul, South

Source: Comissão Parlamentar Conjunta, 1996.

Brazilian Section of the MERCOSUR Joint Parliamentary Commission during the Congress fifty-first term (1999–2002) (Table 12.2).

Again, all but three representatives come from states directly linked to the MERCOSUR issue. Such geographical distribution probably reflects southern states' public opinion's greater interest in subjects related to integration.

We have analyzed the programs of all parties that commission representatives are affiliated to, for these have the strongest say on the issue of integration. By reading through these parties' programs, though, it may be said, none has incorporated the theme of MERCOSUR; only at times is the subject of regional integration mentioned in a generic way.

On the PMDB (*Partido do Movimento Democrático Brasileiro*) program, approved at the 1994 National Convention and ratified for publication at the 1996 Convention, the assertion on international relations' basic principles indicates the party "sturdily defends national interests, understood as Brazilian people's interests in preserving both the territory and national sovereignty, in strengthening cultural autonomy, productive and trading capacity, as well as the defense of other strategic country's goals" (PMDB,

Table 12.2   Brazilian Representatives and Respective Parties at the MERCOSUR Joint Parliamentary Commission, 1999–2002

Party	Representative	Position	State of the Federation, Region
PMDB	José Fogaça	Senator	Rio Grande do Sul, South
PMDB	Casildo Maldaner	Senator	Santa Catarina, South
PMDB	Roberto Requião	Senator	Paraná, South
PMDB	Confúcio Moura	Deputy	Roraima, North
PMDB	Germano Rigotto	Deputy	Rio Grande do Sul, South
PFL	Jorge Bornhausen	Senator	Santa Catarina, South
PFL	Geraldo Althoff	Senator	Santa Catarina, South
PFL	Ney Lopes	Deputy	Rio Grande do Norte, North-East
PFL	Santos Filho	Deputy	Paraná, South
PSDB	Álvaro Dias	Senator	Paraná, South
PSDB	Pedro Piva	Senator	São Paulo, South-East
PSDB	Nelson Marchezan	Deputy	Rio Grande do Sul, South
PSDB	Feu Rosa	Deputy	Espírito Santo, South-East
PPB	Júlio Redecker	Deputy	Rio Grande do Sul, South
PTB	Emília Fernandes	Senator	Rio Grande do Sul, South
PT	Luiz Mainardi	Deputy	Rio Grande do Sul, South

Source: Câmara dos Deputados, 2000; Senado Federal, 2000.

1998:4). For this party, thus, regional integration, hence MERCOSUR, is not linked to the issue of defending national interests; the emphasis on the various aspects of Brazilian nationality (cultural, economic, etc.) is not followed by a concern on building a shared regional space seeking to provide better living conditions for all peoples of the region.

In the party's view, in international relations the national state is predominant and exclusive, hence the party focuses on formulating and accomplishing the national project. Processes of regional cooperation must be taken into account only in so far as they are complementary to national interest; the party's activity leads it to reaffirm differences and specific interests: "PMDB considers that the indispensable, active, and strong Brazilian presence at the UN, GATT, IMF, World Bank and other international agencies, and at the Latin-American Parliament, MERCOSUR, Amazon Pact and other regional organizations and agencies, must seek above all the negotiated solution to bilateral or international questions. But the party will always be ready to face any difficulty that hinders the national project" (PMDB, 1998:22).

Thus, the party declares in advance the supremacy of national interests over any difficulty that might be brought by regional cooperation. Such an attitude narrows the capacity to negotiate and accommodate interests. In other words, MERCOSUR would be a strategic way of consolidating the national project, rather than a process of regional integration that aimed at asserting common interests of member countries in the international scenery. Theories on international cooperation suggest that the insertion of national interest in a regional perspective is a limitation on the success of integration processes.

Part of the reasons for such attitude may be due to the MERCOSUR institutional structure, for related decision making is held by the executive. Thus, a party's standing of autonomy or opposition toward ruling government might lead to opposing the very process of regional integration. By contrast, generally, parties' performance at the national level show that their own dynamics and rooting in society contribute to their own foreign policy formulations. The fact that PMDB is mainly devoted to the national scope, often aiming at tactical aims, hinders the perception of the importance of foreign relations, of which the effects, save on moments of sharp crisis, are mildly felt by society.

The PFL (*Partido da Frente Liberal*) program doesn't mention MERCOSUR or regional integration. The party's pragmatic standing reflects on its view on foreign policy. This is a concise program, made up of ideological norms, principles, and interpretations of the country's political, economic, social, and cultural reality, drawing on what is thought to be a liberal standing. These principles form the party's theoretical framework, from which members draw party directives expressed through concrete actions toward the country's government and social relations. Thus, PFL views on foreign policy, and particularly on MERCOSUR, are only manifest at those moments when party members' interests, or those of the economic and social elites that it represents, are directly affected.

The PSDB (*Partido da Social Democracia Brasileira*) program also does not mention MERCOSUR specifically, drawing only basic directives on Brazilian foreign policy. According to it, attentive to issues of Latin American integration, diplomacy must aim at the country's long-term goals: "Foreign policy has a strategical importance for the country's development. Brazil must keep on fostering dialogue within international scenery, and relationships based on cooperation and non-confront. The traditional long-term goals of Brazilian foreign policy—sovereignty, self determination, security, and territory integrity—must be secured through active diplomacy in issues such as Latin American integration and external debt, as well as in moves toward world peace" (PSDB, 1998:11).

PSDB's standing, as well as that of PFL's, differs from that of remaining parties in as much as these form the ruling coalition under President Fernando Henrique Cardoso's two terms of office (1995 to 1998 and 1999 to 2002), which eventually means they are coresponsible for MERCOSUR negotiations. Both parties' standing is thus linked to that of the Brazilian state. Again, the reason for the MERCOSUR omission on PSDB program is probably because this is not a central theme on the national agenda. While MERCOSUR is not an important matter to social and political life, and, specially, has no potential to bring in votes, its exclusion from the party program tends to be harmless. In other words, it seems integration is not an object of power dispute. PPB (*Partido Progressista Brasileiro*) program, titled *Organizational and Administrative Sate Directives,* establishes at item 18 the party's standing concerning Brazilian foreign policy. According to it, the country must sustain a policy that will:

- maintain respect for peoples' self determination and peaceful solution to conflicts;
- honor UN action and principles (. . .), as well as other documents by which the country is committed to, defending its participation in equal standing in all international bodies;
- avoid automatic alignment, and foster frank dialogue with all members of international community;

- promote increasing political and economic integration into Latin America aiming at strengthening regional agreements and the continental community;
- advocate further participation of developing countries in wealth benefits and a more equitable world political and economic power sharing;
- assure the protection of our country's natural resources, as well as of the prices of our export commodities, with a view to strengthening our currency and bringing wealth to the country. (PPB, 1996:17)

As it may be seen, PPB sketches general, broad lines for Brazilian state foreign policy. Like on the other party's programs, regional integration is generically supported, without mention to controversial themes.

The PTB (*Partido Trabalhista Brasileiro*, Brazilian Labour Party) program, chapter 6, devoted to international relations, reads:

1. Peoples' self-determination, non-intervention and non-interference in home matters of other countries, as well as peaceful solution to conflicts, define PTB standing on this issue;
2. PTB recognizes a new world order and pleads that the country benefits from it;
3. PTB supports all movements that foster world disarmament and elimination of nuclear weapons;
4. PTB supports economic and cultural integration of developing countries an fosters the acceleration of Latin American integration, as well as the establishing of a Latin American common market;
5. PTB underlines the need to an orderly occupation of frontier areas, as well as the need to sufficient funds for improving aerial control, roads and communications of such areas, in order to develop them and to protect national territory integrity. (PTB, 1996:12)

Like the previously mentioned programs, that of PTB includes no specific reference to MERCOSUR, broadly alluding to regional integration processes and favoring a Latin American common market.

The PT (*Partido dos Trabalhadores*, Workers Party) thus states its position on international relations: "As to the relations between the nations, PT sustains a policy of international solidarity among oppressed peoples, and of mutual respect among nations, aiming at more cooperation and world peace. The party clearly states its solidarity to national liberation movements and to all international movements that aim at providing better living conditions, justice, and peace for humanity" (PT, 1998:3).

In spite of the emphasis on cooperative international relations, there is no mention of MERCOSUR in this program. However, it must be stressed that the party has constantly discussed the subject, having carried out internal debate on MERCOSUR's impact onto workers, and at several instances supported initiatives linked to the subject. Incidentally, party members showing strong interest on the subject follow the same geographical distribution according to the state of origin seen on Tables 12.1 and 12.2. Internal debate resulted in further party's documents such as the *Curitiba Letter* (1993), the *Recommendations of the First PT National Seminar on MERCOSUR*, and the *Notes on the MERCOSUR Integration Process* (1995). Furthermore, PT has strong presence at the São Paulo Forum (Foro de São Paulo, 1997) assembling left and center-left parties from all Latin America, having thereby taken part in activities alongside other MERCOSUR country parties. In view of PT keeping a strong and permanent internal debate, a dissociation may be noticed between party office decisions and the position of individual PT members of congress. Whereas MERCOSUR is internally discussed, Congress representatives show a relative apathy to the subject, probably because of the same reason applying to other parties, that is, the subject's scarce electoral returns.

Political parties, both governing and opposing, have in general shown scarce interest in MERCOSUR, dealing with it as a distant process. Opposition parties, though in principle favoring regional integration, criticize some aspects of its current developments, the same occurring at times to nonopposition representatives; such was the case of congressman André Franco Montoro (PSDB, São Paulo), who criticized some aspects but wrote a favorable appraisal of the Ouro Preto Protocol in 1995. Anyway, along the nearly ten years of the Joint Parliamentary Commission, it may be said that the major difficulty has been to gain interest and commitment from political parties and their representatives. There prevails a certain unacquaintance to MERCOSUR negotiations and a distancing from its institutions.

Weberian argumentation may be useful to understand the Brazilian parties' standing on the issue of MERCOSUR. To Weber (1974:26), either the parties are ideological, or they "compete among them by including in their programs requirements from which they expect higher impact." In general, says the author, parties combine both models, hence a political party being, in any case, a grouping of individuals with the aim of seizing power within a given situation. There would thus be a higher probability of involvement in the MERCOSUR issue if the latter's institutional structure were contained in a scenario for gaining power. Another reason for more intense involvement would be the *weltanschauungspartei,* the party's ideologic perspective, in Weber's expression: Party members would struggle to achieve explicit political ideals. Still in this case institutional structure, although linked to better-defined program platforms, would play an important role.

In our view, as long as MERCOSUR decision making remains concentrated on the executive, political parties tend to show little interest on it, driving other social actors to seek different organizational forms to represent their interests in the integration process. No doubt this hinders the process of democratization.

This analysis allows for deriving two conclusions on the issue of democracy in MERCOSUR. On the one hand, democratic values—following Schumpeter's rules—tend to be reinforced within each member state and, as seen, MERCOSUR practices at the same time encourage their consolidation. On the other hand, decision making centered on the executive powers weakens democratic control on the integration process. This leads to relative parties' disinterest, due to the process offering scarce possibility of use for their own political and power goals.

Meanwhile, as their interests outreach national frontiers, some economic and social groups show increasing expectation of participating in the regional bloc. When they do not find an adequate way to do so through the Economic-Social Consulting Forum, they search for other means of intervention in order to favor their interests. At the end of the 1990s, this trend is bringing about serious problems for the bloc, hindering integration; in the last section this phenomenon is analyzed through the example of the sugar issue, when economic and social groups struggle for their interests outside MERCOSUR institutional mechanisms. It may be that such private lobbying strategies are favored by political parties' weak commitment to MERCOSUR, which includes their feckless activity at the Joint Parliamentary Commission.

The Joint Parliamentary Commission

The Iguaçu Declaration, signed in November, 1985, by Alfonsín and Sarney, had established the importance of all society sectors' participation in the process of regional integration, as a grounds for relations between the two countries. This item was nevertheless withdrawn from the June 1986

Argentina-Brazil Integration Act that created PICE, where reference was maintained only to businessmen as the active elements of integration. This has encouraged debate on the process of democratic deficit, leading to the creation of the Joint Parliamentary Commission and, later, of the Task Force 11 (renamed 10 as of 1995) to deal with labor and social issues. Through time, then, there has been scarce room for society's intervention in the integration process, dominated until now by interstate negotiations. The PICE document does not mention the ways by which business leaders might interfere nor articulate themselves to state agencies.

On the one hand, integration was considered by the Argentine and Brazilian governments as an important strategy to consolidate national democratic processes; on the other, high-ranking officials and decision makers' concern with assuring tighter relations between the two countries ended up narrowing society's participation at MERCOSUR. As the process advanced, interest on the issue has grown very slowly, in addition to a certain fear concerning vaguely felt incipient integration effects. This is a general rule to integration processes: political and social mobilization come out from the perception of risks rather than of advantages. Yet such generic interest appeared under variable forms through different regions and social groups.

By contrast, while nationally organized groups and political parties focused attention on internal affairs, neglecting the discussions on regional cooperation, the hindrances to their taking part have led to suspicions about the democratic character of the process and to a reluctance in taking part in negotiations. A rising gap could then be felt between the rhetoric of democratic intentions and actual practice, as economic integration in progress discouraged organized groups' participation except for those specifically interested sectors. Thus the addition of effective concern with democracy to the situation of low participation has brought in a favorable climate for the creation of the integration parliamentary body.

A Joint Parliamentary Commission was set out by the Treaty for Integration, Cooperation, and Development, signed by Argentina and Brazil in 1988. It was made up of 12 representatives from each country appointed for two years by the respective national congresses. Of a consulting nature, its main function was to audit negotiated agreements prepared by government officers and make suitable recommendations before sending them to their respective congresses for ratifying. Thus was sanctioned the consulting role of legislators formally engaged in integration, a role that was inherited by the MERCOSUR Joint Parliamentary Commission created in 1991, now assembling the four countries' representatives. That inheritance, as such, does not fully explain parliament standing in MERCOSUR, for, as seen in the previous section, this is largely because of political parties', especially Brazilian, behavior toward MERCOSUR, which has influenced the commission operations.

From the beginning, in 1991 and 1992, the commission has supported a broad ranged integration beyond trading agreements, aiming at increasing the welfare of involved populations. This integrationist model represents an extension of the internal democratization process onto foreign relations and would have been an effective means of assuring MERCOSUR transition from a practical association into a shared-goals association, following Nardin's (1987) definition. However, while the commission rhetoric clearly supported broad and ambitious integration goals, its action was limited both by the vague definition of its functions and by the determinations set by the Asunción Treaty, having not pressed for enlarging either its role within integration or its power in decision making. We believe this gap between action and discourse is central to understanding the Commission participation in MERCOSUR.

It is worth recalling that, according to chapter 6 of Asunción Treaty, the commission must "facilitate progress of the Common Market constitution" (Almeida, 1998:97): the Commission was and is a consulting forum and did not, at that time, belong to the MERCOSUR institutional structure; its main activity remains to expedite legislative consideration of agreements and treaties. The same vagueness is maintained in the Common Market Group internal statute regulations, which assigns itself, according to Chapter II, "the establishment of the necessary links with the Joint Parliamentary Commission" (Grupo Mercado Comum 1992), without further explanation on how it should do so.

Through the transition period of 1991 to 1994, the commission held a few meetings and issued some recommendations and resolutions, but with scarce results. Its propositions, addressing economic, trade, and infrastructure issues, barely reflected society's general concerns; most sought solutions to facilitate integration as it was being conducted by the executive, in spite of criticism uttered by some commission members.

According to Senator Dirceu Carneiro (PSDB, Santa Catarina), the Asunción Treaty has focused on trading aspects, whereas MERCOSUR should have more ambitious goals (Carneiro 1994). The treaty should be thought of, he goes on, as a preliminary document, to be complemented along the years through the actors' bringing in broader issues into the debate on integration. Such contributions, though, have not occurred. Our research has shown that no relevant MERCOSUR fact or decision through the 1990s was accountable to legislative participation. That is, the Joint Parliamentary Commission has had no influence on negotiations, neither has it proposed for debate major issues aiming at developing and consolidating integration. Most of the time, the commission was concerned with economic aspects of the process, issuing recommendations that were either vague or complementary to what was already being dealt with by other MERCOSUR forums. Hence, commission action has not been significant, for it has not introduced, effectively or specifically, new themes into the negotiations.

It might have been otherwise, though. Following Senator Montoro (PMDB, São Paulo), the commission might have brought to the scope of integration issues that reflected social concerns, creating channels for the expression of society's demands, such as transparency at negotiations, or proposals that expressed regional, sector, and political interests. But the commission role remained weak, consisting merely of ratifying governments' decisions.

Nevertheless, the Joint Parliamentary Commission has always expressed concern with assuring democracy and its institutions, as well as pleaded respect for human rights. This may be observed in several of its documents, mostly from its early operation period (Comissão Parlamentar Conjunta 1991–1998):

a. Resolution #001/92, taken at the May 13–15, 1992, meeting, condemns the continuous freedom, democracy, and human rights violation by Peru's executive government; sends a note of solidarity to the Peruvian people through its Congress; and reaffirms full democracy as a means to uproot poverty, social inequality, and corruption in Latin America.

b. On Recommendation #004/92, the integration process culminating in MERCOSUR creation is said to derive straight from the continent's democratization, particularly in the Southern Cone; following the Asunción Treaty, integration is closely linked to democracy; and, in the face of frequent offence to the constitutional system, judicial institutions must be strengthened. Thus the Commission recommends MERCOSUR governments' signing of an Additional Protocol to the Asunción Treaty, establishing as a condition to MERCOSUR membership the full functioning of democratic institutions and observance of human rights agreements in their respective territories.

c. On Resolution #001/93, the Commission decided:

III. to advise MERCOSUR member-countries' governments to unrelentingly defend democratic system and its institutions, fully aware that interruption of democratic order in any of the signatory countries of the Asunción Treaty will offend the process of regional and continental integration;

IV. to support, by all means recognized by international law, governments issued from the people's will.

d. Recommendation #004/93 reaffirms the Commission's "firm belief that a fully democratic system in member-states is an imperative condition to the achievement of goals set by the Asunción Treaty, in accordance with Recommendation #004/92, issued at Córdoba, Argentina, on May 22, 1992, and Resolution #001/93, taken in Brasília, on March 5, 1993." The same Recommendation further reaffirms its commitment "to work for the interests of societies taking part in the integration process, thus exerting its role as representative body of the involved peoples," hence recommending member-states:

- that the basic principle beneath [their] relations to third countries be to support exclusively those legitimated by people's will;
- to be guided by the highest respect toward workers rights, by assuring them a fair participation in the integration process, as well as in all benefits deriving from it;
- to adopt efficient and rapid measures, among which to form a Common Compensation Fund, with a view to reconversion or adequation of sensitive sectors of every economy, in the terms of Recommendation # 001/93(. . .);
- to proceed as soon as possible to the elimination of non-tariff barriers to the intraregion free trade, following Recommendation #002/93, approved by the Subcommission on Customs Matters and Technical Norms;
- to adopt measures and proceedings relative to the policy for MERCOSUR transport sector, concerning its professionalization as well as control at border customs, documents, insurance policies, zoological control, (. . .), as well as reducing economic and technical asymmetries relative to load and passenger transport (. . .) following Recommendation #003/93, approved by the Subcommission on Transport(. . .).

In spite of innumerable resolutions and recommendations, though, Parliamentary participation has not widened within the integration process.

The emphasis on the importance of MERCOSUR democratization has not converted to effective implementation. Scarce attention was paid to issues interesting to society at large, such as labor and environment policies. The commission has only vaguely alluded to these subjects, having made no concrete proposals.

Answering a question they themselves had asked, on why MERCOSUR has no parliament, Florêncio and Araújo (1997:74) suggest this is due to that MERCOSUR "decision making agencies have no supranational character. All MERCOSUR-related decisions are made by national governments, subject to control by their own Parliaments. Since there is no common executive body, there is no need to a common parliament. Whilst the European Union Commission is not accountable to by the member-state national Parliaments; if there were no European Parliament, the Commission would be subject to no external control." This may be so; but recalling what has previously been discussed on democracy at the root of the integration process, still it must be noticed that institutional political control over the integration process could be much improved. Yet the commission has been assigned no different functions from what had been established by the Asunción Treaty. While the newly created Trade Commission has decisive assignments with effective power concerning integration, the Parliamentary Commission, in spite of its activity during the preceding years, remained a consulting agency, only able to issue recommendations to the council.

Its subordination to the executive power has provoked reactions within the Brazilian Congress. Criticism of the Commission assignments was put forward by Deputy Montoro, who called attention to the risks of the new institutional arrangement: "the future of integration will be defined solely by negotiation among national executives, the populations of the four countries having no direct participation on decisions concerning integration, since their representative bodies, as well as the Joint Parliamentary Commission and the Economic-Social Consulting Forum, have merely consulting functions" (Stuart, 1996). Nevertheless, his report eventually recommended approval of the Ouro Preto Protocol.

Further criticism came from the opposition parties. Deputy Sandra Starling (PT, Minas Gerais) argued for functions similar to those of the European Parliament that, she recalled, exerts rigorous control over the Economic Commission, being entitled to dismiss members, approve of budgets, and so on. On her note of rejection of the Ouro Preto Protocol (Starling 1995), she argues that this institutional insertion "overtly violates the constitutional principle of power autonomy, in as much as congressmen from the four countries are subordinated to requirements and directives issued by an office composed of Economics and Foreign Affairs ministers." Still according to her, "the Joint Parliamentary Commission can only make recommendations to the Common Market Council, through the Common Market Group. Such recommendations may or may not be accepted by the Council, hence the Parliamentary Commission, unlike the European one, will have no control over any Council or Group activity" (Starling, 1995).

Notwithstanding, the Parliamentary Commission's institutional position in MERCOSUR was approved by the member-states congresses. And barely anything had changed in what concerns the control mechanisms on the process of regional integration. The new situation as of 1995 did not significantly mobilize commission members to enhance their own role within MERCOSUR's structures. It may be said that general acquiescence prevailed. The Joint Parliamentary Commission incorporated in 1995 into its internal statute regulations (Garcia Jr., 1997), the same assignments determined by the Ouro Preto Protocol in Article 25: to issue recommendations and contribute to the decisions made by the Common Market Group, the Trade Commission, and the Common Market Council.

The new phase following the Ouro Preto Protocol did not change the Commission's cultural practices; members set out to work in 1995 with no clear goals. At their meeting in August of that year they issued Resolution No.#003/95 determining that the Commission Administrative Secretary "shall establish work schedule and define the subjects to be developed by subcommissions along the coming six months" (Comissão Parlamentar Conjunta, 1995). At the same meeting, the Commission's short-term goals were defined as: "use the Commission's role in MERCOSUR's institutional structure; improve the follow-up of work developed by other MERCOSUR institutional forums; point out the priority themes to be discussed" (Comissão Parlamentar Conjunta, 1995).

The analysis of these goals showed discontinuity from the commission's previous work (during the transition period) and, above all, the lack of a working plan or strategy that might allow for more effective action or the strengthening of legislative power within the MERCOSUR integration process.

Sector Interest and Political Parties: The Sugar Case

We now come down to an example of existing forms of political articulation that some economic and social groups have put into action to support their interests in MERCOSUR—instead of using more participatory, democratic regional structures—by analyzing the issue of the sugar trade within the regional bloc.

Sugar (mainly Argentine and Brazilian) trading has been a source of conflict among MERCOSUR countries. This sector's adaptation to the operation of "Common Tariffs"—that implies free trade and a Foreign Common Tariff (TEC)—has turned from a merely technical issue into a political debate, whereby nationally organized Brazilian and Argentine social and economic groups strive to secure their interests. Their intense lobbying of their respective congresses brought about a confrontation between the two legislative houses, thus generating a diplomatic crisis.

This example may suggest that political parties' participation in MERCOSUR might grow as representatives and congresses are encouraged to actively engage with a view to their electoral interests. By contrast, proposals around local or sector interests might hinder the creation of associations of similar parties from different countries. It must then be kept in mind that an increase in political party participation within the regional blocs may be spurred by an integration-favoring position as well as by opposite motives. The sugar case is an example of the latter.

At the meeting of MERCOSUR presidents in Fortaleza, Brazil, in December 1996, the Common Market Council (CMC) determined that compatibility regulations for the sugar sector would be defined by May 31, 1997. The ad hoc task force did not come to expect results in time, because of disputes on the issue between Brazil and Argentina. The ad hoc group notified CMC of its failure, unleashing a dispute between Argentine and Brazilian negotiators that partially reflected the interests of the social and economic groups affected. Brazilian delegates proposed the adoption of a timetable, starting on July 1, 1997, "for gradual and automatic tariff elimination in the sugar sector" (*Disputa pelo açúcar*, 1997), arguing that it was not defensible that this sector be the only one fully excluded from the process of regional integration.

The Argentine delegates, in turn, claimed that the Brazilian proposal did not take into account the asymmetry between the two countries' sugar sectors, which required special mechanisms to make up for the imbalance. Argentina alleged that Brazilian government policy for the sugar-alcohol sector included government intervention by means of Proálcool, a program that defines the mandatory percent of sugarcane alcohol to be mixed to gasoline and determines that government vehicles be alcohol fuelled. Still following the Argentine argument, Proálcool subsidies encouraged sugar plant owners to produce more alcohol and less sugar, the latter becoming a byproduct of the former, thus reducing its cost, so that the Brazilian sugar price was lower than the other MERCOSUR countries. Worse still, as sugar prices rose in the international market, Brazilians increased its production, placing their sugar in MERCOSUR and the world at more competitive prices, thus displacing Argentine production. In both countries the situation took on political connotations, leading to tension among MERCOSUR countries.

On the Argentine Side

As a result of the impasse, in May 1997 the Argentine Congress sanctioned a law conditioning the withdrawal of MERCOSUR import quotas of Brazilian sugar to the end of Brazilian government subsidies to alcohol producers. Since the law contradicted MERCOSUR agreements, President Menem immediately and successfully applied his veto. According to the Brazilian government, there had been no need to press Argentina, for both countries shared the interest in accelerating integration (*Argentina mantém proteção*, 1997).

The June 1997 meeting of the Common Market Group brought the negotiations no step forward, save an Argentine promise to seek a solution for the deadlock. Argentineans attending the meeting proposed that the issue be dealt with again in 2001, when both countries were supposed to achieve full disregulation of the sugar sector. For the Brazilian negotiators that meant a setback, as they were expecting some progress at the negotiations on this only sector within MERCOSUR of which the taxes so far had not been reduced (*Argentina mantém proteção*, 1997).

On August 6, 1997, the Argentine Chamber of Deputies rejected President Menem's veto, proposing to enact the law while the asymmetry supposedly generated by Proálcool persisted (*Argentina mantém taxação*,1997); the issue was handed in to the Senate, which unanimously approved the law on September 3, 1997. This Sugar Law (#24,822) reads:

> The Argentine Senate and Chamber of Deputies, assembled in the Congress, hereby determine as law:
>   Article 1. The duties applied to imported commodities regardless of origin, are to be applied and must not be reduced on these same commodities' imports from MECOSUR member-countries, as long as persists the asymmetry brought about by Brazilian sugar-alcohol system. (*Senado argentino imobiliza*, 1997)

The law obviously protects Argentine sugar producers, less competitive than their Brazilian counterparts who, by way of the subsidies above mentioned, were able to place their products at lower prices in the international market.

The overthrow of the presidential veto and the new Sugar Law resulted from a broad national political coalition of various party members of congress and sugar producers, mainly from the northern provinces of Tucumán, Salta, and Jujui, who argued that Argentine industry would not be able to compete with Brazil if duties were reduced within MERCOSUR.

As October 1997 legislative elections came closer, the subject gained support from most members of congress; they were told that failure to protect Argentine sugar producers' interest would threaten their reelection. That was a real threat, for if sugar production were stopped, the following unemployment would be accountable to congressmen who would have refused to support the Sugar Law, as well as to the Menem administration's MERCOSUR policy. While Menem's government feared the victory of the opposing alliance between Radicals and FREPASO—which came true—there was temporary room for the alliance between justicialistas and the sugar producers to be able to influence the negotiations of international agreements, which are otherwise a government privilege.

Such conflict came true with the Sugar Law being enacted, causing great alarm to and criticism from the Brazilian government who, in a Foreign Affairs Ministry note on September 4, 1997, urged the Argentine government to "honor the international agreements and the commitment between the two countries, in accordance with the MERCOSUR spirit of understanding and cooperation" (*Lampreia lamenta decisão*, 1997).

Pressures from Brazilian Foreign Affairs led the Argentinean government to adopt a defensive and controversial attitude: Although explaining that the executive branch was not to blame, for Congress had taken fully legal action, it also recognized that the country's laws may not counteract international agreements, for these are validated by the constitution. Nevertheless, top officials openly stated that they were seeking means and pondering alternatives to solve the problem.

The analysis of Argentina's internal situation at that time shows that government had in fact no means to prevent the Sugar Law from being enacted, as its parliamentary basis was heavily sought by sugar producers, who had taken their chances and strengthened their position in electoral campaign times. In order to avoid soiling their or the government's images, Menem-allied senators had left the session before the law was voted. The Argentine government was trapped between binding international treaties and the urge to reelect its own party representatives. The Sugar Law appeared as an electoral tool to reconduct to Congress a number of representatives strong enough to approve the reforms it was proposing; at the same time, it had to appear as unaccountable for the law, in face of Brazil and the other MECOSUR countries. It is then clear that, in this case, Argentine political parties have mobilized around defensive interests, not within a perspective of consolidating the cooperative process.

On the Brazilian Side

Brazilian reaction came in the form of an official Foreign Affairs note issued in September 1997, warning the Argentine government and Congress of the risk of serious diplomatic clash between the two countries. In addition, at the Brazilian Congress Deputy Paulo Bornhausen (PFL, Santa Catarina), then head of the Brazilian section at the Joint Parliamentary Commission, submitted a draft law of retaliation forbidding import of Argentine wheat, arguing that "it is well known that the Argentine export of wheat is heavily subsidized, which makes it impossible for Brazilian producers to compete with it in fair or at least reasonably acceptable ways in the home market" (*Câmara ameaça retaliação,* 1997).

Bornhausen's attitude was primarily political, an attempt to remind Argentineans that the wheat sector in Brazil had undergone a serious crisis due to MERCOSUR but—unlike their own statements—Brazilian government has taken accommodating measures to avoid damaging the regional bloc. The proposed law also aimed at destabilizing the Argentine Congress, by adding another element to the dispute: if it were enacted, Argentine wheat producers would certainly mobilize and press their members of congress, who would then find themselves in a still more uncomfortable position, for wheat and export sectors might withdraw their support for the coming elections. Moreover, a "wheat case" would have still broader effects, for Brazil, as its main importer, absorbs almost half of Argentine wheat exports; hence a reduction of exports, besides affecting a powerful sector, would certainly shake Argentina's balance of payments. Thus the Brazilian threat aimed at mobilizing an Argentine economic sector to intervene by favoring Brazilian interests. In economic international relations, mobilizing other countries' groups in one country's own interest has been an increasingly utilized tactic.

Further reactions followed. On September 8, 1997, the Brazilian Senate president Antônio Carlos Magalhães (PFL, Bahia) addressed the government claiming a stronger reaction to the Argentine congress's decision on Brazilian sugar imports. The President of the Chamber of Deputies Michel Temer (PMDB, São Paulo), in turn, offered his support to Bornhausen's proposal—but was careful to add, "decisions like the Argentine Congress's represent a risk to MERCOSUR" (*ACM cobra reação*, 1997).

Magalhães's position, similar to the Argentine congressmen's, reflected the interests of important economic and social groups from the Brazilian northeast, mainly those of sugar producers, but also including concern for workers who depend on sugar production. As to Bornhausen, though his southern state of origin (Santa Catarina) is not a wheat producer, he spoke on behalf of farmers from its two neighboring states, Rio Grande do Sul and Paraná, the country's major wheat producers.

The Logic of Cooperation

In the case here analyzed, MERCOSUR countries' interests were organized statements within the legislative branches of both countries. A coalition between different groups became strong enough to make the Argentine legislature ignore the international agreements signed with its MERCOSUR partners. In Brazil, originally encouraged by the foreign ministry policy, another coalition in turn began to urge Argentine government and parliament to find a solution that would not threaten Brazilian interests.

Pressure from both sides eventually led the Argentine government to move toward a solution. President Menem's advisors prepared a proposal to revoke the Sugar Law, while others examined the possibility of appealing to the Argentine Supreme Court, expecting a declaration on its illegality, as it countered agreements signed with Brazil in June 1997, when both sides had committed themselves to study the asymmetry between both countries' sugar sectors, aiming at a common policy to fully integrate the sector into MERCOSUR free-trading and Foreign Common Tariffs (TEC). Economy Minister Roque Fernández made public his rejection of his own country's congressional decision, while asking the Brazilian government for some time to find a better solution to the question (*Menem pode apelar*, 1997).

Argentine executive's public standing against its own Congress aimed to prevent possible Brazilian retaliation and gain time for further negotiations. Gaining time was crucial due to Argentina's political moment: From July through October, any error might mean losing votes from sugar producing provinces. The Brazilian government then decided to postpone further measures, although rejecting Menem's claim that he had been taken by surprise by legislative action. According to Brazilian Minister for For-

eign Affairs Luiz Felipe Lampreia, "a Congressional decision can not be
fully detached from the federal government, who holds majority in the
house" (*Em nota oficial,* 1997).

Through the latter part of 1997, means were sought to undo the two
policies at the root of the diplomatic crisis between Argentina and Brazil—
a crisis that was thought of as political rather than commercial. According
to Bornhausen, one of the leading political actors on the Brazilian side, the
crisis had been provoked by the Argentine Congress's risky precedent of
trying to establish a new deliberative forum parallel to MERCOSUR's institutional structure, established by the Ouro Preto Protocol in 1994. If
other congresses in other countries followed suit, credibility of the "Common Customs" would be so shaken as to make it impossible. The Argentine government partially accepted criticism, reaffirming its will to settle
the issue (*Menem reafirma posição,* 1997).

The emphasis on such cooperation is partially drawn from the perception that a sector crisis might threaten all of the advantages brought by the
"Common Customs." Conjunctural factors also contributed, such as the
MERCOSUR World Economic Forum held in the same month (September 1997), where both countries sought to present the image of a mature, united and solid MERCOSUR, ready to attract investments.
Meanwhile, a new round of FTAA negotiations tried to set a timetable for
trade liberalization in the continent, which also encouraged
MERCOSUR member-countries to appear formally as a solid bloc.

From then on, the sugar issue became a matter of negotiation among
government offices, hence bringing it back to the institutional scope of
MERCOSUR. Political parties' participation in the debate decreased. Still,
in September 1997, representatives from both countries' congresses and
export chambers assembled to examine the issue and assess possible developments. There was a consensus that, though against their will, the question would take a long time to be solved; task forces were organized to
study the differences between sugar sectors in Argentina and Brazil and to
later implement common policies so as to integrate the sector into free-
trade and Foreign Common Tariff (TEC) mechanisms (*Exportadores debatem crise,* 1997).

Conclusion

Brazilian policy on regional integration has been a foreign affairs as-
signment, whose minister has thus had a significant role in the process

of integrating the Southern Cone. A closer look at this policy allows for different assessments. Our research suggests that neither within the Brazilian state nor society has there been developed an alternative perspective to the current strategy. It may be said that a classical view on policy making prevails: to advance one step at a time, to consolidate every stage before advancing further. It is worth remarking that MERCOSUR decision-making structure relies on intergovernmental negotiation, there being no supranational agencies such as the European ones. Ever since the 1986 Brazilian favoring of this structure, mostly shared by the Argentineans, efforts aimed at preventing the risk that a supranational structure, if autonomous from national states, might create its own logic and strategy.

Shared fairly evenly among foreign affair policymakers, Brazilian views on the issue are that regional integration, at least for the time being, must progress under the intergovernmental framework. A central element of current Brazilian position is that, rather than redesigning negotiation management tools, members must seek to improve the existing ones. Thus the current structure must be maintained, for current coordination relies on administrative and political forums that have the necessary know-how and are able to point out the issues that relatively or fully meet national interests. That's why Brazil supports the current administrative framework for the integration process.

Our analysis seems to suggest that current forms of public and private interest representation from MERCOSUR member-country societies will become inadequate if integration progresses, for the current structure will not be able to offer suitable channels for those interests to be represented. This leads to hard-to-manage conflicts mainly in ill-defined situations such as election campaigns, a macroeconomic crisis, or tensions linked to sector interests. Economic, social, and political, public and private groups whose interests are threatened within MERCOSUR will search one way or another to make up for their losses in detriment to the whole integration process. That is the lesson of the sugar case.

These persisting difficulties in the articulation of interests concerning regional integration policies suggest the need for better information exchanged and to improved decision-making mechanisms, in order to accommodate national differences. Integration would be favored if the legislative branch had broader participation. The current indifference most Brazilian political parties show toward MERCOSUR; might change if they could enhance their role in decision making, including their role in the Joint Parliamentary Commission. This is not an easy question, in view of the present imbalance among countries, but there are possible solutions that might meet differences and rights. Furthermore, measures must be taken to enhance MERCOSUR agencies—task forces and the Economic-Social Consulting Forum—so that they may encourage private sector participation, thus transferring influence to groups that might otherwise hinder the integration process.

The fact that democracy as a value is shared among the bloc countries, but is formally applied only at national level, and does not pervade the institutional structures may be one of the factors leading to the bloc's negative perception. Thus, a positive valuing of the democratic decision making is crucial.

Bibliography

ACM cobra reação à taxação do açúcar. (1997). *O Estado de São Paulo.* September 9.
Adler, Emanuel. (1997). "Seizing the middle ground: constructivism in world politics." *European Journal of International Relations,* vol. 3, no. 3, September.
Almeida, Paulo Roberto. (1998). *O Mercosur: fundamentos e perspectivas.* São Paulo: LTr.
Archibugi, Daniele, Held, D. and Kohler, M. (eds.) (1998). *Re-imagining Political Community.* Cambridge, MA: Polity Press.
Argentina mantém proteção ao açúcar. (1997). *Gazeta Mercantil.* São Paulo, May 27.
Argentina mantém taxação ao açúcar brasileiro. *O Estado de São Paulo,* São Paulo, Sept. 5, 1997: Diplomacia, A12.
Aron, Raymond. (1962). *Paix et guerre entre les nations.* Paris: Calmann-Lévy.
Barbosa, Rubens A. (1991). *A América Latina em perspectiva: a integração regional da retórica à realidade.* São Paulo: Aduaneiras.
Bonanate, Luigi. (1989). "Osservazioni sulla teoria dei regimi internazionali." In Luigi Bonanate, Anna Caffarena, Roberto Vellano. *Dopo l'anarchia.* Milano: Franco Angeli.
Bull, Hedley. (1995). *The Anarchical Society: A Study of Order in World Politics.* London: Macmillan.
Câmara ameaça retaliação contra Argentina. (1997). *O Estado de São Paulo.* São Paulo, September 6.
Câmara Dos Deputados. (2000). *Deputados.* Retrieved from: www.camara.gov.br. February 2.
Caputo, Dante M. and Jorge F. Sabato. (1991). *La integración de las democracias pobres: oportunidades y peligros.* Buenos Aires. (Mimeo)
Checkel, Jeffrey T. (1998). "The Constructivist Turn in International Relations Theory." *World Politics,* no. 50.
Comissão Parlamentar Conjunta. *Atas das Reuniões,* 1991 through 1998.

Dahl, Robert A. (1985). *A Preface to Economic Democracy*. Berkeley: University of California Press.

"Disputa pelo açúcar." (1997). *Gazeta Mercantil Latino-Americana*. São Paulo. September 19.

Em Nota oficial, Itamaraty manifesta "séria preocupação." (1997). *Gazeta Mercantil*. São Paulo. September 5, Nacional, 4.

"Exportadores debatem crise do açúcar: reunião de brasileiros e argentinos avalia que solução para impasse ainda vai demorar." (1997). *Gazeta Mercantil*. São Paulo, September 17.

Florência, Sérgio & Araújo, Ernesto. (1997). *Mercosur, proyecto, realidad y perspectivas*. Brasília: Vest-Com.

Fonseca Jr., Gelson. (1999). "Anotações sobre as condições do sistema internacional no limiar do século XXI: a distribuição dos pólos de poder e a inserção internacional do Brasil." In Gilberto Dupas and Tullo Vigevani, eds. *O Brasil e as novas dimensões da segurança internacional*. São Paulo: Alfa-Omega; FAPESP.

Foro De São Paulo. (1997). *Projeto de Declaração Final do VII Encontro do Foro de São Paulo*. July 30–31. Porto Alegre.

"Frepaso lidera pesquisa eleitoral." (1997). *Gazeta Mercantil Latino-Americana*, São Paulo, September 27.

Garcia, Jr., Armando Á. (1997). "Conflito entre normas do Mercosur e direito interno." *Informativo Mercosur*. Brasília: Seção Brasileira da Comissão Parlamentar Conjunta; Caixa Econômica Federal, vol. 2, no. 6.

Grupo Mercado Comum. (1992). *Regimento Interno*. From Almeida, Paulo Roberto (coord.) *MERCOSUR: Textos Básicos*. Brasília: Fundação Alexandre de Gusmão; Instituto de Pesquisas de Relações Internacionais.

Hurrell, Andrew. (1999). "Questions on Brazilian Foreign Policy." *Seminário no CEDEC* (Centro de Estudos de Cultura Contemporânea), São Paulo.

Lafer, Celso. (1997). "Relações Brasil-Argentina: alcance e significado de uma parceria estratégica." *Contexto Internacional*, Rio de Janeiro: IRI/PUC, vol. 19, no. 2.

"Lampreia lamenta decisão de parlamentares." (1997). *O Estado de São Paulo*. São Paulo. September 5.

Lampreia, Luiz Felipe. (1999). "A política exterior do Brasil." *Seminário no IEA/USP*. São Paulo.

Lima, Maria Regina S. (1994). "Ejes analíticos y conflicto de paradigmas en la política exterior brasileña." *América Latina/Internacional*. Buenos Aires: FLACSO, vol. 1, no. 2.

Mariano, Karina L. P. and Marcelo F. Oliveira. (1999). *Mercosur: a emergência de uma nova sociedade*. São Paulo: CEDEC.

"Menem pode apelar à Corte Suprema." (1997). *Gazeta Mercantil*, São Paulo. September 5.

"Menem reafirma posição contra proteção a açúcar." (1997). *Gazeta Mercantil*. São Paulo. September 8.

"Ministro argentino condena taxação do açúcar." (1997). *O Estado de São Paulo*. São Paulo. September 8.

Nardin, Terry. (1987). *Lei, moralidade e as relações entre os Estados*. Rio de Janeiro: Forense-Universitária.

Nye Jr., Joseph S. (1992). *Bound to Lead: The Changing Nature of American Power*. New York: Basic Books.

Partido da Frente Liberal. (1998). *Programa do PFL*. Retrieved from www.pfl. org.br/programa.htm. June 23.

Partido do Movimento Democrático Brasileiro. (1998). *Programa do PMDB*. Retrieved from: www.pmdb.org.br/progrm2.htm. June 19.

Partido Progressista Brasileiro. *Manifesto Programa Estatuto do PPB*.

Partido da Social Democracia Brasileira. (1998). *Programa do PSDB*. Retrieved from: www.psdb.org.br. June 20.

Partido dos Trabalhadores. (1993). *Carta de Curitiba*. Curitiba: Primeiro Seminário Nacional do PT sobre o MERCOSUR, September 25.

————. (1995). *Notas sobre o processo de integração do MERCOSUR*. São Paulo.

————. (1998). *Programa do Partido dos Trabalhadores*. Retrieved from: www.pt. org.br/prog-pt.htm. September 19.

Partido Trabalhista brasileiro. (1996). *Programa e Estatuto do PTB*. Brasília.

Peña, Félix. (1998). "Pré-requisitos políticos e econômicos da integração." *Política Externa*, vol. 1, no. 2.

Schmitter, Philippe C. (1998). *How to Democratize the European Union: Citizenship, Representation, Decision-Making in the Emerging Euro-Polity*. Florença: Istituto Universitario Europeo.

Schumpeter, Joseph A. (1979). *Capitalism, Socialism and Democracy*. London: George Allen and Unwin.

"Senado argentino imobiliza Menem na negociação do açúcar." (1997). *Gazeta Mercantil*. São Paulo. September 4.

Senado Federal. (2000). *Senadores*. Retrieved from www.senado.gov.br. February 2.

Starling, Sandra. (1995). *Declaração de voto da Deputada Sandra Starling sobre o Parecer do relator Deputado André Franco Montoro sobre o Protocolo Adicional ao Tratado de Assunção sobre a estrutura institucional do MERCOSUR*. Brasília: Comissão das Relações Exteriores da Câmara dos Deputados.

Stuart, Ana Maria. (1996). "Um balanço político da reunião do MERCOSUR." *Carta Internacional*. São Paulo.

Vigevani, Tullo. (1998). *MERCOSUR: Impactos para trabalhadores e sindicatos*. São Paulo: FAPESP, CEDEC.

Weber, Max. (1974). "Parlamentarismo e governo numa Alemanha Reconstruída." *Ensaios de Sociologia*. São Paulo: Abril Cultural.

Wendt, Alexander. (1994). "Collective identity, formation and the international state." *American Political Science Review*, vol. 88, no. 2.

Notes on Contributors

Carlos Alzurgaray Treto is a former Cuban Foreign Service Officer (1961–1996) with the rank of Ambassador. He is now a professor of International Relations at the Higher Institute of International Relations (ISRI) of the Cuban Foreign Ministry in Havana. He has published two books in Spanish on Cuban-U.S. relations and more than 40 articles on Latin America and the Caribbean. In 2000 he was a Jean Monnet Fellow at the Robert Schuman Center, European University Institute, Florence, Italy.

Luis Fernando Ayerbe is an associate professor in the Department of Economics at the State University of Sao Paulo (UNESP) in Araraquara, Brazil and coordinator of the Group of Interdisciplinary Studies on Culture and Development (GEICD). He has been a visiting scholar at Harvard University and the Autonomous University of Barcelona. He has authored two recent publications, *Neoliberalismo e Politica Externa na America Latina* and *Los Estados Unidos y la América Latina, la Construcción de la hegemonia*.

Sandra Colombo is Professor of International Relations in the Faculty of Human Sciences of the National University of the Center (UNICEN), Buenos Aires, Argentina. She is also a researcher of the Center of Interdisciplinary Studies of International Problems (CEIPI) of the UNICEN.

Armando Lopez Coll is a professor in the Center for the Study of the World Economy (CIEM) at the University of Havana. He was educated at the Institute of Latin American Studies of the Academy of Sciences of the U.S.S.R.

Dorothea Melcher is Professor of Economic and Social History at the University of the Andes in Merida, Venezuela. She has published on a wide range of topics, including Venezuelan history and politics, the Comintern, Sandino, and globalization.

Jaime Preciado Coronado is a Professor and Researcher at the Department for Iberian and Latin American Studies at the University of Guadalajara. He is the former director of the Center for Latin American and Iberian Studies and the Center for the Study of State and Society. Currently, he is the co-Director of the review *Espiral*.

Hector Luis Saint-Pierre is Professor of Philosophy at the State University of Sao Paulo. He is also Group Coordinator for Defense and Security Studies (GEDES-UNESP) and Director of the Center for Latin America Studies (CELA/UNESP). He is a member of several editorial boards including *Revista Critica Marxista* and *Revista Estudios-Politicos-militares.* His major publications include *Entre votos y botas: as forces armadas no labirinto latino Americano de novo milenio.*

Luciana Togeiro de Almeida is an Assistant Professor at the Department of Economics, São Paulo State University (UNESP) and President of the Brazilian Society for Ecological Economics (ECOECO).

Harry E. Vanden is Professor of Political Science and former Chair of the Latin American and Caribbean Studies Committee at the University of South Florida. In addition to a number of articles and book chapters, he has written *Mariátegui: influencias en su formación ideological, National Marxism in Latin America: José Carlos Mariátegui's Thought and Politics,* and *A Bibliography of Latin American Marxism.* He is also the coauthor of *The Politics of Latin America: The Power Game* and *Democracy and Socialism in Sandinista Nicaragua.* He is coeditor of *The Undermining of the Sandinista Revolution.*

Tullo Vigevani is Professor of Political Science at State University of Sao Paulo (UNESP). He has authored numerous books, including *MERCOSUR: Its Impact on Unions and Workers.*

Marilia Campus, Karina Lilia Pasquariello Mariano, and Marcelo Fernandes de Oliveira are researchers at the Center for the Studies of Contemporary Culture (CEDEC).

Robert Weber is an Associate Professor and former chair of Political Science at St. John's University and the College of St. Benedict in Minnesota. He is the author of articles on the U.S. Congress and is a former American Political Science Association Congressional Fellow.

About the Editors

Gary Prevost is a Professor of Political Science at St. John's University and the College of St. Benedict in Minnesota. He received his Ph.D. in political science from the University of Minnesota and has published widely on Latin America and Spain. His books include *The Politics of Latin America: The Power Game,* and *Democracy and Socialism in Sandinista Nicaragua,* both coauthored with Harry E. Vanden; *The 1990 Nicaraguan Elections and their Aftermath* and *Cuba—A Different America,* coedited with Wilber Chaffee, in addition to numerous articles and book chapters on Nicaragua and Spanish politics. His research on Latin America has been supported by a number of grants, including a Fulbright Central American Republics Award.

Carlos Oliva Campos is the executive director of the Association for Our America (AUNA) in Havana, Cuba, and former associate researcher of the Center for the Study of the United States at the University of Havana. He is an adjunct professor of history and philosophy at the University of Havana and has held visiting appointments at the University of Texas and Johns Hopkins. His publications include *La situación actual en Cuba: desafíos y alternativas,* and *Relaciones internacionales en America Central y el Caribe durante los años 80.*

Index

256–60, 264–5, 269, 272; and
  Permanent Arbitration Court, 250
Methylcyclopentadienyl Maganese
  Tricarbonyl (MMT), 73
Mexican-American war, 162
Mexican peso crisis, 72, 101, 228
Mexico Solidarity Network, 75
Monroe Doctrine, x, xii, 7, 8, 20, 162,
  225
Monroe, James, ix
Monsanto Corporation, 74
Moore, Mike, 152
Most Indebted Nations Club, 165
Movement of Non-Aligned (NAM),
  201
Movement of the Landless (MST),
  116
multiculturalism, 32, 34
Multilateral Agreement on Investments
  (MAI), 54, 71, 73, 214
Multilateral Anti-Drug Center, 226

Nader, Ralph, 88
Napoleon, 7
narco-trafficking, 16, 19, 112
National Armed Forces (NAF), 107–9,
  111, 114
National Commission for Mediation
  (CONAI), 115
National Health Care and Pension
  Administration (Cost Rica), 171
National Institute for Learning (Costa
  Rica), 171
National Institute of Ecology
  (Mexico), 225
national security doctrine, 4, 56, 220
national treatment, 71
neoconservatism, 32
Neoliberal, xiii, 43, 49, 52; and liberal
  paradigm, 47, 54, 57–8, 61, 172;
  and neoliberalism, xii, 47, 51, 62,
  218; and neoliberal policies, 54,
  169; and reforms, 52

Neopanamericanism, x, 4, 11, 20–1;
  and free market capitalism, xi
New Strategic Concept, 60
Nicaragua Network, 75
North American Bank for
  Development (NADBANK), 224
North American Free Trade
  Agreement (NAFTA), ix, xi, 13,
  16–17, 19–21, 43, 71, 73–4, 76,
  79–82, 85–7, 97, 99–102, 137–8,
  143, 147–9, 151–2, 155–8, 186,
  189, 193–5, 204, 211–2, 215, 218,
  222–5, 228, 232, 234, 247
North Atlantic Treaty Organization
  (NATO), 50, 54, 60, 108–9, 191,
  245
North/South, 111, 114

Oil Crisis, 184
Organization of American States
  (OAS), 15, 20, 55, 67, 70, 107, 138,
  201; and Group Assembly of the
  Organization of American States, 70
Organization of Caribbean States
  (OCS), 124
Organization of Eastern Caribbean
  States (OECS), 132–3
Organization for Economic
  Cooperation and Development,
  152–3, 156, 190, 221
Organization of Petroleum Exporting
  Countries (OPEC), 40, 187–8, 219
ORIT (Western Hemisphere
  Federation of Trade Unions), 76
Ouro Preto Protocol, 244, 251, 256,
  264–5, 271

Palme, Olaf, 56
Paine, Thomas, 6
Panama Conference, 8
Panamerican Conference, 10, 18; and
  First Panamerican Conference, 18
Panamerican Games, 70